VAMPYRE'S HANDBOOK

5TH ANNIVERSARY - COLLECTOR'S EDITION

THE RITES OF MOROII AD VITAM

VAMPYRE'S HANDBOOK

SECRETS OF MODERN VAMPIRES

written by Joshua Free
with Foreword by David Zibert

First published underground in two volumes:
"The Vampyre's Bible" and "Cybernomicon"

JOSHUA FREE
publishing imprint

©2015–2020, JOSHUA FREE
ISBN : 978-0-578-62344-3

Complete Rites & Teachings of the Moroii and Vitam Paramus
— Living Vampyres Preparing for a Second Life —

MARDUKITE RESEARCH & DEVELOPMENT presents a
CYBERVAMPS PUBLICATION with THE MARDUKITE VAMPYRE ACADEMY
in conjunction with THE JOSHUA FREE PUBLISHING IMPRINT

Mardukite Research Library Catalogue No. "Liber V"/"Liber V1+V2"

Cover graphics assistance by Kyra Kaos.

This material was originally distributed underground to graduating students and Grade-II Mardukite Chamberlains Alumni as a threshold toward work now presented and available as Grade-III Mardukite Systemology.

—TABLET OF CONTENTS—

Foreword to the 5th Anniversary Edition . . . 7
Introduction to The Vampyre's Handbook . . . 11

VAMPYRE'S BIBLE : THE MOROII BOOK OF "V"

– Book I : History & Folklore . . . 17
– Book II : Theory & Practice . . . 41
– Book III : Energy & Feeding . . . 71
– Book IV : Death & Immortality . . . 95

CYBERNOMICON : THE SECOND BOOK OF "V"

– Book V : History of the Dark Covenant . . . 115
– Book VI : The Power of Fire & Blood . . . 147
– Book VII : The Secrets of Merlin . . . 165
– Book VIII : The Future of Chaos . . . 179
– Book IX : Lycanthropic Shamanism . . . 191
– Book X : Ceremonies of Immortality . . . 199

VAMPYRE'S HANDBOOK : EDITION APPENDICES

Appendix A : History Begins With Writing . . . 211
Appendix B : Reality-System Programming . . . 217
Appendix C : The Stele of Revealing . . . 219
Appendix D : Seven Heavens of the Zohar . . . 220
Appendix E : Fama Fraternitas . . . 226
Appendix F : Defense Against the Dark Arts. . . 227
Appendix G : Babylonian Epic of Creation . . . 231
Appendix H : Underworld Descent of Ishtar . . . 240
Appendix I : Moroii Dictionary (v.2.1) . . . 249

Suggested Reading . . . 257

FOREWORD TO THE 5TH ANNIVERSARY COLLECTOR'S EDITION

by David Zibert

LARGELY dismissed by many as simply another pop-culture phenomenon, *Vampires* are a serious esoteric subject—demonstrable by associated semantics found within and throughout every culture and mythology. Yet, it is easily seen how pop-culture—also called "bullshit" in some circles—is a mere fragmented reflection of something very real in the underground.

Eluding the thoughts of those individuals treading on the fluffier side of things, *Vampyrism* is actually a strong, ancient and powerful current within the occult community—so much so, that each and every "occult" group I have ever encountered was found to be led by some "inner circle" that were either:

—referring to themselves as *Vampyres*;

—led by some obscure or invisible *Vampyric Secret Chiefs*;

—or else performed "high magic" workings based on mystical techniques that could, by all means, fall within the semantic of *Vampyrism*, even when not directly stated as such.

And these groups are not necessarily the same as those that cultivate "dark" outlooks, or are of the "Left-Handed" variety, or some other popular "bullshit." *Vampyrism* and the *Vampyres* described in this book—the *Moroii*—proudly stand apart from other "underground vampyres" in a manner best described by *Our* slogan:

> To Evolve — To Become — To Protect.

"*Vampyre*"—variously spelled throughout time and geography as "*vampire*," "*vampir*," "*vapir*," "*opiri*," "*uper*," and "*ubyr*," &tc, —is a loaded and ambiguous word—most purposefully so.[*] And while it conjures to mind—in cowans and mundanes—the image of either a folkloric monster or pop-culture sex symbol—

---

[*] See David Zibert's *Foreword* contributed to "*Elvenomicon -or- Secret Traditions of Elves & Faeries*" by Joshua Free.

these are only outward expressions of this underground culture.

Simply put: the *real Vampyre* is an "energy worker"—characterized by their working exclusively from the "astral," or else techniques of Direct Energy Processing, without requirements of the more mundane "ceremonial magick" trappings. This methodology is not even restricted to *vampyric* terminology, and may be found in all "higher workings" of virtually every tradition—as is the case, for example: in the practical Hermetic philosophy of W. W. Atkinson, the great mind behind the *Kybalion*, among other works.

The *Vampyre* is thus able to causally change reality as *Self* by consciously raising Awareness to the holistic underlying reality—the *All-as-One*—channeling manifestation as vibration and its motions as Energy. When associated *glamour* is removed, be it the "positive Victorian romance" or the "negative monster from antiquity," only that which pertains directly to channeling Energy remains—either "physical" (consuming "charged" bodily fluids as alluded to in some practices) or "subtle" (the etheric, astral "star-stuff" or ZU Life-Energy), both of which are simply termed "*Starfyre*" in *Moroii* tradition.

In this respect, *We* are more accurately "reality engineers" rather than "night stalkers" even if, indeed, *Our* work is rooted in darkness—what is considered: "the Other." Of course, that being said, there are still those who do fall into dark trappings or glamour—or worse: traditions talking about some "predatory spirituality" or other such nonsense (literally "eating up the gods"... *right...*)—but, of course, these others are not of the *Moroii* path and are left to explore their fragmented paradigm outside of Self-Honesty by themselves.

In the spirit of Joshua Free's previous offerings concerning "Mardukite Zuism" (see *The Complete Anunnaki Bible* and *The Sumerian Legacy*)* and other literary contributions on Druidry

---

* Both published by the *Joshua Free Publishing Imprint*.

(such as *The Book of Pheryllt** and *Elvenomicon*‡)—the actual difference between these paradigms being only on a semantic level—*Vampyre* lore is traced back to the earliest inception of written history, through to today and beyond, once more raising the question: "what shall we do with this knowledge so that we may advance further as a species?" And that, verily, is what distinguishes Joshua Free from his contemporaries, from those who are content to simply intellectualize the *fragments*, then move on, *Self-Aware* or not, to the next system which will, just like a vampire, grasp and drain their attentions.

When the first "V" discourse appeared as *The Vampyre's Bible* in 2015, it was an oddity for the author's library catalog—seemingly much different on the surface than anything previously relayed. The same sentiment was carried further, and reinforced, by the release of a follow-up titled *Cybernomicon*, which included related "postmodern" material not exclusively emphasizing *The Vampyre*. But what appears at first glance to be both a candid and weirdish "goth book" is later discovered to hold much more substance when explored by an experienced *Seeker*.

The complete rites and teachings of the Moroii ad Vitam from *The Vampyre's Bible* and *Cybernomicon* are combined for this 5th Anniversary Collector's Edition anthology—and they contain many "unmentioned" or "hidden" *Keys* completing the Egyptian aspects of the "Mardukite" paradigm, for which he author is best known. Any thematic emphasis on a Futurist/Cyber approach is meant, furthermore, only as a literal "Gateway" bridging pop-culture occultism (as already enjoyed by enthusiast Darksiders), to the "Great Deception" (discovered and revealed by the author over the past decade), and finally, with "*NexGen Systemology*," the postmodern futurist applied spiritual technology that can dissolve past glamour in *Self-Honesty*—which is evident now by the present focus of the Mardukite Research Organization as we enter the 2020's.

---

*   Reprinted by *Kima Global Books*.
‡   Also published by *Joshua Free Publishing Imprint*.

Being myself a long time "Darksider"—our live-action games of *"Vampire: The Masquerade"* having been something of an obsession for two to three years prior to my formally joining the "occult scene" and also being your ever dark melomaniac—it is quite a pleasure for me to introduce you to the complete catalog of peculiar discourses of "Liber-V"—revealed to you now as *The Vampyre's Handbook: Secrets of the Moroii ad Vitam & Guide for Modern Vampires.*

—David Zibert
Mardukite Patesi of Canada
Council of Nabu-Tutu
Blue Room Office, Québec
Winter 2019

5TH ANNIVERSARY INTRODUCTION TO THE VAMPYRE'S HANDBOOK

by Joshua Free

To realize that we are *more* than *Human* and to actualize this state of *Awareness*... this has been the ultimate goal of all magical, mystical and spiritual pursuits since the dawn of time. It is perhaps no more blatantly represented and recognized than in one of the most superior occult archetypes ever to emerge:

<u>The VAMPYRE</u>.

When I first developed *"The Vampyre's Bible"* for publication five years ago, I was asked: "What is the difference between *immortal* and *mortal*, and how can anyone claim to be *immortal* in a human body?" I admit that this query caught me off guard as I had never given the matter much thought before as a "semantic" issue. No legitimate answers were available in "New Age" literature—all answers regarded a certain emphasis on "corporeal immortality" of the physical body only.

I kept this problem in mind as I compiled the *Moroii* notebooks for *"Vampyre's Bible"* and *"Cybernomicon."* It wasn't just a semantic issue—it was a real one. What is it that could allow an individual within a human shell to become <u>transhuman</u> in this lifetime without depending on "external technology" and upgrades? Is it possible for us to program—or *reprogram*—our own cells and DNA—and if so, can it be executed using only the mind? Does another existence even await us after this lifetime—and if so, can *Ascension* of the *Self* actually happen from this existence? Or, have we all just been wasting our time?

I considered various ways that "immortal" and "undead" were portrayed in mythographies and catalogs of lore. On a semantic level, both pertained to a state of "not being dead"—an ongoing existence of a superior Identity as *"Self."* This is because the term *"immortal"* carries another distinct quality: it implies consciousness (*Awareness*) that is "not human," "beyond human" or "*transhuman*." This means that semantically, "human" as a synonym for "mortal" *is* a "condition" and *not* a species or race. It is an epidemic disease greatly affecting or "fragmenting" at least 90% of the current population.

To be *Immortal*—as the *Living Vampyre*—is to exist and experience life from a central point of Awareness beyond and exterior to the physical body, realized as a form called the *Etheric Body*. This is what Egyptians referred to as the Body Double in their "*Book of the Dead*." It has an ability to *Live* on after *First Death*, meaning after the "death" of the corporeal body. To accomplish this, energy is sent to a person's *Etheric Body* during this lifetime through conscious Will, Attention and Awareness.

The Eternal or "Et(*h*)ernal Self" is who YOU really are and what YOU could be preparing for when operating beyond the confines and limitations of this world. Hence, the modern name given to Our ancient tradition is drawn from a Latin verse: <u>*ad vitam paramus*</u>, "We Are Preparing for Life," meaning "*A Life Beyond This Life.*"

"*Mortals*" on the other hand, are simply creatures that will die. They have a "terminal" *Awareness* concerning personality and *Identity* without actualizing the True Self, the *Dragon* within. Those suffering from this human condition and which cannot be "*turned*" or "Awakened" will find that their condition is quite *terminal* indeed. Having focused all energy during Life on a corporeal body and existence of inert matter, all they know of and identify with *will* die. For "*Mortals*", all attention and energy is directed only toward the physical body and used only for experiencing sensation in physical existence. This physical body *is* corruptible—so when they are preparing for *First Death*, they are really preparing for *Final Death*. Being "*mortal*" and self-aware of this fact, they try to rake in as much as they can from this material existence, because for them there is no other.

You might notice that there is a general theme growing here—that is all about *Death* and *change* and transformation and *Lives* after existing *Lives*... Of course, this is expected with a book about *Vampyres, Undead* and *Creatures of Night*—but, the other reason is because this *Moroi* system was always intended for those Mardukite Chamberlains continuing on to higher levels of initiation. These lessons were held back from my previous "Grade-I" materials regarding practical magick, Celtic Druid (Elven-Faerie) and the "Grade II" work representing a modern Mesopotamian (neopagan) revival of "Mardukite Zuism"—and yet they closely relate together on one continuum.

When "*Vampyres Bible*" publicly released in August 2015, it was announced that it would be my last book for the Mardukite Chamberlains Grade-II—a notable exception being, of course, the much anticipated "Anunnaki Tarot" guidebook in 2019, an unreleased project first completed in 2009. Presentation of the current *Moroi* work was always intended as a threshold bridge for *Seekers*—those preferring the themes and energy work of "vampyrism"—going on toward Grade-III, only recently made available publicly as '*Systemology: The Pathway to Self-Honesty*' cycle of materials—including: "*The Tablets of Destiny: Using Ancient Wisdom to Unlock Human Potential*" and "*Crystal Clear: The Self-Actualization Manual & Guide to Total Awareness*." This more recent work is now carrying elements first found within the *Vampyre* and *Mardukite* and early *Systemology* materials to new and greater heights than previously achieved.

For many, this present *Vampyre's Handbook* has served as a pivotal turning point of realization toward reaching a true understanding of the essence behind the Great Work.

I hope you enjoy the journey!

—NABU "Zeper" Joshua Free
In the Dark Folds of Winter 2019-2020

BOOK I

HISTORY & FOLKLORE

M - O

—∧Ѵ∧—

MOROII AD VITAM PARAMUS

To Evolve – To Become – To Protect

0. VAMPS, WERES AND THE LIVING UNDEAD
—THE DARKEST SIDE OF NIGHT—

Vampires have a very unique place in human consciousness. Understanding how it get there requires visits to old dusty libraries and days spent with even dustier volumes. *History*, by definition, requires "writing." Everything else archeologists discover are subject to interpretation—usually reliant on the same aforementioned "writings.

Tracing Vampires through history is not difficult. There are key periods of time when, for some reason, Vampires are just *everywhere.* This section of *The Vampyre's Bible* will inform the reader on this—the reader presumably being a Vampyre or a "fledgling" *BabyBat* on their way to mastering the art of Vampyric energy transformation.

Using writings from various periods, the progressive evolution of *Legendary Vampires* and *Living Vampyres* today, it is actually quite clear. From central Europe, the "Traditional Vampire" is described in magical lore and folklore as the *upyr*, from the Latinized "*uampire.*" Later usage by Germanic languages included a "V" – *vapir* and *vampyr*. After this point, the letter "V" even by itself, starts representing Vampires in consciousness, e.g. ^V^, etc.

Darksider genes, diseases and conditions appear to connect traditional *Vampyric* origins in Mesopotamia and Egypt. This very rare sequence of conditions appears more often among "strict" bloodlines, citizens of the court, "blue-blood" royalty and even a few nomadic "gypsy" groups that spread across Europe and Eurasia.

Heightened *psychic* or *psionic* sensitivity and an elevated energetic metabolism requires certain individuals to channel and process significantly higher levels magnitudes and frequencies of energy than what is considered "normal" for the "human" condition. *Energy Vampyres* are naturally "wired" to maintain a balance in the flow of the Universe, *feeding* on *Etheric* energies and transforming with innate "photosynthesis."

Anemic porphyria is a very common blood condition among living Undead. *Porphyria* is the Greek word for "purple." The disease is named for the color often found in urine and feces. Common symptoms include: visual and auditory hallucinations, seizures, and finally, the classic acute light/sunlight sensitivity of the skin and eyes. *Anemic porphyria* can remain indefinitely dormant in the blood system until activated by some triggering condition—whatever that may be. Among general populations today, 1 in 200,000 people (5 *ppm*) have this condition. Modern medicine treats this with *heme injections*, but in prior times, self-medication might have included drinking blood. *Heme* can be absorbed into the bloodstream through the stomach lining.

Pellagra is a "wasting" *darksider disease.* The earliest symptom is hypersensitivity to sunlight. Then, as brain neurons degenerate internally, erratic behavior results, including dementia, insomnia, mood swings and violent outbursts. This condition is often triggered by niacin and *tryptophan* deficiencies from rich diets or overdependent corn diets. *Werewolves*, another *Creature of Night*, do not generally share the same sensitivity to sunlight that occur with *Vampyric* conditions.

As everyone subconsciously appears to be preparing for anyway, we might expect a widespread *rabies*-like virus epidemic of global proportions. It is, perhaps: as yet to be uncovered; is currently being engineered; or is already sitting on a shelf somewhere just waiting to leak out. Unlike genetically carried conditions, this externally introduced agent will interact with and affect each person differently based on heredity, willpower and intelligence. *Rabies* changes physical appearance, personality and behavior. The inevitable final result is death.

The types of animals that usually transmit *rabies* are not likely to interact with humans unless they *do* carry some kind of disease. Wolves (*canines*) and bats have an affinity for transmitting this disease if they are carriers. In fact, significant *Werewolf* activity during the Middle Ages is attributed to rabid bites from wolves and wolf-dog hybrids.

When infected humans degenerate far enough, the virus survives by instilling an instinct to spread the disease. The most common incidents involve feral outbursts of—you guessed it—*biting.* These *Creatures of the Night* often naturally develop "fangs" for biting to transmit blood-borne disease.

Most *Darksider* diseases and conditions appear to be genetic or passed on through personal fluids like blood, saliva, semen, etc, - all of which carry high concentrations of genetic material. Connections between *rabies* and Undead like *Zombies, Lycans* and *Vampyres* is so significant that an entire medical volume could be written on that subject alone.

Many modern organizations and authoritarian "secret societies" exist pertaining to the mysteries of the *Night.* Significant energy is wasted by these groups in their ongoing debates which run rampant about bloodlines, legitimacy of certain lineages and Legacies, etc. Most have adopted a standard that original *Vampyrism* is a product of *Dragon Blood.* This comes from progeny not born of "Adamu" (Adam). We read of a race of Watchers or *OverSeers* in ancient texts and even the Yezidi of Mesopotamia are an example of this.

A prestigious society, known as the *Dragon Court* (now closed due to the death of its founder, *Nicholas de Vere*), traces one bloodline or *Legacy* to the Scythians, original Aryan Overlords and Sum-Aryans. Evidence shows the ancient Mesopotamian vampyric lore of Lilith connecting directly with the Romanian (*Transylvanian*) region. Clay tablets and human remains were found in a fire pit dating back to the proto-Sumerian *Eridu* period c.5500 B.C.—the time of the *Anunnaki*, in which the name of one of them (*Enki*) appears on these "*Tartaria*" tablets.

"The descendents of these early vampires were the sacred Ubaid race who, one millennium later, settled Mesopotamia and founded the Anunnaki religion of the Sumerians in 3500 B.C. Their Transylvanian ancestors were the Anunnaki gods themselves..."

—Nicholas de Vere

Significance of *Blood* becomes more apparent throughout the lore given in the *Vampyre's Bible*, but with Our tradition (*Moroii ad Vitam*) the *Blood* is primarily only symbolic. Other secret fraternal groups, councils and grove nests engage in physical *Sanguine Starfyre Rituals*. The purity of an Elder's *Blood* is celebrated and then shared. Some, of course, believe heightened *Starfyre* power can be distributed to a congregation by blood.

Christ famously performed what is known as the "Gnostic Mass" during the Last Supper. It comes complete with a Starfyre transference (which they call the "Holy Spirit") using blood symbolism. Physical *Blood* is not necessary and is in some ways limiting. Christ was an Ascended Master, so he was able to tap the actual energy within the *Blood* and share it by direct contact. "Laying on of hands" is something that will be addressed further in *Book III: Feeding*.

—LYCANS & WEREWOLVES—

Werewolves and Vampires appear together quite often in myth, stories, and among real modern-day populations. In ancient times and all throughout the Dark Ages, very little distinction is made between the "*vampyres*" "*werewolves*" and "*witches.*" The same name can apply to all three, such as with the case of the V*rykolokas* of Europe. Russian lore states that if a witch mates with a *demon* or Werewolf, then the resulting child will be a Vampyre.

Prejudice and biases between living *Vampyres* and *Werewolves* appears to be learned behavior and not genetic programming.

Racial distinction here is not a rule; it's tradition. Hostility and discord is more prominent now than in ancient times. Modern traditions and occult practices around the world have become an elitist means for mental masturbation by those who would do well to stay far away from these mysteries.

For purposes of Our tradition presented here – the *Moroii ad Vitam Paramus* – a preferred and proper name for these *Children of the Night* is "*Lycan*." They are technically not Undead. However, they do share many vampyric attributes, including an alignment to the moon with their natural energetic biorhythms synchronized with lunar cycles. Significant class distinctions between the two are not just another cultural stereotype. *Lycans* are viewed as a subservient class to the *Vampyre*. In fact, Wolves are the Vampyre's animal familiar, once respectfully guarding them and their territory by day.

Vampyres and Lycans are channels for energetic transformation on some level—meaning the exchange, transference or alchemy of the Universal Stream. As *Creatures of Night* go: *Vampyres* present themselves with aristocratic etiquette; Werewolves are typically more wild, rough-housing and often more interested in physical and athletic activities.

"*Newbies*" *or fledglings* are referred to as "*pups*" (for Wolves) or "*BabyBats*" (for *Vampyres*). This nickname "hazing" continues until they master Self-control of innate monster-like urges. Responsibility for this discipline falls on the pack or clan (for wolves), and a family-coven or personal *Maker* (for Vamps).

"*Lycans*" are the Werewolves most commonly associated with *Vampyre* culture. These are not the same as tribal shamanic priests or indigenous *shapeshifters*. It is, however, true that the wolf carries a very ancient tradition of warriors throughout Europe—including *berserkers*—who transform (or revert) into primitive animal states. Such "warriors" are thought to be possessed with the spirits of wolves or bears. Lycans receive public attention in central Europe around the same time that accounts of vampyrism rise. *European "Lycans"* appear first on public record in the 1500's when Church records start classifying *Vampyres*, *Werewolves* and *Witches* all synonymously as *"of the Devil"*—requiring excommunication and extermination.

That Werewolves would turn into Vampires after death was not an uncommon belief in medieval times. Lore of a hybrid *Were-Vamp* also appears. But, hysteria caused suspicious humans to focus on each other rather than actual Vampyres and Werewolves. Not unlike the Salem Witch Trials.

Different wolf-traditions present unique beliefs concerning their origins. Those observing traditional Romanian/Etruscan lore hold that they are descendents of *Lupercus*, an ancient *transhuman* entity depicted as a wolf. Another tradition, from Greece, refers to *King Lycaon* who attempts to murder *Jupiter* (*Zeus, Marduk, Enlil*) while He is on earth (disguised as a wayfarer). He is cursed with *Lycanthropy*—a condition for him—and so are his generations. Many werewolves today are not *shapeshifters*. They still carry an instinct to *shift* into *wolf-mode*. This primal, feral and predatory state demonstrates the wild nature of instinct remaining from distant genetic memory.

1. MESOPOTAMIAN VAMPYRISM – (c. 4000 BC)
LILITH : THE MOTHER OF VAMPYRES

Lilith – the ultimate archetypal prototype of the *Vampyre* that lurks in your subconscious. She is the original *Mistress of the Dark, Queen of the Night*, the First Vampyre and Mother of All Vampyres. She is also sometimes regarded as Goddess of Death, Disease and Disaster in traditions outside of her personal cult. Records of her first appear among ancient Sumerians, graphically depicted with owls, serpent-snakes and dragons.

To the prehistoric *Cult of Lilith*—her own *Children of the Night*—she is the Mother Goddess, the Isis, the Kali, the Inanna-Ishtar

—a supreme corporeal representation of Divine feminine energy in the Universe. Her cult predates *all* known religions. Her legacy survives in Babylon and the Babylonian influence on early Semitic Judaism and Hebrew Mythology, particularly during the "Exile."

Mesopotamian traditions of ancient Sumer and Babylon were rooted in pragmatism and civic functionality. Later newer Semitic beliefs spread like wildfire. They were more superstitious, even when borrowing lore directly from Babylonians. Consider, for example, the Talmud of the Jews—written by them in Babylon during the "Exile."

Original lore and traditions preserved in ancient Babylon are borrowed from, then bastardized and finally replaced by the Hebrew paradigm. In some pre-Christian versions, Lilith becomes "Adam's" first wife. According to ancient Rabbinical lore, it is Lilith who is banished from *Eden* (E.DIN in Sumerian) and returns later as the serpent-snake (dragon). Early religious traditions blamed her or her *Vampyric* spawn—the *Lilu* (called *Alu* in Hebrew)—for deaths of babies, impotency in males, infidelity and infertility among couples, and yes, believe it or not, even nocturnal emissions.

Original lore of the *Alu* describe physical *Children of Lilith*. Later religious traditions treat them as "etheric spirits" that are restricted to use animated human corpses as a means of interacting with this world,. As Vampyres, their qualities include draining men of their "vital" energies and/or feeding on *Blood*. Rabbinical lore lists Lilith as Queen of the *Succubi*, a type of Undead female representing a *Vampyre* far better than later Christian interpretations of non-corporeal "demons."

Most dream-encounters with Vampires are sexual in nature. Sexual activity *can* "raise" or heighten personal energy levels by changing chemistry of the Blood. Removing blockages and replacing static energy improves the natural flow. This is _not_ the only way to clear personal energy pathways. In fact, Sexual activity, if misaligned, can be more psychically damaging.

Humans satisfied their confused sexual curiosities throughout the Dark Ages with *Demonologie*. This field of "study" exclusively began with sexually charged *Vampyric* beings—classified as *Incubus* and *Succubi*. These descendents of Lilith animated dead bodies to inhabit for sexual purposes. They drained vital energies from men and impregnated women.

Religious traditions of later cultures develop *Demonologie* further with *changelings, alien babies* and even *virgin births*—such as with Jesus Christ and Myrddin (the historical Merlyn) born of a virgin by an ethereal entity. Lilith's lore remained widely known among general populations until around the 17ᵗʰ century. Today, many people are very surprised to learn about this "occult" information.

Historical researches suggest that Lilith's cultists and followers are among the first detractors from the *"Realm"*—meaning original "rebels" within society or the world of Lights. Considered *outsiders* in ancient Mesopotamian tradition, *Vampyres, Lycans* and *Witches* are all permanently labeled *"Wanderers of the Night"*—those beyond the Realm. To rival a cultist's mystical powers or malignant witches operating outside the system (outside the Realm), ancient Sumerians and Babylonians developed elaborate counter-efforts, such as the *Maqlu Ritual*.

Sumerian *Utukku* and Babylonian *Edimmu* (*Alu*) are described on the cuneiform *Surpu* tablet series as "suckers of blood and eaters of flesh." The name *Edimmu* translates to mean "what is removed"—literally "that which, taken away"—indicating a person who died "before their time." Those who had violent deaths, died in the desert or were turned away from the *House of Death*, become the *Edimmu*, wandering the wastelands for an eternal Existence. The immortal part—the ascended, *etheric,* "godhead," "shade" or *egregore* part—of Lilith is kept alive by those still honoring this tradition, including cults of Her own *Children of the Night*, for at least 6,000 years unbroken.

—CAIN'S LEGACY : THE CHILDREN OF NOD—

Cuneiform tablets from Mesopotamia—written thousands of years before Judaism and Christianity—reveal our most ancient accounts of hybrid humans cohabiting earth alongside "gods." These "gods" engineered humanity and seeded civic systems for their civilization.

A standing rule kept the *Anunnaki* from procreating (mixing any additional genetics) with the humans (*adamu*). Such an act represented bestiality, inconceivable within the "*Realm.*" As a safety precaution, the engineered race of workers were unable to procreate, lest their numbers overpower the *Anunnaki*. So, when Adamu and a hybrid female, Ti.Amat ("*Mother of All Life*"), proved unable to procreate, they are brought to *Eridu* and given forbidden additional DNA "life essence" from *Enki*, *Adamu* and *Anunnaki* 'goddess' *Ninmah*. This upgrade made reproduction possible.

Adapa ("*Found*") and TiTi ("*Life*") are the first born with an ability to procreate. Adapa is "human," but more than this he is a direct descendent (with bioengineering) of *Enki*, son of *Anu*, whose progeny on earth are always shown as "men of renown" or more than human." Enki's own heir son—Marduk —established Babylon: "*The Gateway of the Gods.*"

Adapa and TiTi are the parents of KA.IN (*Cain*)—"Father of Vampyres" in later traditions. The *Talmud* and *Genesis* regard Cain's bloodline as separate from the rest of humanity. The scripture speaks of "enmity" between his race and the progeny of Adam. Thereby, a separate *Blood Legacy* is credited to Lilith and Cain. Eventually the Church removed all references to this from their own sanctioned scriptures.

After killing his brother "*Abael*," Cain is exiled from *Eden* (E.D-IN or *Mesopotamia*). He then goes west to the Lands of "Nod"— literally, the region of "*Wanderers*" existing outside of the Realm. Standard scriptures reveal that in the "Land of Nod" he is united with his cousin, Lilith. Although Lilith bore off-spring with others, It is Cain's Legacy with Her that takes priority in modern matters of the *Living Vampyre* tradition.

"Children of Nod" are born into an eternal covenant as *Children of Night*—*"Nodites,"* the *Eternal Wanderers*. These *Wanderers of the Night* are often later reclassified throughout history as demons, dark fallen angels, the damned, elves and fairy fey, dragons, the light or white or "fair" people, and as of recently, extra-terrestrial aliens. For the purposes of this current study, *We* will consider all of these to be referring to the same thing.

2. EGYPTIAN VAMPYRISM – (c. 3500 BC)

Egyptian Vampyrism descended from a prehistoric Ur-cult of Lilith in Mesopotamia. In spite of this, Egyptian symbolism—the *ankh, scarab* beetle, *winged discs and so forth*—are the most often used cultural connections for Traditional Vampyrism today—also called "TradVamp." There is good reason for this—and yet... the one thing we do <u>not</u> actually find within the Egyptian paradigm: animated "Undead."

Egypt—as a collective civilization and religious culture—is made up of citizens that are, themselves, true *Vampyres*. Their mystical system offers both the most elaborate and complete preparations of the dead, but more importantly, interactions after *Death*. These teachings also describe a "star" (*astral*) source of humanity and all Existence, and that a "Gate" to a *Heaven for* "gods" connects this *Otherworld*.

Mummification is a very unique tradition rooted in a belief that *Etheric Bodies* can be aided in the *Otherworld* by preserving the physical form after *First Death*. The body itself is actually buried with an *Ankh*, specific *scarab amulets*, and texts from the *"Book of Dead."* Each of these are meant to provide specific assistance to the True "I" or Self in the afterlife.

Precision of Egyptian burial practices eliminated any concern of animated corpses or walking Undead. Physical bodies are systematically deconstructed during the mummification process in such a way that a body does not come back to this life. Not only do the *dead stay dead*, Egyptians were masters in the Vampyric ability to survive *First Death* with an Identity in tact.

3. GREEK VAMPYRISM – (c. 1000 BC)
LAMIA OF LILITH AND THE VRYKOLOKAS

Traditions drawn from lore of Lilith and her children—the *Lilu* —migrated from *Mesopotamia* to *Greece* by way of *Libya,* or more specifically: the first *Libyan Vampyre Queen, Lamia.* Lilith and Lamia both share a taste for child-eating and symbolic association with serpent-snakes, according to their lore.

Greek historian Diodorus writes of her distorted features: a penis hidden by the snakeskin covering most of her body; and the furry paws of a cat. Lilith is also considered to have been covered in hair and clearly "hermaphroditic"—each self-produces a horde of "demon-spawn" named after their maker. Lamia is cat-like (with abilities to even transform into a cat), and Lilith is often depicted flanked by a lioness on each side.

Eventually the name Lamia (and her "Lamos" hordes, plural) is equated with the *succubus.* In this form, the Lamia is able to reanimate corpses to interact with the material world and feed off living humans. The Greeks eventually discovered the solution to their Undead problem: *proper burial*—something the Egyptians already mastered thousands of years earlier.

The Greeks did not believe that all Undead were necessarily evil or malignant. Christianity impressed that belief later on. Greek lore does however refer to reanimated Undead blood-drinkers with an potential to harm humans. And—activity of this nature was observed to increase during the full moon.

While not restricted to a strict nocturnal existence, Vrykolokas prefer to sleep in tombs during the day and be "*wanderers*" at night. Such lore contributes to the first verifiable connection made specifically between Vampyres and Werewolves. From this point on, they often appear together in lore, even by the same name, names related to the Slavic word for "*wolf*."

Adriatic – *Vrykolokas*	Albanian – *Vurvalak*
Balkan – *Volkodlak*	Bulgarian – *Volkudlak*
Crete – *Kathakanas*	Serbian – *Vukodlak*
Greece – *Vrukokalas, Vrykolaka*	Turkish – *Vurkolak*

4. CELTIC VAMPYRISM – (c. 1000 BC)
THE SIDHE AND EUROPEAN SAMPIRO

Celtic Vampyres reflect something between a fairy and a ancestral spirit. The *Sidhe*, pronounced "*shee*,"are associated with lore of *Elves, Dragon Blood* and *Faerie Folk.* They could drink blood, drain vital energies (*Starfyre*), use hypnotic powers, not to mention expertise in enchantment and glamour. Another type of Celtic Vampyre—*Gwrach y Rhibyn*—are evil crones that drink the blood of innocents. They are described in lore as "a fairy, a warning and a vampire" all at once.

The Sidhe are *People of the Mounds*, dead ancestral spirits residing in burial sites and tombs. They may be hidden in trees, woodland forests and are commonly encountered at crossroads. There are specific types, like the *Leanan Sidhe* ("LeAnn shee"), the Celtic Sidhe Vampires of love and death. A Celtic *succubus*, she is a "*fairy-lover*" to men. She also appears at crossroads and will attack travelers, leaving them on the side of the road, drained of vital energy.

According to ancient Celtic Druidic lore, true *SidheVamps* are emanations (or descendents) of the ancient Mother Goddess—*Druantia.* She is "Lady of the Oaks," "Queen of the Druids," and progenitor of a Celtic Vampire legacy among the fey. As time passed, darker *Vampyric* elements of fairy lore were stripped down to become fluffier child-friendly *Disney*-style bedtime story versions.

A different shambling *Darksider* appears in lore from Albanian tradition—called the *Zampyro*. Similar accounts can be found throughout Europe and Celtic countries under various names. It is most identifiable by the "pucker kissing sounds" it makes in anticipation for a *Feed*—meaning, of course: drinking *Blood*. European *Sampiro* do not always kill its victims, preferring to leave them physically drained and energetically discarded—similar to what the *Leanan Sidhe* does.

Sampiro's can sometimes be seen lurking in shadows around residences or as faces peering into windows late at night. During Ottoman Empire influx, local vampire lore is eventually used as racial prejudice propaganda. Rumors were spread that "anyone born to Turkish parents is a vampire." This politics did not restrict itself to Turks. As intolerant religious ideals gained strength, many believed that anyone leading a life deviant from the norm could possibly rise from their tombs, returning to the land of the living as a Vampyric Undead being.

European Vampyre lore from this era introduces the wooden stake as a primary means of giving a Vampire *"True Death."* This must be attempted only when they are sleeping—and with only one chance. If you fail, the Vampire awakens. Different traditions in Europe favored specific wood for stakes: in Hungarian and Romanian regions, mountain ash or rowan; in Russia, the oak or ash; and in Celtic traditions, mystical applications of Death energy often involved the Yew tree.

5. ROMAN VAMPYRISM – (c. 50 BC)
THE LAMIA AND THE STRIX

Greek lore of Lilith's *Lamia/Lamos* is found in Roman mythology as the *Strix*—specifically the *"owl"* that is associated with

Lilith. These nocturnal, bird-like, blood drinking, flesh-eaters were named *Strix* after the Greek word for "owl." The name for this creature remained in Roman-Latin vocabulary.

Any type of encounter or interaction with a *Strix*—its appearance or even the sound of its call—indicates death is near. Other than the *serpent-dragon* and *wolf*, it is the *owl* that stands apart as a significant totem or power animal for Vampires throughout history—even more than the bat. This tradition sparked semantics for "night owl"—a way of telling someone they act like a Vampire. One famous group of Vampyres did derive their name from the *Strix*—The *Strega* and *Strigoi*.

6. TRADITIONAL VAMPYRISM – (up to 1816)
ITALIAN STREGA AND ROMANIAN STRIGOI

"TradVamp" in Europe emerges in Rome, Romany/Romania, Etruscan/Tuscany and Milan regions of Italy. "*Strega*" is an Italian name for "*Gypsy*" witch. They called themselves *Romani*. Some have entertained that gypsies are named for their origins in *Egypt*. It has since been determined that many were actually also from India, the Middle East and Mediterranean.

During this period of history, lore regarding the traditional *Creatures of Night* emerges—typically types conjured to mind (before the days of *Twilight* and *True Blood*...anyway). FamTrad division becomes apparent between "*Strega*" shamanic wolf-clans and aristocratic "*Strigoi*" priests—meaning very literally between the *Lycans* of Italy and *Strigoi Vampyres* of Romania. The word *Strig* is a Romanian equivalent to Italian "*Strega*"—both of which are derived from evolving lore of the legendary Mediterranean *Strix Vampyre*.

Most contemporary *Werewolf* lore is derived from shamanic wolf clans—*Lycans* that practice *Old Ways* and folk magic commonly revived in the "New Age" today. The word "*Strego*" means "to enchant, glamour, or fascinate." As shamans, their practices incorporate many natural tools, reflecting a primitive nature-oriented tradition. In contrast: *Vampyres*, prefer elaborate ceremonies and also to conduct their ritual dramatics in tombs, crypts and/or highly decorated chambers.

According to wolf-cults and their priests, called the Luperci. Lycans are the descendents of (or in religious service to) *Lupercus*, the emanation of ALL (*"God"*) represented in wolf form. The primary Lycan holiday is *Lupercalia*, Festival of Lupercus, on the eve of February 2nd. This timing coincides with the Celtic *Imbolc* and Christian *Candlemas festivals*. Modern Lycan lore is obscure due to European semantics used during the Dark Ages, often referring to *witches, vampires* and *werewolves* with the same word.

Strigoi are not just any *Vampyres*. They are the archetype of Transylvanian Vamps—the Cursed Ones, the Damned. They are the ones never finding rest in material death and eternally wander the earth unsatisfied. They *Feed* on mortals without reservation or respect and are the base-model of 20th century "vampires"—starting with *Dracula*.

Anne Rice's portrayals in the "*Vampire Chronicles*" represent some *Strigoi* elements. *Strigoi* are directly referenced in *Vampire Academy* as "a destructive anarchical malignant sect of vampires, opposite benevolent mainstreaming *Moroii*." In addition to *Vampire Academy*, ethical mainstreaming vampirism (representative of *Moroii ad Vitam* ideals) are depicted in *Vampire Diaries, Hemlock Grove, True Blood, Twilight* and *Daybreakers*.

By Church standards, the *Strigoi* are treated as victims of a religious disease. Certain conditions seem to carry it: a seventh same sex child in a family; to lead a life of sin; to not attend church services or receive the Sacraments; to die without being married; to have participated in Dark Arts; to have performed "unnatural" acts; sexual deviation; to be executed for perjury; being cursed by a witch; and suicide—all of which lead to a "troubled soul" for the deceased.

Strigoi emphasize power of Blood and recognize Bloodlines as FamTrad Legacies. They encourage "*Sanguine*" vampyrism and reflect the usual traits: pale skin, blood drinking, inhabiting tombs and haunting crypts. Ancestors remain a significant part of their religious traditions—Undead Elders called *Strigoii Morte*. *Starfyre* energy continues to be exchanged (or passed down) within the family Legacy even after *First Death*, as a means for perfecting the *etheric body*.

Now we come to lore of the famous Vlad III, Vlad Tepes, Vlad the Impaler—the one called Vlad III Dracula, meaning: *Son of Vlad II Drakul*. A prince of southern Romania is celebrated as a national hero and not as a "vampire." Although Vlad is often considered some character basis for Bram Stoker's famous work, aside from some names and locations, there is actually very little similarity connecting the two. There is also nothing in lore or history connecting Vlad specifically with any true *Vampyric* or *Strigoi* religious traditions.

One of the first sanctioned *Vampire Hunters* in history is none other than his father, Vlad II Drakul. He is instated as a member of the Order of the Dragon, and while that might sound cool and esoteric, it is a religious fraternity similar to the Knights Templar during the Crusades. Their primary goal: to protect the integrity of Christianity from the Muslim Turks—which they called "vampires."

Vampire Hunters, Holy Orders of the Church and Dragonslayer Knight factions all suddenly appear in the Realm as if from nowhere during the Dark Ages, a time of significant vampire activity. Lore of crosses carried as amulets, wooden stakes, garlic necklaces and holy water all develop during this time.

It is curious that mundane outsiders would have such a problem with Vampyre culture. By *Moroi* standards, Christianity is simply another tradition that, like Vampyrism, focuses on an *Undead* deity—one containing elements of both *Living Vampyre* and *Living Zombie* traditions. Consider the "*Last Supper*" where their deity upgraded his human followers by exchanging power through transhuman *Blood*. This is exactly the same as the esoteric tradition of *Sanguine Starfyre* practices.

Modern use of the word "*Strigoi*" is <u>not</u> restricted to any one FamTrad Legacy. It is widely used; made popular by practitioners and members of a particular contemporary group: *Ordo Strigoi Vii*—just one tradition out of many *Living Vampyre* Legacies emerging from the Underworld.

—ORDO MOROII AD VITAM PARAMUS—

In the description of the *Strigoi*, a second tradition or path is mentioned: the *Moroii* (a name derived from *mora*, meaning *nightmare*). In all of history and traditional lore, the *Moroii* are the only true "*Living Vampyres*"—*Vampyres* that have not yet experienced *First Death*. They are not *Undead*—they are *Living Undead*—and it is from the hereditary perspective (paradigm) of <u>this tradition</u> that the current author has presented "*The Moroi Book of V: Vampyre's Bible*" to the public for the first time.

Moroii dedicate their "mortal" lives to mystical, magical and *Vampyric* pursuits, called "Energy Work." Using innate and practiced skills, a *Moroi* cultivates energies and processes them inward to enhance their *Etheric Body* for their *Ascension*.

The *Etheric Body* is the part that survives *First Death*, but it must first be prepared as a proper vehicle to achieve true *Ascension*. Your total conscious *Ascension* is <u>not</u> imminent—it is not guaranteed after *First Death*. Many "religions" fool their followers into thinking so, as to reinforce artificial dogmas.

Thousands of years ago, the Egyptians knew and mastered the science of *Life After First Death* as they understood it within their own paradigm. True *Ascension* allows you to retain your consciousness intact and experience a new *Self-directed* Existence after this lifetime. The alternative is to be recycled back into this world, usually forgetting all you have learned—or even become a true Undead after *First Death*, eternally "*wandering*" this plane of existence.

> <u>MOROI</u> : *n.* [*Romanian*] a vampyre with a conscience, known for feeding respectfully; a person possessing magic and vampyric affinity for energy work prior to *First Death*; alt. "*Moroii*" plural or collective ("*the* Moroii").

Sanguine-aligned *Moroii* may *Feed* on Blood, using willing donors who are rewarded or paid for their services. *Moroii* can also eat human food, but they are highly selective about their diet. They tend to require more fluids for nourishment rather than heavy "corporeal" foods and often use supplements to treat anemia and other Darksider diseases. It is very uncommon to find a full-blooded *Moroi*, and *Dhampir Moroii* are born from one Human parent and one carrying a *Vampyre* gene.

"Psi-Vamp" *Moroii*, with an affinity for energy manipulation, will learn how to *Feed* using *Starfyre* energy. The *Sanguine Vampyre* does the same, but *Starfyre* concentration and purity is much more highly refined when only the precise essence has been extracted. Psi-Vamps use this energy on the astral plane, for *Etheric* transference and other *Starfyre* work.

As a spiritual tradition, *Moroii* lore refers to the *Grigori.* an ancient race of *Watchers*—metaphorically, stars and planetary bodies that watch over us. The *Watchers* appear in the lore of all ancient cultures. They have specific names in each language, but representing the Planets every time.

For *Moroii*, the *Grigori* give new *Life*, the star-power "magic" of *Blood*—and a map to follow them *home*. Of this map: half is hidden in Ancient Mesopotamian on cuneiform tablet writings, and the other half was revealed in prehistoric Egypt. And, to make it simple for modern *Moroii*, the knowledge of <u>both</u> come by way of a Book of the Dead from each culture. [Those who, in preparation, have worked through the *Mardukite Babylonian*

Ladder of Lights as a means to directly reach their *Etheric Body*, just smacked their head and said: "Ohhhhhh, now I get it."]

Therefore, in conjunction with previous work by the present author, "*Vampyre*" cycle of material represents the final "*level*" of *Outer Circle* teachings that bridge a *Seeker* to higher Grades of work as an extension of the modern *Mardukite Zuism* movement. Understanding comes quickest when preliminary *Light Work* from the "Mardukite Core" is performed, but it is not a prerequisite to understanding the <u>*Moroii ad Vitam*</u> ("*Living Vampyres of Life*") tradition: and the "grade" of NexGen Systemology bridged to, from within *this* book.

7. VICTORIAN VAMPYRISM : 1816–1897
LORD BYRON'S "VAMPYRE"

By the end of Medieval times, Vampires had all but become extinct in society. FamTracs of Eurasia simply went underground and were forgotten. This began an Underworld social network of cultural exchanges independent of *humanity*. The legends evolved into Victorian Vampyrism, where they were welcomed into a new fiction genre: *Gothic Horror*.

On the 16th of June 1816, at Lake Geneva, Switzerland, Lord Byron began reading to a small group of his intellectual friends from a book called *Fantasmagoria*. Attendance included John Polidori and Mary Shelley (who receives inspiration for her masterpiece *Frankenstein* on this same evening.)

The Vampyre by John Polidori appeared in the April edition of *New Monthly Magazine*, in 1819. Two decades later '*Penny Dreadfuls*' start to appear, pulp fiction for the price of one penny. An example of this being *Varney the Vampire -or- Feast of Blood* (1845-1847) featuring the <u>first</u> Vampire to shape-shift into a bat. Even the origins of *Sweeny Todd* may be found among the original '*Penny Dreadfuls.*'

John Polidori's *Vampyre*, inspired by an outline from Lord Byron, is the first male "Vamp" to demonstrate charisma, charm and a seductive use of sexual prowess. This classic novella initiates a shift in public attitude toward Vampires. *Vampyric* portrayals move away from demonic monsters depicted by the church and evolve into traditional "aristocratic" elitist family-styles that we often associate with them today.

—"CARMILLA" : THE VAMPRESS—

In 1872, 26 years before *Dracula*, a magazine called *The Dark Blue* published a Gothic novella by Sheridan le Fanu, titled: *Carmilla*. Named for its main character, *Carmilla* is a true Vamp-Vampress presented as a sexually alluring woman that seeks the love and affection of mortal human young lady, Laura. As a proper "Lady"—and a Christian—Laura does not return Carmilla's sexual advances; finding them repulsive and sinful. Yet, Carmilla becomes her romantic stalker, visiting each night, eventually "leaving the girl wasting dangerously away."

Camarilla is never actually addressed as a *vampire*. But then, that word is not ever used to describe the *upyr* family of the fictional "Hemlock Grove" saga either. However, in *Camarilla*, there numerous key stereotypes cannot be overlooked: sleeping during the day; never needing to eat; bi-polar personality; spending nights out; hating the sound of Christian hymns; and in the end, she is eventually staked and decapitated.

8. AMERICAN VAMPYRE MIGRATION : 1897–1979
BRAM STOKER'S "DRACULA"

The release of *Dracula* on May 26, 1897 marks a turning point bridging the social consciousness of Victorian Vampyrism into the neo-Vamp, modern and eventually pre-Punk roots of the early GothVamp styling.

Bram Stoker, born in Ireland 1847, is most famous for his literary contribution – *Dracula*. Stoker, a member of the *Hermetic Order of the Golden Dawn,* is the <u>first</u> to use the term *"Undead,"* a name that almost became the title of his novel. He dies on April 20, 1912, two decades before *Dracula* debuts on Broadway and film.

Nothing captures the essence of *Dracula* like Stoker's novel. Yet, since then it has been remade, revised, dramatized and bastardized countless times. The basic themes have even undoubtedly influenced countless other creations that do not even incorporate the name *"Dracula."*

9. ESTABLISHMENT OF HOLLYWOOD VAMPYRES
THEDA BARA AND BELA LUGOSI

The world is introduced to the first American *"Queen of the Vamps"* in 1914. Her signature style is a prototype for modern female *"Vamps"* and *"Goths."* Born in Cincinnati, Ohio, actress Theda Bara is the *original* alluring, sexy, seductive, exotic-Hollywood-California "Goth chick prototype" of the early 1900's.

> <u>VAMP</u> : *n.* [*slang*] a *femme fatale*; a woman who uses sexuality (and enchantment) as a weapon to prey upon men.

In *A Fool There Was*, Theda Bara is debuts as a *"Vamp"* that seduces men into ruin before discarding them. Bara is also famous for the line, "Kiss me, fool." The term *"Vamp"* is coined for the first time to promote her work as an actress, appearing in 40 films over five years.

This period marks the public introduction of black Egyptian-like liner-mascara for the eyes. Inspired by Cleopatra, this is the preferred style of Gothic musician Siouxsie Sioux. Russian-born Hollywood make-up artist Helena Rubinstein assisted Bara in highlighting her eyes and contrasting ultra-pale skin. Rubinstein introduces America to "mascara."

It is unanimously agreed that Bela Lugoisi definitively brought Bram Stoker's *Dracula* to life on stage and screen. Born in Hungary, October 20 1882, Lugosi is globally famous for appearing in the Broadway play of *Dracula* starting in 1927 and its 1931 film version by Universal Studios. He is the iconic prototype, "in the flesh," of what the world considers a real "*Vampire.*"

Bela Lugosi appeared in *261* New York Broadway performances before Universal Studios purchases rights in 1931. *Dracula* is the first *vampire* movie made after the silent-film period. Lugosi later appears in sequel films: *Dracula's Daughter* (1936) and *Son of Dracula* (1943). Although many would swear on their life it was Lugosi—it is actually Christopher Lee, decades later, that portraying the first *Dracula* on camera to have *fangs*.

During his lifetime, Bela Lugosi was married five different times. He produced one male heir, *Bela George Lugosi* (born January 5, 1938). As is the epidemic of Hollywood's Undead, Lugosi fell into depression later in life. He used pain medication and morphine to satisfy a growing opiate addiction. Issues erupted when heirs were not given rights/royalties to his work post-mortem. As a result, his son, *Bela George Lugosi*, decided to pursue a legal career. In 1966, the trial *Lugosi vs. Universal Studios* began, resolving over a decade later in 1979. Lugosi won the trial, but Universal won an appeal. George Lugosi is, however, responsible for successfully getting the *California Celebrities Rights Act* passed in 1985.

Bela Lugosi died in 1956 while living in Hollywood's Culver City. He is buried in Holy Cross cemetery there. Then, 23 years later, a "Gothic Rock" band called *Bauhaus* sing of his Legacy, officially ushering in a new era of the modern "*GothVamp.*"

BOOK II

THEORY

&

PRACTICE

M ~ 1

–ΛVΛ–

MOROII AD VITAM PARAMUS

To Evolve – To Become – To Protect

0. PERSONAL DEVELOPMENT

*"All that we have accomplished today
is what we thought and dreamed of yesterday..."*

Vampyric Power comes from *"Mastery of the Self."* Charismatic charm and a powerful persona require complete control of the *Self*. Of all *Creatures of Night*, the *Vampyre* is the only one that makes *Self*-mastery a priority. *Lycans* carry a more wild nature and can barely control their own primitive animals side. And *Zombies*, well... *Zombies* lack all self-control, operating solely on one basic instinct: *to feed*.

Self-mastery is multifaceted: *Self*-control, *Self*-awareness, *Self*-sufficiency and *Self*-reliance. Within and of these things, we discover innate "psionic" abilities that aid in first gaining and then maintaining corporeal and material independence. This helps keep your Awareness focused on *Ascension*.

Glamoury is a byproduct of personal empowerment over the material Realm using willpower—the strength and integrity of WILL. You must give the "I" (or *Self*) freedom to master the physical environment. As master, you gain responsibility for your own survival: personal preservation and the continuation of *Self-determined* Existence after *First Death*.

Corporeal *Self*-mastery is the first step toward *Immortality*. *Moroii* tradition refers to the *Self*—the "One who IS"—as the "_Dragon._" It is the deepest point of the "I" residing in a human shell; the true perspective of the *Eternal Self*—a point of *"godhood,"* the *Dark Flame* within. The *Vampyre* is a master of *energy manipulation*. For this you must learn how energy operates and how it affects the human condition—which is relevant for your conscious experience from a corporeal Human body. For an *Identity* to Exist—to have a state of *Being*—in the Realm, his realm of lights, the corporeal and *Etheric Body* must function together harmoniously as a systematic machine.

Specifically programmed functions form personal energy concentrations (energy centers) of *Starfyre*—called *astyr* in some
traditions; *chakras* in others—where the corporeal and *Etheric
Body* "meet"; are energetically connected. Each *aster* processes
specific energy frequencies. The *astyr* system also emits a field
of *electromagnetic* "waves," known as the *astra* or *aura*.

Contemporary science does recognizes auric fields as a *"biomagnetic"* property of *Life*. This indicates that maintaining
personal control of <u>thought</u>, <u>emotion</u>, and <u>effort</u> is critical.
These conditions cause personal *neurological* and *biochemical*
reactions in the brain and body. Reactions immediately affect
your energy frequencies and intensities.

To be an *active* creator and engineer of their environment and
reality, *Vampyres* choose to be <u>not</u> *reactive* to others. It is *We*
who inspire the emotions of others. *Moroii* spend their lives
collecting, cycling and condensing the energies they interact
with. Much of this is sent inward to the *Etheric Body*—a Ethereal Et(h)ernal *"subtle body."* This is accelerated by reducing the
personal fragmentation of "reactive programming" (see also:
*The Tablets of Destiny: Using Ancient Wisdom to Unlock Human Po-
tential* and *Crystal Clear* by Joshua Free).

As the *Moroii* feed, refined Universal "vital energy"—called
Starfyre—is consciously directed toward strengthening the
Etheric Body by will and intention. This is the only way one can
be sure to remain intact—and achieve *True Immortality*—after
First Death. And this does not *just happen* automatically.

Effective "energy work"—*True Magic*—is conducted from a specific state of *Awareness*. Rather than b*of* the *"corporeal body,"*
consciousness is transferred to its true perspective and central "point" of view—"I"—Divine Self or *"I of the Dragon"*—the
seat of consciousness often referred to as the "Third Eye."

"I am" is the central point of *Self*. It is exterior to the body, but
for our present purposes, we shall use the *Third Eye* to connect

its "vision" with motor-functions and sensory faculties of the body. Thoughts generated here force an *energetic potential* into existence. When these thoughts are directed with definitive purpose, then we can see its expression of, and communication as, "*Power.*"

Spend time "in phase" as Observer: *observing* your thoughts. How often are you thinking of things you *don't want?* Practice only bringing to the *Mind's Eye* what you want to see reflected in your reality—nothing else. Emotional stimuli and thoughts create chemical reactions that do affect your interactions with the Realm and progress (or lack thereof) on your Path.

A lack of programmed preconceived responses are required for the *Vampyre* to truly trust their own "*self-honest intuition.*" Condition yourself through repetitive experience (reinforced observation) to know that what you are feeling or sensing is intuitive. Simply eliminate all thoughts, emotions and behaviors based on judgments or a *dead memory.*

"Judge not, lest ye be judged..."

1. MODERN VAMPYRISM : DARKSIDER LIFESTYLES

Modern-"Vampire" symbolism is fictionally and functionally quite different than propaganda spread throughout history and folklore. From "demons" and "devils" to beautiful sparkling in sunlight Vampires... suddenly, mainstreaming among "mundanes" has never been easier for the real Living Undead.

In many ways, "Modern Vampyrism" is practically inseparable from "Goth" subculture. There is, of course, a big difference between "interests" in vampyrism and actually "practicing" it. Psi-Vamps and modern *Moroii* practice a living spiritual tradition that they are personally inclined toward naturally. "Goth-Vamps" may carry only the outer "vampire" image to supplement an underground "Gothic" lifestyle. Some writers distinguish between roleplaying-type "<u>*Vampires*</u>" and practiccing "_Vampyres_," with the "spelling." But, these two categories are not mutually exclusive. One can easily lead to the other.

As Psi-Vamps awaken they may feel drawn to certain "Gothic" subcultures or styles as an outer reflection of their inner work. Then there are those who fit the categories but despise the labels attributed to it—"I'm not a '_Goth_'!" or "What do you mean, '_real_ vampires?'" Many basic aspects of the culture— music, makeup, fashion style, books &tc.—all qualify as Goth-Vamp. Of course, not all _Goths_ are _Vampyres_ or even interested in the practice of vampyrism at all. Our purposes here is not an attempt to define _what_ "Gothic" culture is as a whole—nor are we to limit what can be considered "vampyric." As much as the "Indies" and "Punks" hate all things that could carry a stereotype, there simply are certain tendencies and patterns fitting of the _Vampyre_ lifestyle, and these are best distinguished as "_Goth-Vamp_"—as they seem to share much of the same music, clubs and styles. Common elements: artificial fangs; blood; sanguine practices; creepy contact lenses; dark makeup; black clothing; and naturally, avoiding the sun.

Goths and _Vamps_ often follow Vamp-Culture—a plethora of books, movies, television series and music. The _original_ 'sect' of _70's_ "Gothic Punks" responsible for launching the movement were enthralled by a rising Vamp-Culture. Today, with the influx of futurist _CyberVamps_, a movement with a history of unique eclectic eccentricity can now expand indefinitely. It's no secret—Modern Vampyrism is responsible for effectively launching the entire contemporary Gothic movement and all of its influences. This inception primarily occurs in 1979 when the band _Bauhaus_ plays an anthem sparking a new era of _darksider_ post-Punk subculture: "_Bela Lugosi's Dead._"

This new brand of "Dark Punk" did not carry the same vibrant colorful angry antics of its predecessors. These lonely "_Wanderers of the Night_" were more methodical, darkly introspective and reserved—with the more "emotional" ones, even reaching points of total misanthropy, nihilism and apathy.

"The vampyre has long represented the fear of both life and death, representing humanity's darker inclinations and embodying the trepidations of those in fear of losing their lives to the Darkness..."

– Raven Digitalis

As *Darksiders* grew their numbers and exposure, something else dark and forbidding lurked just beneath the surface, waiting to incorporate and alienate GothVamps even further: the *Occult*. A 1980's cultural rise in fantasy, witchcraft, magic, increased public acceptance of alternative lifestyles... basically by just shoving it in their faces over and over again.

Prior to the 21st Century, people were often fired from their jobs if anyone knew they were "pagan" or a "witch." Now, even the U.S. Army uses a pentagram-marked headstone for Wiccan veterans. Regardless of alleged acceptance, Vampyres do not usually go into public, loudly advertising *what* they are —unless, for example, it's a *"Goth" Club*. But even in such an environment, there is likely to be much social ambiguity.

The loudest ones usually do not practice Vampyrism, do not participate in the "Goth" scene are immature and make general nuisances of themselves. Then there are recently *Awakened BabyBat fledglings* with uncontrolled immature recklessness. Responsibility falls upon *Makers* or *Families* to control this.

Many modern *Living Vampyre* traditions treat acquisition of artificial customized fangs as a Coming-of-Age Rite of Passage. *Vampyres* and *Lycans* might use *fangs* to assimilate a different mindset for energy work and ritual theatrics. But, any *"mask"* allows its wearer the ability to take on new forms—to literally *"trans-form."*

Religious and magical ritual dramatics all globally have one key factor in common: persons and/or spaces are temporarily perceived as something other than *ordinary*—being outside or above the ordinary. The individual assumes a *"Godhead,"* then performs symbolic gestures, mirroring a desired transformation in the Realm, even if only to shift perspective/mind-sets.

If literary cues embedded throughout *this book* trigger successful Awakening, the "Vampyre's Bible" *may* serve as a tool of self-initiation into a *Living Vampyre* tradition—"*Moroii ad Vitam.*" According to true Romani-Transylvanian lore, the *Moroii* are *Living Vampyres* residing in a mortal body that have not yet physically experienced *First Death* during this lifetime.

—YOUR "IMAGE" & OTHER ARTIFICIAL PERSONALITIES—

Using image as *Identity* affects interactions with the Realm. You are not changing because you "care what people think"— you are changing because you are aware that projecting a specific masked *Image* is among the initial steps of successful *Glamour*. Some refer to it as the *Outer Glamour*.

> MASQUE (mask), *n.* [see "mask"]
> 1. masquerade.
> 2. unique dramatic entertainment with a mythical theme.

> MAS*QUER*ADE (mas'ke-rad'), *n.* [see "mask"]
> 1. a ball or party at which masks and fancy costumes are worn.
> 2. a) a disguise.
>   b) acting under false pretenses.

> MASK (mask) *n.* [Arabic – *maskharah*]
> 1. a covering to conceal or protect the face.
> 2. anything that conceals or disguises.
> 3. a) a molded likeness of a face.
>   b) a grotesque face representation, worn to amuse or frighten.

Enchantment means <u>charging</u> with intention, using concentration, will and energy. This is an important skill for *Glamoury*. To "*Charge*," *Vampyres* gather and direct energy toward something. This changes our perception, which *biomagnetically* affects the "*Charge*" as you interact with it in the Realm.

Personal Glamoury requires <u>intentional</u> "*Charging*" of a specific appearance. A persona is selected for its conductivity with a chosen energy (*frequency*) type: "*Enchanting*" people, places and objects transforms perceptions. Something seems different than before. Your empowerment affects others.

The key to *vampyric power* is living deliberately. *Every* intentional act *is* a magical one—so make every act intentional. "*Charge*" your makeup with an image, persona or mask you seek to project as an *Outer Glamour*. Most *Vampyres* take their presentation in public and to others very seriously—*We* are always in character.

Black often dominates a *Vampyre's* (or *Goth-Vamp's*) wardrobe. Black clothing enacts a metaphysical ability to absorb and hold ambient energies. The color represents nighttime, unknown mysteries and "*Infinity*" as alpha and omega. *Living Undead* look as if having just crawled out of a coffin or grave—but, with *style*. *We* make *Death* look good.

For environmental and some other forms of public *Feeding*, it can be more beneficial to not attract unnecessary attention. Of course, *Light Feeding* can be achieved through minor public attention. *BabyBat fledglings* who are not able to *Feed* properly will instinctively use *Outer Glamour* and attention to attract energy—sometimes called <u>Attenergy</u> in NexGen NewSpeak.

Glamours are a sequence of enchantments and intentionally charged energy collected around yourself. Biomagnetic vibrations are sensed unconsciously and affect your physical appearance. Energetic interactions occur with contact and attention. People then attach "attributes" to you without even knowing why.

All intentional acts can be enchanted. Accessories you use—makeup, masks, eye liner, eye shadow, goggles, lipstick, nail polish, boots...—all of these can be *Charged* for intentional use. TradVamp styles tend to be monochromatic, dark and contrasting, especially black eyes against true pale white skin.

Vampyres work with *vital energies* of Existence. There is only one kind, but it varies in degree. *We* call this energy *Starfyre*. It is cycled and transformed through "*astyr*," energy centers relatively running down the spine. *Our* system recognizes seven of these *aster*. These *astyr* (*plural*) are also known as "*chakras*" (the Sanskrit word for "*wheel*").

Quality, type and circulation of *Starfyre* through *astyr* produces major *biomagnetic* auric fields around lifeforms, called *astra*. All life has a similar personal energy system; not only the *Moroii*. The energy being passed through the system is the same *Starfyre*, but processed to different degrees at each *aster*.

> HEAD : throat, third eye and crown
> BODY : navel, solar plexus, heart
> BASE : root

It is easiest to classify *astyr* by relative positions in the body: base/root, navel, solar plexus, heart, throat, third eye (*pineal gland*, also "Dragon's Eye") and finally the crown. *Starfyre* transformation is unique to each *aster*, which emit certain frequencies (vibrations) often described or distinguished by color.

> CROWN (violet → ultraviolet...) : top, hair, hoods,
>   accessories, color style.
> THIRD EYE (indigo) : the eyes, style and color of
>   your mask.
> THROAT (blue) : mouth, neck, lipstick, fangs, chokers.
> HEART (green) : chest, pendants and necklaces that
>   hang, symbols.
> SOLAR PLEXUS (yellow) : stomach, upper clothing, capes
>   and cloaks.

NAVEL (orange) : eliminative waste system, belts,
    the waist, some lower clothes.
ROOT (...infrared→red) : reproductive system, under-
    garments, lower clothes, boots.

Charge makeup with intention before and while putting it on your face—creating your mask. Eyes are a *gateway* to our true *Self*, the *Dark Flame* burning within. Eyes allow you to see and direct your energy in the Realm. For *Surface Feeding* and forming energetic links, they are used to direct our attention.

"Energy flows where attention goes."

Many styles of eyeliners, shadows and mascara exist. This is a chance to bring out your uniqueness and individuality. Try *Enchanting* eye-makeup before application. Uses might include an increase in *"psychic vision,"* to *see* a situation more clearly, or to *fascinate* and draw something—or someone—to you.

Liquid eye-liners are superior to liner "pencils." Consider experimenting with color or incorporating dark gray in some instances, rather than strictly black. Spend time perfecting and practicing the application of your *"trademark"* look. With a little effort, you can observe how different highlights and shading fit a purpose, specific lighting, the time of day, etc. Monochromatic and contrasting black-and-white contrasted with small touches of red are classic *vampyric tones.*

Organic hair and nails contain *all* of your genetic DNA coding. PsiVamps see their hands as a "magic wand"—extensions of will and reach. Females generally wear nail polish "properly," while males "rough it up" or leave it incomplete for effect.

2. "DARK MAGIC" : STARFYRE & BLOOD MAGIC

Darker colors attract or hold energy and light colors project and direct it. The mundane world is the "Realm"—"of the Light"—a visibly material world that corporeal bodies interact

with. All magic, but especially *vampyric*, is not of the Realm—
not "*of the Light.*" It originates in the *Other*.

Mortals fear *Darkness* and these powers are not for them. They
came to *Us* from Ancient Ones revered as "*gods.*" Dark Magic is
"*daemonic magic*" as defined by the ancient Greeks to mean:
From the Higher Genius, "I" or *Self.* This has been greatly mis-
understood in the modern "New Age" and alleged "Left-hand
paths." Transhumanist magic puts *Awareness* back into "I am"
—the *Dark Flame or Dragon*—who is the *Et(h)ernal Self*, rather
than binding our energy to the Realm and to the material
body. Cain and Lilith passed this specific knowledge of *Ascension* on for *Us* using various secretive sects around the world.

Moroii tradition predates a post-Zoroastrian dualistic world of
"Gods" versus "Devils." *Moroii* tradition is also not *Satanism*. It
is not *devil-worship*. And further—it should not be confused for
what mundanes call a *Left-Hand Path*—because from our clear
vision in crystalline unity (from the *Dragon's Eye*) we must ask:
"Left of *what*"?

True *Darksider* magic, especially concerning Living Undead, is
not explored in contemporary or mainstream mysticism.
Those with a natural affinity to using innate skills of pulling
and transforming energy receive no support. Others only reinforce a normative belief that it is "wrong" to be what they are.

Living Vampyre and *Undead* (or "*Darksider*") traditions focus
primarily on energy work. A unique personal relationship de-
velops between the experience of the "I" and the energy fields
the "I" interacts with on this plane. This is all "magic" really is
for a *darksider*. The doom-and-gloom projected by mundane
outsiders is actually comforting, calming and fearless to us.

—THE SHADES OF DARKNESS—

EARTH – Black, shadows, underworld, hidden knowledge, descent, protection, grounded, solid firm ground

AIR – Purple, wisdom, power, nightside, psy-energy,
work, the mind, mentalism
FIRE – Red, dusk, comets, lifeforce, sex, essence, passion,
blood darkfyre
WATER – Silver, lunar, twilight, stars, emotional
exchange, astral and etheric connections

We do not approach our work with fear of what is "out there..." There is nothing *out there* that is not *in here*. Stay focused and keep up. You just might unlock the *Moroii ad Vitam* secrets of *Blood*, *Death* and *Immortality*...

Our work is direct and deals specifically with raw energy— *Starfyre*. *We* have no incantations; *We* operate our magic silently and unobserved with no banishing spells. *We* transform energy as needed. Nothing truly "comes in" or "goes away" as everything is of the same *Starfyre*—only differing in degree.

We do not approach the *Portal-to-the-Other* while simultaneously waiting for what might be lurking to bite us right outside our Magic Circle. There is no reason to be a conduit for anything that is *"negative"* or tied to *"fear."* We only bring into *Awareness* what is desired to manifest.

The *Starfyre* spectrum a *Vampyre* taps directly is really one and the same energy making up all of what we call *Spiritual Life* and/or *Awareness* . *Moroii ad Vitam* represent this with the *Egyptian* glyph for "Life" and "Living"—the *Ankh*. Sometimes this cross is depicted with a second bar, representing *"spectrum fragmentation"* as *Starfyre* fields interact and change.

Working with raw energy requires an ability to have an *inter-dimensional* perspective. You cannot *see* power potential in a varied rainbow of degrees with the naked eye. It's there whether we see it or not. Gaining *"Awareness"* of this natural "biomagnetism" allows one to work with it by simply knowing it is there.

Energy must be allowed to flow freely and naturally. Its tides are critical for balance and harmony of all Existence. Much of what people deem as "bad" or "negative" is actually a product of blocked currents and static energy. This will need correction/transformation by someone that is skilled with such abilities. *And, hey, that's you!* —You may also benefit greatly from additional assistance in this "department," which is the subject of the "Grade III—Mardukite Systemology" materials.

Each *aster* filters, cycles and transforms energy uniquely. Different types of programming and perspectives are like a prism. Singular invisible white light is sent into it. The size, shape, purity and total design will transmit or produce different results. In Systemology, distortions in this "crystal of Awareness" are called *"fragmentation."*

Creatures of Night are divided into three primary categories: *Vampyres, Lycans* and *Zombies.* Certain traditions recognize hybrid combinations and other labels altogether. Mystique and personality invoked from each one is quite distinct from the others. These attributes could be plotted on a wheel.

> VAMPYRES : *psychic, immortal, blood, refined, sexuality*
> LYCANS : *shamanic, mortal, rock & roll, unstable, shapeshifting*
> ZOMBIES : *toxic, rotting, brains, dangerous, feed feed feed*

Fascinations and obsessions with certain fictional and musical themes can be indicative of a natural affinity for some type. It may be that current Undead trending between these types reflects the condition of mass consciousness in Our World. Or, maybe for some, this is just good fun. As with all things; it is what you make it.

Living Vampyre tradition is the ONLY known system, or methodology, that legitimately concentrates on the afterlife. *Moroii* collect specific energy during their lifetime and direct it to the *Etheric Body* so it may survive after First Death. *Ascension* doesn't *just* automatically happen. Most people are simply recycled back through a "white hole."

—"THE POWER IS IN THE BLOOD"—

The Fire & Blood Axiom
The *Power* is in the *Blood* and *Blood* is *Starfyre*.

Universal Energy—*Starfyre*—vibrates various degrees and patterns as it interacts with energy and matter across space. These streams produce different particles and wave fields that allow Existence to... well, *Exist*. It is this power of *Life*, the essence of being: *ZU, qi, chi, prana*... And, it is, of course, found in *Blood*, the substance we associate as the vital "fluid of Life."

Clockwork gear systems of the *astyr* pull *Starfyre* in, then process and project it throughout the system and outward. It is personal biofeedback system directed via thought and biomagnetic resonance. These types of emissions are also known as an aura or *astra*. Most *Moroii* find that vital energies of a person can be accessed directly with Psi-Vamp energy work.

Sanguine practices are <u>not</u> necessary for effective results.

Personal bloodshed significantly empowers energy workings or "rituals." But, not much is needed—a single drop of your blood caries the potential energy of an atomic bomb. So don't waste it. As a closed system: in order for the body to make *new blood*, it should be understood that it has to discharge some.

Vampyres "cycle," process and refine potential or *latent* energy. A small amount of blood loss symbolizes personal sacrifice and the circulation of energy. No further benefit is gained in mass bloodletting; a single drop holds all the possible *Starfyre* potential available. More of the same type does not increase power.

Psychologists determined a chemical discharge, from an unconscious emotional release, occurs in the brain simply by the sight of Blood. *Vampyres* use Blood and Breath (and other *vital* fluids: saliva, semen, menstrual blood, vaginal sweat, &tc.) to *Charge* an object or *Enchant* a ritual dramatization.

Blood Magic—even without physical Blood—is not for all purposes. Using personal Lifeforce *does* get results. Like a *Blood* drop being diluted in clear water, power unleashed will spread indiscriminately with the force of an atomic bomb.

"Don't use dynamite where a shovel would suffice."

Mystical qualities and magical correspondence of Blood and *Vampyric Magic*, including: mars; iron; red; black; life; Aries; ram; Leo; lion; tigress; strength; war; sex; lust; passion; leadership; ceremonies; Ereshkigal; willpower; fire; transformation; action; dragons; discord; chaos; destruction; and reformation. *Vampyric Power* comes from the *Awareness* of *Self* and proper flow of energy processing. Energy work requires concentration. One main difference between practices of neo-Goths (Goth-Vamps) versus futurist *CyberVamps*, is emphasis on an ambiance wrought with "*electro-industrial*" themes—some of which lead directly toward *21st Century* energy work, spiritual technology and contemporary Millennial New Thought.

3. THE GLAMOUR

GLAM*OUR (glam'er) *n.* [Scottish – *grammer*, "magic"]
1. seemingly mysterious allure.
2. bewitching charm.

Baobhan Sith are female Vampires of Celtic Mythology, (where "glamoury" semantics originate) that seduce and discard men after first draining their vital essence. Some European lore of *Lycans* and *Vampires* explain they are weakened by silver. Celtic *Fey*, on the other hand, are repelled by *iron* – although the metal does appear in certain "Faerie Dragon" rituals.

Glamoury is an art of Celtic origin. To work the magic of *Glamour*, personal energy and intentional acts are used to *Charge* any *Enchantments*. *Glamour* is classified as Enchantment since it does change some *perceived* facet of reality. In Scotland, *Glamoury* is a form of magical hypnosis or "charm" dating back to the prehistoric *Age of Faerie*.

Children learn seduction early in life. We innately charm those that might help us get desired results. *Glamoury* affects other people on a subconscious level—their perceptions. Below the surface communication (energy exchange) between us and environmental ambient fields is automatic and constant.

Vampyric emphasis on *Glamour* started with *Dracula's* modern neo-Vamp revival. Simply become aware, remain aware, and maintain hyper-vigilance. Watch for visual cues and reactive body language from both you and the energy field that you are communicating with. Seeing people as *fields* can help—particularly once you can detect (or "sense") *gradients* of black and white in these field-flows.

Bio-chemical reactions to external stimuli cause *micro-expressions* and personal energy shifts—which are detectible. Listen and be *aware* of *everything*. Observe yourself. Observe how you project onto who or what you are observing. As an Observer, you are exchanging "information" data energy with them/it. You can even *read* choices they've made and who they decided to be based on their projected "energy wave-signatures."

Vampyres are known for their powerful trademark personalities. Even without knowing why, others may pick up on energies projected from those around them. Strong wills command reality and generate charisma. Charismatic types are generally more successful due to the process of *biomagnetism*, even when they don't understand how it works themselves.

Influential personalities can help make the world a better place—if executed properly by the right people correctly. Persuasion does not always have to be direct. It can even be more effective if you do not present yourself with the stereotypical "salesman" approach. You have to read a person to see what method will work for them and their personality on a case by case individual basis.

Some people only argue and debate as a means of sorting out their own thoughts. Others require practical examples of "empirical evidence" or proof. To these mundane types: If they can't see it; it doesn't exist. Then there are those who cannot accept anything that does not come from their own mind *first*. It *has* to be their idea. Indirect suggestion and "leading" them to the desired conclusion are often required. Consider interactions not as a battle of wills, so much as energetic "fields" reacting to each other. *Glamoury* establishes a link or pathway for energy flow. *Starfyre* can be sent out, amplified by the target, then pulled back to continue cycling and condensing. This is called "harmonic resonance." These skills are important for successful *Feeding*.

As a global caste system, *all* mortals ("mundanes") are beneath *Vampyres*. This is typical of those in command of the Human Condition and other forms of *Homo Novis*. Other Undead and Creatures of Night appear to be subservient to *Vampyres* too. *Lycans* are familiars, assistants and warriors—but wolves are not considered "stronger" than *Vampyres* individually, since Wolves are notorious pack hunters. Solitary *Vampyres* resembles a "lone wolf" path.

Vampyrism—even if under another "name" or mask, such as Mardukite Zuism or NexGen Systemology—may very well be the next *non-sectarian* global religion of a futurist transhuman generation (NexGen). *Vampryrism* is not a "superstition." It is based on Cosmic Law and explicable by quantum physics and energy flow patterns. The *Moroii ad Vitam* focus on transcending the "game" of "Deity and Dogma," preferring a holistic melding of physical and spiritual needs on a practical and predictable degree. In that state we find *Gnosis*.

4. VAMPYRE MAGICK AND "ENERGY WORK"

As a magical system, *Vampyrism* is concerned specifically with management of raw *Starfyre*. All mystical systems observe some use of energy by willpower. *Vampyrism* is set apart because it works <u>directly</u> with *rays* and *streams* as they are, <u>without</u> overlaying a specific mythology, flavor or cultural pantheon.

VAMPYRISM : a natural science of "subtle" energy work and its conscious transformation using *biomagnetism*.

Starfyre is cycled at what *Moroii ad Vitam* call *aster* individually and *astyr* system collectively or plural. There is actually no difference between *aster* and *astyr* when spoken out loud. This is purely a literary conception. There is some *Living Vampyre* and *CyberVamp* terminology and language appearing in this book for the first time to the public.

Astyr produce electromagnetic radiation in the form of an *astra field* encasing the corporeal vehicle (body). This field is tied directly to all faculties used to experience and <u>sense</u> any "outside world." Fundamentally, this experience is a result of wave interference when fields interact. This is directly tied to our energetic exchanges with others.

<u>Everything</u> we see, hear, feel, smell and taste in the Realm is only *particles* and *waves* of information received by appropriate sensors. Quantum physicists only now realize there is no "out there" independent of "in here." We constantly reinforce our version of reality with energy by our participation and attentions.

Our *aster* radiation leaves resonant imprints on whatever we come into contact with—objects we touch, places we spend time—and the more personal; the greater the *Charge.* You should also be aware that your *energetic signature* is marked on <u>all</u> your energy imprints.

Consider your energy like putting up a piece of graffiti art. It will have its own unique style. An energy imprint of your most grievous time will be a different energy pattern than another person's most grievous time. The energy signature itself is like a "tag" of our name left at the bottom of every work. It is as unique as a fingerprint.

Common energy exchanges between individuals in the Realm are not consciously engineered. Just like projecting a *Glamour*, it requires energy and concentration on your part to maintain it. Energy exchanges between individuals naturally occur during field interaction. These exchanges have an effect on how we think and feel, because all energy contains information and latent potential. It becomes *some-"thing"* when it interacts with some other information (and fields).

When you have communication between two sources of data, each is changed by the other... permanently. It can be transformed again, but there is no reversing or undoing the information exchange. There are no backups, no mulligans—the drop of *Blood* has been released into the pool of clear water. All energy is <u>*information*</u> and we are constantly exchanging energy as *data-communication* using *astra fields.* Unwanted energy streams and fields that we come in contact with *are* still information. For us to have sensed it at all, we have to process that frequency through our system—which is changed by it.

Once energy is changed it is not returned to its previous state. Morality is not a factor here. Discharge from the transformation is "ionized" (charged) residual. You cannot "unlearn" something, or keep away something found unpleasant totally "out" of your mind once it has left an imprint.

<u>All</u> *emotional emission* carries a "static" charge. It is immediately inactive with no additional latent power potential upon release. It is still mutable, as with all energy, but it is best likened to the "char" around something or trying to restart a fire from already burned up ash. There's nothing else to really do, but *clean it up. Cleaning up,* like taking a shower or bath, makes you *feel better.* Scientifically, the water *is* actually neutralizing ion states of your outer shell. Yet, this is one example

of how the *Vampyre* can benefit from simply understanding conceptual basics of metaphysics.

You do not need maths, logic proofs and complex equations to make an "energy function" *function.* Cosmic Law is just as effective whether you know how energy works or not. You do not need to be a car mechanic, work for a tech company or be an appliance assembler in order to *make use* of technologies. Each of these technologies does come with a guide or manual that provides an elementary conceptual overview, usually one that is poorly written by some engineer, usually of the exact opposite demographic than what is intended to read it. But the important part here is: a manual *exists.*

The "flavor" or "type" of energy primarily described thus far is an indication of frequency. This is only one axis line of our theoretical graph. Strong resonant *Charges* and Imprints are result from amplitude—meaning *intensity.* Energy exchanges are enhanced by the strength of the link and the integrity of the imprint. All *Etheric Links* are energetic pathways that can later be reactivated with simple thought and even tapped for *Feeding* at a distance. These links are permanent. They are the original pathway energy traveled. They can shrink through intention or inactivity, but they will immediately activate, and may be stimulated again, from *Attention to "recall"*

—SENSORY SENSITIVITY—

Vampyre Magic requires understanding and using *"psychic energy"*—*"subtle energies"*—we call *Starfyre* in *Moroii* tradition. People thought of magic differently in ancient times. The true magic has been all but completely lost or bastardized in the *Realm* today. If it exists at all, it is to be found in the *shadows.*

PSY*CHIC (si'kik) *adj.* [Greek, *psyche, soul*]
1. pertaining to the psyche or mind
2. a.) beyond knowable physical processes

      b.) apparent sensitivity to forces and energy fields
      beyond the physical world.

Inadequate understanding and application of inappropriate terminology caused the Realm to ignore "*ether*" as imaginary... But, who cares? We are going to see how it works anyways, using knowledge We have available about *Starfyre*.

Starfyre creates its own field that it requires to exist. The invisible background *matrix*—meaning these fields collectively— holds infinite potentiality. The word "*matrix*" comes from a Latin expression for a "mother's womb." This *matrix* interacts with frequencies that vibrate manifestation as "matter." All "things" only exist because at their core, they are in motion. Vibrating particular frequencies and intensities determines the type of manifest matter. String theory attempts to apply mathematics to these vibrations. The *Vampyre* does not need to know how it works in order to realize what it works for.

> "Magic is a process to become more than human, to unveil
> the potential that resides and operates within each of us."
>   – Ted Andrews

Humans often take things apart, separate them into as many parts as possible and give each a fancy label. After all that effort, they believe they *must* have learned something. They have learned only that they possess incredible abilities of creating and projecting and storing their own bullshit.

Heightened Sensitivity is really a degree of Awareness, a heightening of our own reception to physical sensation. Unlike mortals, the *Living Vampyre* is able to recognize what and why they sense what they do. Experiment with seeing how your energy field responds to another field, object, person or place. Shift conscious *Awareness* to your *astra field*. Visualize many arms radiating outward from your field. Use these hands as you might if searching for something in the dark. Significant results may occur by simply increasing sensitivity to frequencies just a little beyond normative human sensory awareness.

The most important tool is the *Mind's Eye*—the *Ghost in the Machine*, the *Dark Flame of Self*, the *Dragon* that is "*I am*." Those with heightened sensitivity or any degree of "mystical" abilities can extend or transfer conscious *Awareness* to sense beyond their shell. Such an ability is required for "*Deep Feeding*" techniques.

Sight and touch are two meta-senses that prove valuable in most practical applications. Focus on those two. You aren't necessarily striving to become a "Madame Zelda" here. Small increases in skills of *energy*, *touch* and *sight* sensitivity will develop further with repetitive experience.

You can practice heightening sensitivity in your hands—rubbing palms back and forth for thirty counts. Mortals count *heartbeats*; yet given the audience of this book, I figure... But, seriously now, this technique raises *Awareness* and "*personal energy*," stimulating electrical (EM) activity. This is taught in a variety of ritual magic traditions.

Pull your hands apart about two feet with palms wide. Begin slowly moving them toward and away from each other repeatedly in clapping motions. Keep your hands from touching, If your hands touch each other, the energy will "ground" out from a "short circuit" and you will have to begin again. Gather energy in this way 30 times, then pull your hands 6 to 8 inches apart and direct your Awareness to the ball of accumulated energy formed there by will. You may *Charge* it with a certain "color" (*frequency*) if you choose. You can use it to *Charge* an object or area. Directing this in a neutral state condenses and compresses basic ether (*Starfyre*).

Develop sensitivity in this way as you practice "sensing" and "reading" the varied energies around you. You can easily develop sensitivity in your day-to-day life. Note the people. You can sense *astra fields*, *astyr* and conduit blockages. Sometimes this requires a very small amount of applied energy.

In the beginning, you may find more success by first increasing sensitivity in your hands before using them. Focus <u>all</u> of your awareness on your hands and use them to *"feel"* fluctuations. It can take time and practice to literally *"read"* the encoded information. But, like listening to a radio in a foreign language—you still know and sense *something* is there.

To see or feel—to sense anything *self-honestly*—you must cancel or quiet the other "noise" waves that may interfere. This is just like clearing an obstruction of view to watch an event. Clear out the debris from the gutter so that it may function as intended, *allowing the water to flow freely...*

5. GOTH-VAMPS OF THE 1970's AND 1980's : THE ARRIVAL OF THE "BATS"

Over forty years ago, global social consciousness began to shift about *Vampyres.* Many people credit this to author Anne Rice and her debut novel in 1976: *"Interview with the Vampire."* A new literary genre bridged "nostalgic" *Dracula*-like *Vampyres* with the *post-modern* and *futurist* ones that humans are more familiar with today. In between: the "TradGoths."

Popularity of Anne Rices's *"Vampire Chronicles"* grew alongside the rise of a modern GothVamp scene. For decades, until fairly recently, *Vampyres* maintained a strictly covert underground Existence. Using a guise of "quality fiction" and "fantasy gaming," they met secretly to coven with other *Vampyres.* By the 1980's an entire "Gothic" *Vampyre Underworld had* formed.

Historically, *Gothic Christians* were heretics. Although they did not view Jesus as the only path to *salvation*, they *did* see him as an embodiment of the *Spiritual Warrior, Magician-Priest* and *Healer* all in one. These just happen to be the *Three Archetypes* of traditional *Vampye* society: a subjective division of energetic personalities found among many *Living Vampyres* today. *Vampyre* culture has now completely blown up, uniting Old

School Goth-Vamps with the "*Twilight*" Generation. Yet, there are still a few that clearly remember how this era began...

The headlines read: "*Punk is Dead.*" It ended in January 1978, San Francisco, California, when Johnny Rotten quit the *Sex Pistols* at their last live show ever. A new *post-Punk* evolution in counter-subculture was germinating, driven by music inseparable from the history of the *Living Vampire*. This new post-Punk underground scene earned itself a name—because of the <u>music</u>—and that name was "*Goth.*" Apart from the trademark look and fashions of "*Gothic*" subculture, nothing so defined, united and then divided traditional Goth lifestyles and Goth-Vamp personalities as the <u>music</u>.

Traditional "Punk" culture represented anarchy in a very angry, loud and rebellious display of dissatisfaction with the Realm. Then suddenly, "*Dark Punks*" appear replacing the popularity of the former. This new breed carried darker, moodier and more reserved auras than their Punk predecessors...

Bauhaus and *Joy Division* lead the scene by defining the post-Punk Gothic sounds and tones of this "dark, exotic new force dawning on the U.K.'s subcultural horizon..." Most TradGoths and *Vampyres* in the *Community* today agree that the "first true VampGoth Rock song" ever performed is "*Bela Lugosi's Dead*" by *Bauhaus* in 1979. Historically, this new "Gothic" sound is first described by interviewer Steve Keaton for the publication "*Sound.*" He refers to *Joy Division* as "dancing music with Gothic overtones," then later adds "could this be the coming of punk-Gothique, with *Bauhaus* flying in on similar wings..."

Bauhaus and *Joy Division* were both highly influential at the inception of the movement—but also very short-lived. *Bauhaus*, a band already dealing with internal tensions, are asked to appear during the opening credits of 1983 cult-classic Vampire-genre movie "*The Hunger.*" This seemed like a great chance to reignite the unity of the band, working together on something significant.

Live scenes of *Bauhaus* playing *"Bela Lugosi's Dead"* did technically appear in the movie—but only footage of front-man Peter Murphy actually appeared. This only confirmed what the band was already having internal issues over concerning their image—and that was the end of *Bauhaus*. But... by then, a whole scene had emerged for Gothic music, beginning with opening the first Goth-club in 1981—the <u>Batcave</u> in London, England.

As soon as a unifying concept of "Goth" formed, an uproar over terminology began. Remember: these are nihilistic types that don't want to be *classified* as *anything*. Out of sheer independence, many shun the actual movement as soon as there is one. This proves you can never truly organize *Chaos*. You tend to see this mentality much more often with the *UberGoths*—who are like snooty *Puritans* of the *Gothic Underword.*

Every time successful underground movements begin to meet unique needs of a generation, it is eventually assimilated into the mainstream. *Marilyn Manson* and *Nine Inch Nails* (or technically just *Trent Reznor*, since no NIN band members exist) are perfect examples of this. "Outsiders" attribute all of what they know of Goth to these more public examples. They popularize what becomes a stereotypical image to the Realm that does not actually represent the Underworld movement that inspired it. TradGoths and VampGoths will often consider these types as corporate mainstream or *metal*, but not technically "Goth" and borderline on the *Electro-Industrial*. Another perfect underground example is the esoteric band TOOL, which like Nirvana once upon a time, was pulled kicking and screaming into the mainstream.

Do not misunderstand: Performers provide incredible entertainment and catharsis for their audience, especially live. But! They should not be treated as a benchmark of Gothic subculture, fashion or its music. There is <u>no</u> existing benchmark to this movement; there never has been. The true *Underground* is dynamic and ever-evolving to meet the needs of the times— never static—as *We* clearly see with the futurist <u>Cybers</u>.

In the 1980's *Vampyre* culture remained mostly underground, bonded together through a "New Wave" of *synthpop* and *electronica*. A few Gothic Rock bands retained their original or "traditional" Gothic sound. Most began to increasingly recognize and use the power of the synthesizer.

—VAMPIRE : THE MASQUERADE—

It is most generally agreed among the "*Community*" that *Our* era of NeoGothVampyrism begins in 1991, celebrating its 25th Anniversary in 2016—for which *The Moroi Book of V: Vampyres Bible* and *Cybernomicon* were released—in addition to serving as a bridge toward Mardukite Systemology. However, in 1991, Mark Rein-Hagen's publication debuted—a tabletop "fantasy role-playing game" system produced by White Wolf company: <u>*Vampire: The Masquerade*</u>.

The Masquerade developed into literally a *masquerade.*

It provided a new mutual forum providing discretionary "cover" for "certain kinds" of people coming together on neutral ground. This is the first time since Anne Rice's work that "Vamp-fiction" coincides with a huge spike in interest from a new generation (called *BabyBats* or *KinderGoths* by TradGoths).

The peak point of modern "Goth" and GothVamp culture occurred in 1995. Around the same year—1995—the "New Age Movement" was solidified and integrated into mainstream. A "live action" version of *Vampire: The Masquerade*, called "*Mind's Eye Theatre*," was also released, including its condensed guidebook: *Laws of Night: How to be a Vampyre* and *The Book of Nod*, explaining a history of Lilith and Cain. *We* even had a "V:tM" television soap opera for a short time (long before the *Vampire Diaries*) called *The Kindred*. And remember the show *Forever Knight*? ...It all seemed so obvious and yet *Vampyres* were able to maintain covert practices while increasing popularity of their image—right in public view.

Even now, *Darksider Culture* has been on the rise for the entire 21st Century. *Vampyres* and *Witches* and *Zombies* and *Werewolves* —one cannot look anywhere in society right now and not see these elements. Population of the *"Creatures of Night"* are increasing, naturally, as part of a social need. A cultural division is also taking place: Old School TradGoths that carried the movement this far are being replaced by new *Cyber-Goths* and *CyberVamps* of an *electo-tech*-empowered generation. Futurist *Cybers* use <u>electronic music</u> with <u>Gothic vocals</u> (or no vocals) and <u>dark overtones</u>, which are often *distorted* or *synthesized*.

The *Futurist post-Modern neo-Goth CyberVamp* era is upon us.

6. CYBERVAMPS OF THE FUTURE :
CYBERVAMPS & NEO-GOTHS

Obsessions with the Undead; a fascination with Vampires; meta-human evolutions... these are the things *We* can expect to see all throughout the 21st Century. *Futurist Darksiders* continue to grow in numbers, particularly in denser metropolitan areas. *Neo-Goth* and *Cyber* fashions and music reflect a cross between *Mad Max*, *Tron* and *Tank Girl*.

This culls to mind two relevant iconic themes really stand out to futurist *CyberVamps*:

Firstly, *radioactivity*—A symbol of <u>*Three Rays*</u> radiating from a central point. (*Some readers will find irony in that.*) There are countless conditions of dangerous *radiation* possible. It is assumed that in the future, destructive solar effects will be shared by all—not just *Vampyres*. Wearing UV-protective *Cyber*-clothing is a "reflection" of this ideology.

Secondly, and perhaps even more applicable, is *biohazardous*—represented with a cthonic *Dark Crystal*-esque symbol prominently symbolizing the "Undead" and future apocalypse among CyberVamps and Cyber-Goths. It is sometimes paired with direct *Zombie* references or to fictional organizations such as: Z.A.R.T. *"Zombie Arrival Response Team."*

Whether more *Zombie-like* in nature or *Vampyric*—it is a *fact* that recent generations believe it "very likely" that a *manufactured* biological chemical will cause an epidemic among the population and result in a worldwide "*Zombie Apocalpyse*." Even mutated versions of very real *Darksider Diseases* could actually do this.

Now, in the 21st Century, <u>*Children of the Night*</u> remain bonded through a chain of *books*, *films* and *music*. Having no authoritarian system in place, and no "large *public* secret societies" to destroy individualism of this path, *GothVamp* and *CyberVamp* lifestyles remain loosely connected to *Gothic*, *Occult* and/or *Dark Media*. Except now... there is *a lot* more to choose from.

Whether under the guise of *Undead Zombies* or *Mystic Vampyrism*, recent shifts in "Gothic" and "Vampyre" subcultures just prove how dynamic the Underground really is in keeping relevant with the times—and how successful they've become at pushing it up into the Realm.

The same year that *Vampire Masquerades* and *Neo-Goth* movements enjoyed their apex, another part of this current trend sparked into existence. *We* already had *Vampires* and the *Occult* in *Our* pocket, so the next logical step of the system: to change human consciousness about *Technology*—how to get new generations to ignore the warnings of a *Terminator*-generation and line up around the block to join the "*Singularity*."

—A DARK ELECTRO GENERATION—

In the early-1990's, a minority group of bullied nerds from the 80's, blaze a trail for a paradigm shift as <u>A</u>merica goes <u>O</u>n-<u>L</u>ine. We enter a *New Age* where *CyberPunks* gain more influence in the *Community*. In the summer of 1995, *CyberPunks* receive a huge public spotlight for the first time, featured simultaneously in several films: *Hackers*, *Johnny Mnemonic*, *Strange Days*, *Dark City* and *Ghost in the Shell*. They couldn't have made this subculture look any more appealing to the new generations if they tried. The movie *Hackers* alone is probably responsible for inspiring many of our top young computer experts today.

Coinciding with the release of the *Matrix* franchise (1999-2003), the *Cyber* community exploded. When everyone took off their masks for a moment, it seemed that many of these same neo-*Goths* and *GothVamps* were also *Cybers* interested in dystopian futurism, alternative technologies and using personal computers. A new flavor of *Vampyre* culture starts to reflect modern or futuristic environments and styles, rather than distant past and "Victorian" ones.

This new generation of *Millennial Vampyres* received an influx of inspiration. Bestselling books like "Twilight" (2005-2008) by Stephanie Meyer and "Vampire Academy" (2007-2010) by Richelle Mead reached millions, not even taking into account exposure from *film* versions. The Sookie Stackhouse "Southern Vampire Mysteries" (2001-2009) by Charlaine Harris is responsible for "*True Blood*," one of the most successful HBO series in television history, alongside *Game of Thrones.* Not surprisingly, and following the tradition of Anne Rice, all of these bestselling "Vampire" novels are written by females.

The Voices from the Underground; the Faces of *Our* Generation; the modern Heroes of True Revolution; From the origins of "Goth" with *Joy Division* and *Bauhaus,* through the "classic" era of *The Cure, London After Midnight, Sisters of Mercy* and *Siouxsie's Banshees,* and the German evolution of "electronica" with *Kraftwerk*'s "8-bit sounds" inspiring Dark Electro-Industrial: *Blutengel, Clan of Xymox, Skinny Puppy, Depeche Mode, Frontline Assembly, Angelspit, Velvet Acid Christ, KMFDM, Thrill Kill Kult, Combichrist, Rammstein, Lords of Acid, Faderhead, Grendel, Eisenfunk,* Mardukite CyberVamps *DJ Nabu & DJ Kyra Kaos, Inkubus Sukkubus,* Rachel Haywire's *Experiment Haywire,* the curiously named *Alien Vampires* and a Mardukite favorite: *Zombie Girl...*

...And, Yes, We use MUSIC as *Our* weapon.

BOOK III

ENERGY

&

FEEDING

M ~ Z

—∧Ψ∧—

MOROII AD VITAM PARAMUS

To Evolve — To Become — To Protect

0. ENERGETICS : BASIC KNOWLEDGE

EN*ER*GY (en'er-ji), *n.* [Greek *en* "in" + *ergon* "work"]
1. expressive action
2. potential and effective power
3. the capacity to do work and overcome resistance

Polarity in the universe allows for <u>motion</u>, allows energy to vibrate, oscillate and exist. This is a basic property of energy. It has nothing to do with moral "dualism" or forces at war with one another. Energy is not and can never be classified by the human expressions of "good" and "evil"—or "bad." Humans base moral experience on superficially structured dogma and relative self-serving consequences. If you irrefutably insist that energy is "bad" just because of "discomfort" or "pain," close this book, put it down, walk away, and maybe give it to a friend later. You might master entropy in your next life, but may be too caught up in the "game" this time around.

There are only two causes for these disharmonic experiences: a.) disruptive interference of wave patterns during field interaction—that unbidden feeling that something is "wrong" and requires *adjustment* by a powerfully willed entity; and b.) energies are too static or inactive, wherein the solution is, again, a *transformation* into something else, motion and randomity. If you only consider *Death* and entropy as *bad, negative,* or *terrible* things—then, I'm not even sure how you could have made it so far in this book... Until you can <u>clear your fear</u>, *Vampyric* work may end up hurting you or someone else from erratic, unfocussed or wild energy, even if you "mean well."

Improper handling of any device or machine can cause "accidents," particularly when uncomfortable or inexperienced in its handling and use. Finding fault with and demonizing these "things" because of misuse is completely illogical. But, this is how "*Vampyrism*" has been treated for the past century.

IM*PRESS*ION (im-presh'en) *n.* [Latin *premere* "to press"]

1. to stamp, mark or imprint
2. to 'fix' into memory
3. to strongly produce an effect on a person's mind or emotions

Real Vampyric Magic and energy work is part of a *Living Philosophy* based on real Universal Laws of *Physics*, the *Axioms* of metaphysics, and observation of "Cosmic Law." The only variable is the *Vampyre* and their interactions with *Starfyre* energy. Naturally sensitive to energy, *Vampyres* spend their lives practicing and developing innate skills.

Basic information regarding *Imprints*, *Charging* and *Enchantment* are given in [a previous section] titled: *Practice*. Energetic fundamentals are a constant. The same principles of energy handling always apply even as the level of knowledge and use progresses. To reduce paper use, book cost and reading time, any basic concepts that continuously apply, once introduced, will not be repeated.

An *Impression* (impressed association) is a more permanent imprint than simple *Charging* and *Enchantments*. Such are only manifested for short term use. An *Impression* might occur during an initial meeting or first contact. A transmission of *astar* energy is interpreted and used as a baseline for further experiences. Changes in perception alter energy fields that another individual will project (and you interact with). Consider the phrase *"first impression"* and how important you already know that to be. If basic *Enchantments* are like "stamped ink"—then *Impressions* are made with a chisel and hammer.

The *Vampyre* is the key variable in these situations; combining *Awareness* and *Willpower* to *Create*.

AWARENESS	→	*To Be +*
WILLPOWER	→	*To Act =*
HAVINGNESS	→	*To Have*

To Have is to behold some concentration of energy manifested and agreed upon in your reality. Energy is potentiality and energy is everywhere as everything—whether you are seeing and experiencing it directly or not, everything is an energy. Transformation occurs when you interact with energy, which changes the way YOU see and experience it. And without your "processing" of energy to give it meaning and experience the information, there is nothing actually going on "out there" but an infinity of potential energy patterns...

...and it is YOU that chooses to see it in a specific way.

1. STARFYRE

In the first degree of knowledge transmission—*Book II: Practice* —basic prerequisite skills are described concerning preliminary uses and natures of *energy*. And *"energy"* often seems like too broad of a term—as if we are not being accurate enough in using it to reference so much; but, this is not the case.

The term *Starfyre* has already appeared in this book, but is not directly explained. Contrary to beliefs that it is solely "blood," *Starfyre* is actually synonymous with *"energy"* when referring to the raw fundamental core essence in and of all things. Calling it *"Starfyre"* just makes it sound cooler. Many names for this unifying energy have been found throughout history and in various esoteric texts—all of which describe this singular "Universal Energy" or "Universal Agent" that composes the totality of Existence. Other names for this "energy" include: *Zu, Chi, Ether, Ki, Odic Force, Orgone, Prana, Qi, Ruach, Vril...* all of which are describing the same *Starfyre*.

One visible phenomenon of measurable *Starfyre* that you are probably familiar with is *Lightning*. In this form, *Starfyre* is vibrating its most pure "material" state as *"Plasma"*—the most fundamental composition of *all stars*. And as it turns out, we are <u>all</u> made of *"Star Stuff."*

"We are all made of *stars*..." —Moby

"Every man and woman is a *star*..." —A. Crowley

English language of the *Western* world is incredibly vast in expressions; yet no word exists to properly describe the various *"vital energies"* and *"energy centers."* The closest is *"Lifeforce"*— and even this seems pale compared to the language of Eastern paradigms or esoteric traditions previously listed.

"Existence" is just a name we give to the wave-functions carrying information for the human condition to transform what we perceive into a sensible Reality. *Starfyre* radiation is caused by unseen vibrations. These vibrations compose all forms and types of matter and energy. It is this force that allows Life, the Universe and Everything to have any "Existence."

All that there is, was and will be came from a single expression—from an Infinity of Nothingness—a *"packet"* of infinite potentiality, frequency and amplitude. Whatever label you use to describe this phenomenon—an explosion, a *Big Bang*, the rupturing of membranes—see, *string theorists?* I got your back —it a point of *complete unification* that <u>all</u> is connected to.

Reality exists from the experience of "relative motion." The "expansion" of the Universe we observe as it cools, is what provides the experience of "time" in space. We are already entering a domain when where begin to "quantify" waves and fields. *Frequency* is the "measure of movement per time period," for example: Miles *per* Hour; Feet *per* Second... Oscillation of the wave propels it forward as the Observer: *observes*. The raw *Starfyre* separates itself into more parts. More parts mean creating more fields for interaction. Each *field* produces a new progressive level of complexity in the meta-system of *Life*.

IN THE BEGINNING, Energy radiated out from a single wave function. As the energy cooled it began interacting with itself and creating wave patterns of varying *conditions, states* or *degrees*. The concentration and density of *Starfyre* changed as it expanded... and this continues even today.

As *Starfyre* "cools" in its expansion: concentration of raw energy decreases; compression increases; a "Point in Existence" becomes cumulatively *less ethereal* and more *material*.

1. The unified point of all Existence.
2. The Universe moving through its own space-time.
3. The fragmentation into "smaller and smaller" sub-systems.

The central core or "heart" of a system is responsible for the circulation (flow) of its vital energies, particularly in relation to motor functions. In addition to the "heart," there is the *"Dragon's Eye"*—the seat of consciousness referred to often as the *"Third Eye"*—the *Dark Flame* burning within; the Observer that is the "I-AM."

In the Moroii tradition, there is also the concept of *eloya* (*Star-Heart*) or *"Dragon's Heart."* This seems to possess more of a "genetic" quality rather than a "spiritual" one—tied specifically to the "star-stuff" that the physical energy and physical matter of the physical body is made of—and naturally tied to a long descent of "genetic memory" as an ongoing physical existence. *"Eloya"* is another name for the *Heart Aster*—but as a *crystalline prism* that processes light that we "see on screen" as Reality. The many rays of physical manifestation come from one core energy type. This unified *Starfyre* contains potential for all fragmentation. The written sign for a *prismatic effect* is the sign for *Fire, Change* and *Transformation*: an upward-pointing triangle—whereas the "Dragon's Heart" of "Dragonblood" is represented by a downward-pointing triangle, often divided into three equal triangles.

By participating in *Life*—by being an *Observer*, radiating personal fields that interact with other fields for sensation—you are changing the nature of Reality, simply by having Awareness. There are no *Passive Observers*... Your *"Identity"* is a unique combination of *"Being-ness,"* multiple facets that allow for individuality and perceived separateness of the "I"—the "eye"!—to exist. Your *"Being-ness"* is composed of all the energy types and information for your actual "true Self" in addition to your "programmed" personality. This is equivalent to a uniquely cut and shaped *crystalline prism*. It processes the same unified ("white") incoming light-energy; but it displays the light differently, specific to its variant design.

Today, scientists have discovered that crystals make the best material for dynamic information (data-energy) storage; and the *Vampyre* is not surprised. If you can take the examples above and imagine your *Awareness* as the *prism* and the visibly projected light as the range of your Reality—then you've grasped this lesson and are ready to know *exactly* how this works (...so that you can use it to your benefit!).

2. THE ASTYR AND ASTRA

Astyr are personal energetic focal points or "centers." Each have their own facets, properties and sub-systems, which we simply call their *function*. As described previously, we are continuously processing *Starfyre*—and *astyr* are the processing machines. They function together as a system. Like interlocking gears, they are not truly separate from one another.

> DY*NAM*ICS (di-nam'iks) *n. pl.* [Gr: *dynamis*, power]
> 1. relating to energy or physical forces in motion.
> 2. the various forces operating in any field.
> 3. conversion of on energy "type" for another.

"Dynamics" are variables that correspond to a person's operating energy levels (or signature) relative to the degree of over-activity and/or under-activity of each aster. Your astra is a radiation shell-like field produced by the motion of energy through *astyr* transformers.

> The condition of the astra is entirely dependent
> on the activity of the astyr.

—ASTRA : STAR LIGHT—

ASTRA—The Luminous Body—often called the "<u>aura</u>" by many New Age practitioners—is the result of radiation from the energy cycling processes of *astyr*. Any energy that you come into contact with is being pulled in, processed and then projected out through *astyr*. As new energy flows into the system, other previously processed energy flows out. Consider water running through a household pipe. As you use it, drawing it out, water fills in from the Source to replace it. Innate faculties exist to circulate *Starfyre* through our system.

Energy and potential of the Universe is limitless. And even if it isn't actually infinite but only recursive (repeats like an "8"), using energy is like dropping your personal water pipe into the ocean; you're never going to tap it all, regardless of all the possible uses and degrees of water.

When someone's *astra* field is dim or fragmented—or they say "they feel drained" or have "no energy"—their *astyr* are not functioning at the proper frequency and amplitude. There is NO shortage of energy in Existence. But, there IS counter-energies and restrictive blockages that cause resistance to flow.

Astyr function automatically, but until you actually look at them to "see" and be *aware* of them, they are not fully in your range of control—they are not, as we say, in your *Awareness*. It is only when an Observer *observes* that there is conscious interaction between. After that, it is a matter of visualization and willpower—the application of intention to start, stop or change a variable in the systems of energetic interaction. This is entirely within your conscious control.

Astra fields are the part of you that does energetic "feeling" or "sensing"—your personal reach, like the surface of your skin. It is the part that interacts with the Realm and all *fields* subjectively considered "outside" of "I" or Self. Mental attentions affect how you feel and experience Reality and also how others "feel" when they are around you. *Fields* such as the *astra* are often described as "*spherical*." They radiate and cycle outward from a central point—the *astyr*. But, there is more than one central point involved in a personal system or *field*, which makes this *field* more "elliptical" or egg-shaped in nature.

When "clearing" (or "cleansing") energy fields of an area, or even your *astyr*, you are *not* to try pulling out energy or creating a vacuum in time-space or banishing anything back up the pipe against the flow. Like the water pipe example, it is simply a matter of "moving" unwanted energy out by *pushing* your processed and charged *Starfyre* in to replace it. It is not much different than opening a "flood gate." Didn't anyone ever tell you: "it's easier to push rather than pull"? *Starfyre* flows fluid like *water*; it burns and transforms like *fire*; it permeates in all spaces of *air*, and can condense to a slow vibration solidifying like *earth*. Eastern Traditions refer to this as the quintessential state of *Akasha* – the "Fifth Element."

Since your *astra* shell is your means to experience the Realm, there are times when you may wish to change, enhance or alter its state to meet specific needs. Additional uses of *astra* are better served in the next section: *Rays of Starfyre*. The uses are literally only limited to the extent of imagination driven will— a combination of the ability to *Be* and the ability to *Do*. The remainder of this section is not a standard of terminology or a complete authoritarian guide to technology of energy work; but merely some suggestions from the author.

Any possible use of the *astra* falls under two main categories: *active* and *passive*. Passive enhancements are more common due to simplicity and range of use. "*Shields*," "*Filters*," and "*Cloaks*" are all forms of *auric projection*. These require a familiarity with *Rays* and abilities to channel enough energy into your enhancement during its initial activation, so that it will continue to function on its own. *Cloaks* keep energy in. *Shields* are minor protective enhancements.

Filters redirect undesired frequencies from churning in with the energies being cycled by *astyr*. You never project an idea that you "don't want such and such type of energy"—that's a surefire way of having it express shipped right to your doorstep. *Filters* operate on the principle of "negation by polarity." Restrict its ability to Exist by emitting a *Charge* of an opposite polarity. If you can hold the consideration that the white light energies are beautiful and the murky fragmentation is ugly, the attraction and repulsion of proper energy will become natural. The key with any type of energetic protection is to selectively block or transform certain energies, rather than simply restricting *all* incoming energies like a static *Shield*.

"*Circles of Protection*," "*Bubbles*," "*Walls*" *and Blood-Fire* are all *active enhancements*. These require the continued concentration of a *Vampyre* (magician-wizard) to keep them functioning. All of the protective examples given prior are actually effective defensive skills taught as *Dark Arts*.

3. RAYS OF STARFYRE

Working with *Rays of Starfyre* is the main prerequisite for all further energetic applications in this book. These classifications are drawn from some of the most ancient mystical and magical traditions. What is presented here demonstrates the greatest consistency across all surveyed examples. *Rays* are manifestations of *Starfyre* that move away from its unifying source. They represent 10+1 dimensions of Existence that self-perpetuates itself at its own degree and condition. Streams of this energy are everywhere, generally unnoticed and just beyond the range of normative human senses.

True Magicians perform magic by *calling forth* ("evoking") *Starfyre Radiance* using their *Awareness, Will, Intention* and *Emotion*. Modern practitioners find that identifying *Rays* by <u>color</u> is the easiest and most accurate way to differentiate their relative degrees on a continuous "spectrum."

We develop energetic links and ties to practically everything we encounter. Conscious use of these conduits allow energies to be directed in a stream or Ray. Spend time preparing for deliberate uses of projected Rays, such as *Feeding*—the *vampyric photosynthesis* method of transforming *Starfyre* to affect change in a visible Realm of Lights. Traditional correspondences for the primary *Rays* are given below. Any "gemstones" mentioned have long-standing use in *Eastern* and *Western* traditions for equalizing *astyr* imbalances.

THE SILVER RAY

Polarity: Female, dark, passive, lunar, left direction.
Quartile Element: Water (some aspects of Earth)
Physical Manifestation: The Mineral Kingdom
Threshold Time Period: Dusk, sunset, autumn.
Light Bands (Rays): Indigo, violet and blue.
–Violet Ray (*Saturn*): Astral vision, darkness,
   Otherworld, wisdom, wards.
   Manifestation: Element of Vapor/Cloud
–Indigo Ray (*Jupiter*): Beauty, enchantment, emotions,
   love, music, play.
   Manifestation: Element of Rain
–Blue Ray (*Luna*): Compassion, dreams, healing,
   peace and understanding.
   Manifestation: Element of Sea

THE GOLD RAY

Polarity: Masculine, light, active, solar, right direction.
Quartile Element: Fire and Air
Physical Manifestation: The Animal & Human
   Kingdoms
Threshold Time Period: Dawn, sunrise, spring and
   summer.
Light Bands (Rays): Yellow, orange and red.
–Yellow Ray (*the Sun*): Knowledge, intellect, confidence

and inspiration.
   Manifestation: Element of Skyfire
–Orange Ray (*Mercury*): Communication, courage,
   being aware, wishes.
   Manifestation: Element of Star
–Red Ray (*Mars*): Transformation, healing, strength,
   will and leadership.
   Manifestation: Element of Flame

THE CRYSTALLINE RAY

Polarity: Neutral, crystalline, reflective, akasha,
   middle position.
Quartile Element: Earth (also Akasha or
   'Quintessence.')
Physical Manifestation: The Plant & Tree Kingdom
Threshold Time Period: Twilight, midnight, winter.
Light Band (Ray): Green
–Green Ray (*Venus*): Life-force, balance, healing,
   growth, true love.
      Manifestation: Element of Earth

THE VIOLET RAY—CROWN

Spiritual Element: Fire of Spirit (Nwyvre of Akasha)
Gemstone: Amethyst specifically.

THE PURPLE RAY—THIRD EYE

Spiritual Element: Water of Spirit
Gemstones: Quartz, quicksilver, silver, sapphire, and
   turquoise.

THE BLUE RAY—THE THROAT

Spiritual Element: Water
Gemstones: Hematite, Pearl, Topaz and Lapis Lazuli.

THE GREEN RAY—THE HEART

Spiritual Element: Earth
Gemstones: Amazonite, Aventurine, Emerald, Moss Agate
  and Serpentine.

THE YELLOW RAY—SOLAR PLEXUS

Spiritual Element: Air of Spirit/Akasha
Gemstones: Citrine, Diamond, Gold, Tiger's Eye and Topaz.

THE ORANGE RAY—DIGESTIVE

Spiritual Element: Air of Fire
Gemstones: Amber, Carnelian, Jacinth and Opal.

THE RED RAY—REPRODUCTIVE

Spiritual Element: Fire
Gemstones: Red Jasper, Red Agate, Ruby and Rose Quartz.

4. LINKS, CORDS AND BONDS

Etheric (ethereal) links, cords and bonds form as a result of <u>any</u> energetic wave interaction that takes place. This happens between romantic couples, friends, peer groups, co-workers, extended family, past lovers, and even the clerk at the convenience store, who you don't even know anything about... Some of the most significant bonds you will experience can begin with a simple energetic exchange. These conduits are pathways by which energy is transmitted and received from two sources. Energetic pathways strengthen from increased time "together" (frequency) and its intensity (amplitude).

Encounters may trigger you to assume a different frequency to meet some "relationship role." This is where there is flexibility in consciously altering our energy. Transformations are going to happen anyways. So, be in charge of yours and choose the mask you wear for impressions very carefully.

There will always be a cord once the connection is made. Even ones in the distant past we are connected to through memory. As soon as our *Awareness* falls on to our past memories, the conduit becomes active again and conscious energy will be feeding an aspect of your life that can no longer benefit you.

If you notice, people use "recall" and "memories" to *bring forth* (literally "*conjure*") a particular state or mood when desired for a purpose. Rather than sending energy backwards, you can more effectively alter present states by intention and will, producing increases of energy in the *present!* A negligible amount of energy is always "bleeding" off through every one of your links once they are formed. Even a *thread* is still a link. These are instantly reactivated and reinforced with *Awareness*.

People get caught up in past social lessons or stuck in old emotional cycles when energy is being sent to something that is no longer in the "present" to reciprocate as a closed circuit. It is true that you can use old "abandoned" conduits later on to feed at a distance, but this is not a preferred practice.

When you *Feed* for energy work, a link for the exchange is necessary. As intensity sought from *Feeding* rises, the link has to penetrate deeper into both energy fields. *Deep Feeding* actually goes as far as to tap the *Etheric Body*, the one that survives *First Death*. Connections can also be formed unconsciously through casual interaction and then reinforced with repetition. Existing links become stronger and the threshold increases. As the pathway increases in its size, cumulatively more energy can be passed through at a time. Even the smallest bit of contact, like a hug or a handshake, will create links—yes, even pushes and shoves. This is one reason why *sensitives* avoid all unnecessary physical contact. Use discretion concerning who you surround yourself and interact with—and especially who you have *romantic encounters* with.

In the case of *Feeding-partners*, connections become stronger with each *Feed* and can be reinforced with casual contact. Beware: connections formed through *Feeding* can be mistaken for attraction and love. Relationships formed as a result of *Feeding* reach unhealthy states more often than not. One must tread carefully when working with partners. Obsessive and potentially dangerous behaviors can ensue. They taste our energy just as we taste theirs. Separation or distance can become torture for a donor—and sometimes for us as well—causing a distraction to our work. This all generally ends with their hatred and resentment. ...And you will still have a consciously fed link with this person afterward to boot.

"Energy flows where attention goes."

Starfyre is the ultimate psychotropic drug of *Life*. Each variation of energy changes how we process Reality experience. As with anything else that causes a sensation, alteration of perception, and/or a "head-change," addictions can form to specific energy signatures—to specific *types* of energy.

There is a reason being around certain people and places causes a specific kind of sensation. At a physical level, we interact as chemically energetic beings, so when we are taken away from some aspect we have developed a dependency toward, we are always going to go feel the "kickback" or retraction wave. As long-term relationships develop, exceptionally strong bonds and permanent ties are made. Where some situations call for *Feeding*, Energy exchanges (*"cycling"*) can be particularly powerful between familiar partners who are both aware of energy work and are actively participating.

Starfyre pathways are linked with a cord. These *"astral cords"* can stretch infinitely. You can't cut them or tear them. If an "abandoned" conduit is a problem, there are two properties of energy that you can influence: *frequency* and *amplitude*. You can use will and intention to reduce the *amplitude* of flow to "shrink the link" or you can use shields, blocks, filters and dampeners based on *frequency* at the incoming connection to your *astra*. The best option, however, is always preventative:

be careful what you come in contact with in the first place. You can take the "charge" off of a "cord" or "imprint" but the very imprinted impression itself will always remain.

5. PSI-VAMPYRISM : FEEDING BASICS

Creatures of Night feel a *"need to feed."* They are compelled to enact energetic equalization. This "perfect balance" is never actually reached, but like the pendulum swing, it is simply a theoretical zero-state that keeps things in motion. Psi-Vamps use processed energy from the *astyr* for magical work or to strengthen their own *astra*. The most advanced and lofty use of highly refined *Starfyre* is to project it as the *Dark Flame* to strengthen and solidify an *Etheric Body* for after beyond this life. Doing so raises a "<u>Light Quotient</u>" (*LQ*) to near 100%— a state that is never actually achieved in this physical existence, but we aim for it. The 100% "<u>*akh*</u>" state is issued if we are pure enough to rise above material existence: this is the only "Judgment" or calculation that takes place after *First Death*.

Feeding in secret is a priority. Some have specifically called this part of Vampyrism: "the *Masquerade.*" You can use your charisma, charm and *Glamour* to persuade and bond with a donor. You may be drawn to specific sources of higher quality energy. Select only the best choices to use in your energy work. Those who are poor sources of energy or whom you do not wish to *Feed* from, you should avoid <u>all</u> contact with—including eyes and thoughts. You must think of the *Starfyre* as *Blood.* Hence, you would never *Feed* from someone carrying a blood-borne illness as a donor, either.

Most people would consider it a violation to *Feed* on them without their knowledge. Some *Living Vampyre* traditions go so far as to equate such acts as molestation and rape. Always observe *Feeding Etiquette*—especially where other *Vampyres* are concerned.

Due to *Our* natural energetic nature it is traditional for a *Vampyre* not to allow themselves (the *astra field*) into a private dwelling unless specifically invited. But, regardless of what people may believe due to the terminology used, the process of circulating energies resulting from *True Feeding* is healthy as stagnant energy can be freed up as a result of *Feeding*. The flow is increased by *Feeding*. The body is forced to cycle new energy to replace it—unless there are blockages, in which case the *Vampyre* will be clearing those as well. So, in the end, donors actually benefit from healthier energy systems—and the Realm benefits from healthier people.

Since the publication of Dion Fortune's *"Psychic Self Defense"* in 1930, nearly everyone—even those allegedly open-minded—seem to freak out at the mere mention of any *"psychic vampyrism"* in vocabulary. This was not improved, when Anton LaVey reinforced this premise in his *"Satanic Bible"* during the 1960's. *Moroii* prefer not to view *Feeding* as predator violence, but instead call it for what it is: a form of *photosynthesis*. People assume by the term *Psychic Vampyre* that a person is selfishly preying on peoples energy. There is, indeed, an incredible difference between <u>*Energy Vampyrism*</u> and <u>*Psychic Parasitism*</u>.

UNCONSCIOUS FEEDING

One *Darksider Disease* that can even occur even in humans is *Sympathetic Feeding*. *"Unconscious Feeding"* is a particularly unproductive form and not uncommon for *Vampyres* to be afflicted with it. This occurs for *Vampyres* that are not fully awakened to who, what, and why of their nature; or they are unable to control their nature. *Sympathetic Vampyrism* can occur if someone with a High-Etheric-Metabolism is not *Feeding* properly or does not know how. Suction pressure caused by this depletion pulls energy from surrounding sources. Unconsciously, the *Feeder* will influence events or put themselves in situations that produce the energy they need. This can have disastrous social implications.

6. ENVIRONMENTAL ENERGY AND AMBIENT FEEDING

The first type of *Feeding* taught to fledglings is *environmental*. Some call it "atmospheric" or "ambient"—meaning what is on all sides or surrounding you. *Environmental Vampyrism* is a very light and broad *Feeding* technique, tapping the collective energy of a group consciousness (*synergy*). Large groups and gatherings in public have an ability to raise and channel large "quantities" of energy. Religious services involving a singular synchronous focus can form a powerful *group consciousness*. The next time you are in a shopping mall or attend a party, pay close attention to the energy around you.

> *Active Ambient Feeding* – When all eyes are on you as center of attention. Performer, Entertainment, &tc.
>
> *Passive Ambient Feeding* – Tapping energy that a group is sending to an Active Ambient Feeder.
>
> *Radiant Feeding* – Absorbing directed attention when large amounts of "*Attenergy*" (*Attention-Energy*) are present. Media, Hobbies, Personal Excitement.
>
> *Environmental Feeding* – Skimming amplified group energy or "Synergy" (Synchronized Energy) from interaction, celebrations, shopping malls, &tc.

Passive methods do not require involvement, participation or interaction. For this type of *Feeding*, you want to blend in, not stand out. (It is difficult to tap energy unnoticed if you are in full Goth regalia.) Watch for significant discharges of emotional release peaks of emotive "EM" *Starfyre*. Emotive resonance takes place when intensity (amplitude) increases from *positive wave interference*—field interactions cumulatively "growing" off each other like an echo; tones ring out like a note of music. As a result, environments take on a charge with an affinity for different degrees, as a "resonance." Like attracts like energy...

"Nothing is good or bad; except thinking makes it so."
—William Shakespeare

Emotions of crowds and groups will "*color*" their Synergy. This type of *Starfyre* is absorbed by the environment. It may leave some residual, but it dissipates fairly soon after an activating event is no longer present or being fed. Intensity, longevity and repetition will all increase the relative resonance. Consider differences in frequency and amplitude: when the home team wins; when they lose; Black Friday sale at the mall; a widespread alert of a terrorist attack; a moment of silence for 9-11... The list is endless.

7. SURFACE-CONTACT FEEDING

Heat, much like *Starfyre*, is of a singular nature. Heat fluidly moves from an area of greater concentration to an area of lower. The transfer of heat in the Universe is very similar to how all energy is transferred—so much so that an understanding of some basics concepts about its science seems beneficial. Just as a human sentiment of "good" and "bad"—we observe no dualism in thermodynamics. There is no "hot" and "cold" in the Universe. This is another human convention. There is only "heat" and the transfer of heat—or removal of it from somewhere and transmission of it somewhere else.

As an example: an "air conditioner" does not provide "cold" air. It removes heat from air in a space as it processes the air. The heat is quickly collected by a refrigerant filled surface and directed elsewhere—usually outside. The same "air" in the space is returned back to the space with the heat removed; it is has been "conditioned."

As a *Vampyre*, *Our* body temperature often tends to be one extreme or the other. Friction (*motion*) is a way heat is created. To keep things simple, we will say that energy creates friction as it moves and interacts with other energies. As energy is transformed to perform work, heat is being generated from that work. Rather than saying "hot" or "cold"—the body's relative temperature rises as it projects high frequency, high intensity energy. Since *all* physical contact creates a link initiating energetic exchange, a *Vampyre* touches with intention. This helps to maintain conscious control over the links and transfers using Will.

For a *Vampyre* to *shake hands, hug, kiss...* self-control must be maintained over any emotional and electrical discharge. This would *Feed* other people in a way that they are unable to process—unless, perhaps, it is another *Vampyre*. Many *Vampyre* couples benefit from the strength gained from each others ability to build and cycle resonating energy between them.

Surface-Contact Feeding operates by the same principles above. This moderate level of *Feeding* uses simple "contact" to create conduits for energy. Even an "accidental bump" into someone will suffice. All that is needed is contact and maintaining conscious control over the *links, cords* and *bonds*. Threads of energy linking *Us* to everywhere *We* go and everyone *We* meet. The effects of this occur unconsciously and are significant. If the *Vampyre* does not maintain control over their own energetic discharge, they may be influenced by energy from someone else without realizing it.

The conduit used for *Feeding* is like a drinking-straw—usually connected to the <u>Solar Plexus</u>. It is retractable—but the pathway for it remains open and more easily accessed each time it us used. At the end of any deliberate energy work, it is a good idea to retract all conduits opened. Although a pathway still remains, residual bleed through is minimized.

The first deliberate "*Bite*" requires more concentration and willpower to succeed in making an initial conscious link. All aspects of *Feeding* are a communication and exchange of energy—*yours* as well. However, after links are formed properly they can always be accessed again through intention.

Surface Feeding does not require "touch" (distinguished from *Surface-Contact Feeding*, or simply *Contact Feeding*). You project a conduit or *"etheric fangs"* (whatever imagery works for you), penetrating the outer *surface* of *astra* radiation. *Deep Feeding* goes much further—all the way through the *astra* and linking to the *Etheric Body Double—The Et(h)ernal Self*—the part of the *Vampyre* that survives *First Death.*

Without "touch" you lose benefits of physical contact to initiate a link—but you gain advantages doing this unnoticed from a distance. A *Vampyre's* effectiveness is dependent on skilled concentration and Will. To form a link suitable for *Feeding*, the conduit must penetrate the *astra* like a needle or drinking straw. For this, and other obvious reasons, many Psi-Vamps prefer to see the cord as long *Etheric Fangs* that puncture the *astra* skin like... well, like a *bite!*

Females Vampyres—I don't think anyone uses the word *Vampress* any more with all this P.C. gender stuff...—seem naturally wired for this last method. It is simply called *Sensual Surface Feeding.* This specific erotic method does not involve physical contact or sexual intercourse. It is similar to absorbing energy by being the center of *someone's* attention. *Sensual Feeding* is often naturally occurs with people and their *Attenergy.* It may be encourages or drawn out. Various types of people—from the entertainment industry to exotic dancing—consciously and unconsciously use this to get their *energy fix.*

8. FEEDING: DEEP & DIRECT

FEED (fed) *v. t.* [Anglo-Saxon *fod* "food"]
1. to give food to.
2. to provide something necessary for the growth, operation, etc. of a system.
3. to gratify, nourish or encourage.
4. to supply material to a machine/function.

Deep Feeding offers the highest concentration of refined energy accessible from human star-energy systems. This concept carries the potential for the most energy—but it also comes with some cautionary warnings. This type of energy work links two *Etheric Bodies* by a cord. You *are* able to penetrate deeper into someone's energy than the *astra*—but you use a *like energy* to initiate it—meaning your personal *Etheric Body*. Incoming energy is then processed at the Root/Base *aster* for *Deep Feeding*.

Bonds formed through *Deep Feeding*—including casual sexual activity—have a potential to remain connected spanning lifetimes. This is also where couples/partners in *Awareness* have an ability to work together with *Etheric Energy*. The strongest bonds and links possible in the human form occur through *Deep Feeding* when both partners are skilled in energy use. *Deep Work* can include a complete *astyr* alignment. Partners each bring their *Awareness* to their own *astyr system,* making certain that they are functioning healthy enough for this exercise. Face your partner. Focus on your base *aster*. Project a cord from there to your partner's base. Do this for each one.

Deep Feeding merges the fields of two people at an *Etheric* level, and not simply the outer *astra* shell. It literally is *blending as one*, because the links that form are very special, called *Ecstatic Links*—which means, "I stand outside myself." *Deep Feeding* gives a part of your-*Self* away in exchange for part of someone else's *Self*. All that we have described here is what some call *Direct Feeding,* because it is mutual and between partners who are aware of what is going on. Some prefer to reserve the name "*Deep Feeding*" to mean penetration of an *Etheric Body* that is not mutual or unaware. This is all semantics.

This type of energetic exchange is detectible by highly sensitive people. If they are a *Vampyre* and they sense this intrusion, you will most likely find yourself in the middle of *magickal warfare*. Chances are very good, since they detected you, that they're more experienced, so be careful. Energy—and the energy work described in this book—is very real. So treat is so.

BOOK IV

DEATH

&

IMMORTALITY

M – 3

–∧∀∧–

MOROII AD VITAM PARAMUS

To Evolve – To Become – To Protect

0. STAR-DRAGONS AND THE KEY TO LIFE

After making the journey of *Selfhood* and environmental mastery, a *Living Vampyre's* final mission or objective of existence is to establish a *Legacy* and walk the *Twilight Path* toward *Etheric Immortality*. In many instances, this level of development is frequently represented by the ANKH and SCARAB.

The *Ankh*, an ancient symbol famous in Egypt as the glyph of *"Life"*—composed of the Omega and Tau in Greek Hermetics— is often combined with the *scarab*, a sign for *Immortality*. Even without the *scarab* beetle, *Ankhs* represent not only corporeal *"Life,"* but specifically *Eternal Life*. Many other key elements of Egyptian Tradition—*Mirror of Hathor*, the *Sistrum* and *Caduceus* —all resemble the *Ankh* shape.

Ankhs are commonly worn by *Vampyres*, *Goth-Vamps*, and many others in the *Gothic* subculture. The *Ankh* carries very ancient symbolism connected to a winged serpent or dragon coiled around a cross. Many have associated the symbol directly with Queen Lilith—the Mother of Vampyres. It also represents the DNA of Enki—through Cain. All of this symbolism, along with the *"Oroborus"* sign of Eternity, may be found on the *"Star-Dragon Ankh"* of the *"Moroii ad Vitam."* Since ancient times, the cross is religiously associated with what is "above," "beyond" or "outside" a terrestrial existence on Earth. In fact, the original "cross" as a *cuneiform* sign from Mesopotamian language indicates either "god," "sky," "star," "planet," "heaven" and "deity" all in one. Ancient mystics clearly believed that these aspects were connected.

1. THE EGYPTIAN BOOK OF THE DEAD : COMING FORTH BY DAY AND NAVIGATING THE AFTERLIFE

The name-title *"Book of the Dead"* is a misnomer, instilled by early academicians. This same thing happened with the term

"Assyriology" as an applied term for study of all Ancient Near East cultures. The actual title—REU NU PERT EM HRU—translates to: "*Chapters of the Coming Forth by Day*." Most folk today simply refer to it as "*Coming Forth by Day*," or else the *Egyptian Vampyre's Guide to the Afterlife*.

Of all the possible "occult" materials available, the Egyptian "*Book of the Dead*" is probably the singular most popular book among *Living Vampyres*. You will most likely find some edition hidden away or on a shelf "*just in case*." The potential for *Immortality* is among the oldest beliefs on Earth—in Egypt and Mesopotamia. For this reason, passages from it also appear in the "Mardukite" recension of *Necronomicon: The Anunnaki Bible*.

Technically there has never been any actual "<u>book</u>" of the Dead. The work for the Mesopotamian "*Necronomicon Anunnaki Bible*" is derived from *cuneiform* <u>clay tablets</u> in Sumer and Babylon from various collections. They guide the "*dying*," not the *dead*, in accessing the *Etheric Body*. In Egypt, the "*Chapters of Coming Forth By Day*" are compiled from *hieroglyphs* on <u>pyramid walls</u> and numerous <u>papyrus</u> fragments found buried with the dead to aid the *Etheric Body* in the Otherworld after *First Death*. The Egyptians apparently wrote secret knowledge withheld from the <u>clay tablets</u> of Mesopotamia.

The Egyptians buried their dead with this *Guide to Immortality* so it could be used by the *Etheric Body* in the *Otherworld.* In the 2nd Millennium B.C., the "*Chapters*" found on pyramid walls and inside coffins were collected by Thebians and transferred to Papyrus. The *Papyrus of Ani* is the most complete recension we have today—dating back to 1500 B.C. Its translation from Hieroglyphic Text into English is credited to E.A. Wallis Budge, responsible for the most widely published of all versions of the *Egyptian Book of the Dead*.

As described throughout the present text, Egyptians acknowledge distinction between the *Material* and *Etheric* bodies. They called the corporeal, corruptible, eventually mummified body

—the *khat*. The non-corporeal, non-corruptible, etheric body—the "*sahu*." They believed the *sahu* had the ability to survive *First Death* and continue on if strong enough and pure enough. In another translation, there are five divisions of the *Self:*

—the *Reh*, one's name or personality (*Identity*);
—the *Kha*, a physical corruptible body;
—the *Ka*, the aura or *astra* of the physical body;
—the *Ba*, an *Etheric Body-Double*; and
—the *Akh*, a refined immortal spirit that *Ascends*.

2. KHEPERA AND THE ANCIENT BEETLE CULT

"Homage to thee, O thou who has come as Khepera.
Khepera, the Creator of the Gods."—*Papyrus of Ani*

Coming Forth By Day reflects a prehistoric theology propagated by early priests of RA, an ancient deity known as *Marduk* in Mesopotamia. This is before Egyptian religious emphasis shifts to Osiris. The material also contains incantations to invoke "*Khepri*"—one of the most hidden gods—to protect against the deterioration of the *Etheric Body*.

CHAPTER XLV

The *Chapter of Not Rotting in the Underworld*—
Thou did not decay;
Thou did not become worms;
Thou did not whither;
Thou did not rot;
Thou did not putrefy;
Thou did not turn into worms;
I am the god *Khepera*, the Everlasting;
I shall not decay;
I shall not rot;
I shall not putrefy;
I shall not turn into worms...

The rendition of an ancient Secret Doctrine—related via Egyptian language—explains how the ALL assumed the form of *Khepera* (represented by the *scarab* hieroglyph) to "create" *Life* —represented by the *Ankh*. This mythos mirrors many aspects of Mesopotamian lore, specifically the Babylonian Epic of Creation and the modern Standard Model of *Mardukite Zuism* and its applied spiritual technology known as *NexGen Systemology*. First ALL was *The Deep*—a watery ocean *Abyss*. The One "comes into being" by pronouncing its own name: *KHEPER*, meaning "to become," "come into being" and "*to transform.*"

> I myself am *Khepera*;
> I shall possess my flesh forever and ever;
> I shall not decay;
> I shall not crumble away;
> I shall not whither away;
> I shall not become corruption...

In prehistoric Egyptian Tradition, long before later religions of Isis and Osiris, *Khepera* is the most ancient emanation of Creation, the Realm and *all* of *Life*. It is written that *Khepera* is formed from "*Essence of primeval matter.*" This is similar to the prehistoric "*Eridu*" system of *Enki*, who emerges from the sea —from the *Deep* or "*tehom*," "Ti.Am.Tu," TIAMAT—to seed *Life*, humanity and civilization. The earliest lore of *Lilith*, *Cain* and the *Vampyres*, originate from this same *Eridu* system of *Enki*, c.5000 BC—where southern Babylonia met the Persian Gulf.

A symbol of transformation, *Khepera* and the *scarab* are linked to the *benu*-bird, which is like a "*phoenix.*" They are perceived as self-made, self-produced—the *asexually self-generated Scarab* and *Ankh* symbolism connecting exoteric use of "O" and "T" signs composing the hieroglyphs, including the "*Sign of Khepera.*" Later Egyptian systems recognize *Khepri* as one of the "forms" or "faces" of RA—specifically the "face" at dawn, a time of rebirth and new beginnings; with RA, the face of noon; and *Atum* at dusk.

—ZEPER : THE POWER OF STARFYRE—

The concept of *Starfyre* is discussed at length in previous levels of knowledge in *The Vampyre's Bible*. It is a raw primordial substance carrying information for virtually infinite potentiality. There is another word connected to this, one that appears in the highest levels of esoteric learning: ZEPER—at least, this is how the *Moroii ad Vitam Paramus* spell it (phonetically).

Light is projected onto a screen of Reality—"*Coming into Being*"—literally: becoming in the Realm—*manifesting* and transforming from out of space. Where <u>*Starfyre*</u> is ALL potentiality, <u>*Zeper*</u> is an active form, or manifest expression of *Starfyre*, occurring when the highest potential is turned into the highest power. This "*Power of the Highest*" is what is sought at the finale of every esoteric, secret, fraternal and otherwise "occult" system in Existence. According to medieval *grimoires*—next-to-useless books of codec mystical lore—it is "*by the Power of the Highest*" that the "priest-magician" has any authority at all, especially in their alleged "commanding" and "blasting" of arcane spirits, which is just pure megalomania. *Vampyres* dabbling in such things should understand this, which most mortals don't know: It is the magician's own consciousness of *Self* that is being trapped in the *Triangle*...

Zeper is specifically <u>the</u> concentrated energy type that *Moroii ad Vitam* must cycle toward the actual I-AM "Self" to develop and strengthen the will and intention of the *Etheric Body*. We must do this over the course of our lives. It builds up as our complete Identity and provides us *Charge* for the present *Life* as well. It is never too late to consciously do this. This evolution of the *Self* or the *Coming into Being* (*Coming Forth into Light*) actually defines *Zeper* in many traditions. But it is treated wholly different by various factions. One sect of the *Temple of Set* based in *San Francisco*, known as the O.V. (*Order of Vampyres*), spells this "*Xeper*." A more publicly visible tradition, *Ordo Strigoi Vii*, refers to this force as *Zhep'r*. They also encourage a *Legacy* by using this energy to earn *Immortality*.

Remnants of the *Beetle-cult* of *Khepera* survive today, inspiring the name of another *Living Vampyre Legacy*—probably one of the most highly respected in the *Community*, particularly as an "educational system"—the *Kheprian Vampyre Legacy* developed by Michelle Belanger. Her magnum opus—*"Psychic Vampire Codex"*—reached the surface world in 2004. However, it actually existed in the Underground for a quarter-century—since 1991, which is the first year of the modern neo-*Vampyre* era, also coinciding the the release of *Masquerade*. Many in the *Community* consider *The Codex* as the single most influential literary contribution to date for post-modern/futurist *Vampyre* culture.

3. TRANSFORMATION & TURNING :
MAKING & AWAKENING PROGENY

"Vampyrism is a unique black magical condition that in and of its very nature requires a posture which enables a natural and effortless exchange of power from the lesser to greater."   – *Order of Set, OV – Appendix 88*

As soon as the topic of "Vampires" is raised, everyone quickly starts in with the *"How do I become a vampyre?"* and *"Can you make me a vampyre?"*—it seems that the effects of media conditioning have succeeded, because this current i-Generation can't seem to adopt the *"Dark Gifts"* fast enough!

Psi-Vamps are generally born and not made in the way that *Gothic Horror* stories suggest. Of course, an acute "science" of psi-Vampyrism no longer actually exists. It is then difficult to say what combination of genetics and environment allow potential *fledglings* and *BabyBats* to come into being. Many are drawn toward *Vampyre* culture—however Awakened they may be. This natural inclination to *Darksiding* is considered genetically encoded and as a means of personal *Awakening*.

—METHOD ONE : THE AWAKENING—

This is "officially" the only "ethical" method recognized and condoned by the Community. Therefore, it is generally not numbered. Responsibility for Awakening of a *fledgling* is not to be taken lightly. *BabyBats* require a lot of attention from their "*Awakener*" or "*Maker*," particularly in the beginning. If the *Progeny* is not taught the "Way" by their *Maker* after being *Awakened*, the creation of an *Unconscious Feeder* may result—an affliction that will only get worse and progressively more uncontrollable with time. If someone is truly sadistic enough to intentionally do this against a person's own choice—and the will of the Community —they should at the very least give their poor abandoned *BabyBat* a copy of this book, so they might have a chance to figure things out for themselves.

True Awakening for others will not require a lot of "technique" from an experienced *Sire* to be effective. Most effort is spent directing Attenergy toward their potential *Progeny*, stoking their "*Dark Flame*." We can test their nature by seeing if they appear to be consuming the *Light* within. Since *We* know and understand best the characteristics of *Vampyrism* first hand, *We* should be able to better recognize these traits in others. Bringing them close around *Us* and keeping them in close proximity as *We* go about *Our* lives, the consistent field interaction will either trigger an *Awakening* for them or drive the person away.

—METHOD TWO : THE TURNING (MAKING)—

Turning is not taught in the *Outer Circles* of *Living Vampyres*. It is not even recognized by the *Community* as legitimate. Numerous energetic precautions are required: some too complicated to mention and some approaching the utterly ridiculous. "*Turnings*" create strong permanent empathic bonds between *Sire* and *Progeny* that extend beyond *this* lifetime. Only skilled Elders usually attempt this, and often only when approaching

102

First Death, contributing to solidifying a Legacy for their Immortality (should one not already be in place.) This method is not a substitute for establishing a Legacy. It qualifies mainly due to an ancient practice called *"Laying On of Hands"*—passing on important information as coded energy from the electrical charges (fields) generated from our body.

This method of "turning" or "making" *Progeny* does not rely on a natural *Awakening* process—or if the potential *Progeny* has demonstrated no signs of *Awakening,* but are obsessed with "Vampires" and just *really really* want to be one. The process is deceptively simple, but may require an undesirable amount of time, energy and patience to be successful. There are some ethical concerns; but we are focused on the mechanics here.

The process is questionable but relayed simply: *Progeny* must be "victimized" by *Deep Feeding,* until the last point of vital essence remains. Even if they exhibit somatics—cramped or sick —the *Sire*/Maker cannot stop; you cannot take half-measures with this process or the results may become unpredictable. Bringing someone intentionally to this point of *emptiness* naturally creates a "vacuum state" with suction pressure. This basically is a description of *Sympathetic Vampyrism.* Energy must immediately be fed back to the *Progeny* by the *Sire* to equalize the "energetic trauma" necessary for a *Turning.*

4. MOROI : THE LIVING VAMPYRE TRADITION

MOROI : *n. pl.* (moroii, *sing.*) [*Romanian*] *Vampyres* with a conscience; *Vampyres* that feed respectfully; *Living Vampyres* who possess magic and vampyric affinity prior to *First Death.*

Moroii ad Vitam Paramus is a modern solitary *Living Vampyre* tradition drawn from a variety of hereditary Romanian and Italian FamTrads of Europe. The current text, *V: The Vampyre's Bible,* is intended to both: provide resources necessary for personal self-dedication and provide inspiration to celebrate futurist *Moroii-CyberVamp* subculture—literature, music, film, fashion style and philosophies (both those influencing and influenced by).

Moroii ad Vitam Paramus means: *"Living Vampyres who are Preparing For Life."* Moroii dedicate their "mortal" lives to magical and vampyric pursuits, cultivating energy from this Realm and intentionally direct it to their *Etheric Body*—to essentially rehabilitate the power and authority of the True Spirit within. By empowering the true *Self*, all that is connected as *Identity* is empowered. Millenniums ago, the Egyptians mastered this art. However, *Chapters* from the *Book of the Dead* predate dynastic Egypt. Its origins are attributed to unknown sources existing even earlier, and from elsewhere, than Egyptian civilization.

Modern *Moroii ad Vitam* study traditional *Vampyrism* as described in this book. We are interested in the effects of media and subculture on *Vampyrism*—also how Underworld *Vampyrism* has influenced the Realm. As *Chaos Magicians*, We are open to studying many related mystical traditions, including those observed in ancient Mesopotamia and Egypt in the Near East and the Germanic and Celtic systems that dominated Europe.

There are <u>no</u> sanctioned orders, organizations or groups for *Moroii ad Vitam*. It is a wholly individual path – a *Cult of Self* – and there is no authority but *Self*—the *Dark Flame* within. Likewise: Thou shalt never use this book or tradition to order and organize *Individuality* or to confine *Identity* to structure. Other *Living Vampyre Legacies* already exist that offers more partitioning, ranks, titles and vocabulary than you could dream of bringing into your paradigm. The only exception permitted is to use the material of the *Moroii* as bridge to the materials of *Mardukite Systemology*—relayed in *"Systemology: Original Thesis," "Tablets of Destiny: Using Ancient Wisdom to Unlock Human Poten-*

tial" and *"Crystal Clear: The Self-Actualization Manual & Guide to Total Awareness."*

As a stand-alone tradition, the *Moroii ad Vitam* maintain no "degrees" of ranking—for an individual that is on a individualized path, what basis do we have to gauge it? *Vampyres* are as advanced as their understanding and experience allow. So, *We* shall have no ranks; no buildings for empty protocols or meetings good for nothing but conspiracy. No moneys should be collected for the exchange of teachings and/or assistance involving any social or group activity in the name of the *Moroii*.

The material costs for books and amenities are discretionary to individuals involved and should be handled as private transactions <u>away</u> from *Moroii* energy work. These guidelines provided should suffice to answer any of the *"Why"* questions concerning these *suggestions*. It is actually more beneficial for the affluence of personal energy to pass on this knowledge (in book form) as a *gift*—sharing it with friends and loved ones. Never forcing or evangelizing these mysteries!

Funerary services are used to commemorate and observe the one significant *Moroii* "Rite of Passage"—*First Death*. *Moroii Vampyres* of the modern era are traditionally buried with:

     —an *Ankh*,
     —appropriate *Scarab Amulets*,
     —a personal symbol or *pendant*,
     —a copy of the *"Egyptian Book of the Dead,"*
     —a copy of the *"Vampyre's Handbook"*
     —a copy of the *"Necronomicon Anunnaki Bible"* *

The last item is only included if they are observers of "Mardukite Zuism" as well. The entire concept reflects an ancient tradition where priest-magicians taught that the *Etheric Body* could benefit from tools and tomes buried with their corporeal body.

---

* To this some researchers and Mardukite Zuists have now also mentioned the inclusion of the *"Tablets of Destiny"* volume.

The *Moroii Legacy* is a unique product of the *Crystal Ray*. The *Middle Pillar*. The *Lifeblood of Lilith*. Its "sterwardship" fell onto —*Jehshiv ah Vii*—(*Nabu, Joshua Free*)—who prepared this book to preserve the "*Zeper Legacy*" of the *Moroii*. The <u>Sign of Our Entry</u> (a *Legacy signet*) is the "*Star-Dragon Ankh*." This appeared previously in "*Mardukite*" literature, simplified as a "double-barred" *Ankh*—the cuneiform sign "PA" used to denote the god NABU. *We* also have an emblem—an abstract logo predominately featuring an "M" wherein letters "A" and "V" (<u>M</u>*oroii* <u>a</u>*d* <u>V</u>*itam*) can also be drawn out. Crossover initiates tend to equate the "M" with previously adjourned "Mardukite" work or the continuation of Mardukite Zuism—and... *that's just fine.*

The *Crystal Path* is direct and unforgiving and not for everybody. Luckily, the Universe is always in motion. To our right, there is a reflection of the *Golden Ray*, the quite masculine and intellectually-driven *Zhep'r Legacy* maintained by *Ordo Strigoi Vii*. The *Strigoi Vii* call their *Sign*, the "*Legacy Ankh*"—a tall, thin, "sharp" *Ankh* resembling a knife or dagger, which actually matches their rigid structure of ranks, levels, degrees, new vocabulary that some folk prefer for their practice—and... *We're totally cool with that.*

On our left side, the *Silver Ray* shines on a *Twilight Path* that is more fluid and intuition-driven. Focus is strictly on "energy work" without overemphasizing a physical *Vampyric Lifestyle*. The *Kherete Legacy* is not surprisingly represented by slightly more feminine energy... that of Michelle Belanger. Her famous "*Psychic Vampire Codex*" has seeded countless traditions over 25 years, and is considered by the *Community* as the definitive textbook education for the *Silver Path*. The *Sign* of *House Kheperu* is the classic *Ankh*, with *wings* for *bars* emerging from behind a centrally located *scarab*.

5. DEATH & IMMORTALITY
THE HARBINGERS OF CHANGE AND DEATH

Change and Transformation—what is there to fear? To Exist, all things must remain in motion, in a state of vibration; all things must evolve to Exist in time. *Death*—is another change in state, a transference of energy. Just as the *Vampyre* learns to manage energy from a *corporeal* perspective, so too can the nature of *this* "transference of energy" be influenced.

Entropy is constantly at work, slowly expanding the Recursive Material Universe back onto itself—like the Circle of *Our* symbol: an *Oroborus* snake swallowing its own tail. From wherever it originated, Energy concentrations that once were "things" begin to break down and return to their most fundamental "level" or state. *Moroii* utilize this knowledge of *Legacies* and of directing *Starfyre* or *Refined Zeper* into their *Etheric Shell* (both while still in a mortal body).

The difference then, between *mortal* and *Immortal* conditions of *Self*, is ability to overcome *Entropy*—a natural tendency of all things in the Universe to break down. *Vampyres* stand apart from all others; they defy the "*natural order*" as mortals perceive it by maintaining an *Identity* after *First Death*. In spite of recent religious propaganda over the last two millennium—for most humans, *First Death* will be *Final Death* (also called *True Death*), with no preservation of actualized "Identity." This occurs when *Entropy* successfully shatters the integrity of the *Etheric Body*.. Then the breakdown of the *Etheric Self* follows as the "Dragon"—the "seat" of the *Dark Flame*—dissolves back into the Abyssal Nothing from which it came.

—THE MEANING OF LIFE... IN TWO MINUTES—

The "*Purpose*" or "*Meaning*" of *Life* is simple: purely, absolutely and completely: to _Exist_; to _Survive_ as *Life*. That's it. That *other* stuff is "meaning" that you have given it—or allowed someone else to apply "meaning: to your Reality for you. The true primary function of our Existence is to maintain a condition of that Existence. Our secondary function, having established the primary: To survive as errant catalysts—*agents* of the Universe. *Our* Existence is necessary to maintain the balance of the Universe. And this purpose is not restricted to these corporeal bodies. They are "vehicles"—a means for *Self* to get from A to C by trailblazing through B.

Most "mortals" are not able to "free" themselves from the "gravity" of this corporeal Existence, even after experiencing *First Death.* The brain releases a chemical compound called DMT and there is an illusion of seeing "life flash before your eyes" as your conscious Existences is immolated back into pure *Starfyre* energy.

You must utilize a "vehicle" that meets the requirements of your environment. The purpose of *Astral-Etheric Life* is no different than the *corporeal*—just at different *degrees.* Without a strong *Etheric Body* for *Self,* you may see "Light" but you will be unprotected from its stellar radiation. You enter the White Hole—from which ALL things come—but for the unprepared: it is basically a *meat-grinder* for your Existence; dosed with amnesia; and a one-way ticket *back* to a corporeal Realm.

...and then you'll be stuck having to buy this book again...

—HOW TO LIVE FOREVER... in a NUTSHELL—

Ascension and *Immortality* are similar but not the same. *Ascension* is a <u>state</u> of *Being* beyond the *astral plane* of mind and consciousness. *Immortality* is a <u>condition</u> of *Existence*—the ability to maintain sufficient *Etheric* energy after *First Death.* It is logical: an *Etheric Body* is *really* how to survive on the *astral plane*—also called the *Other, Otherworld, Underworld, Heaven,* &tc.—and no religion will tell you because they want you to *Feed* your *prana, lifeforce, Starfyre* to <u>them</u>. You won't benefit from that in *any* kind of "after"-*Life*...much less "this" one.

Since *Vampyrism* is a philosophy of *Self-Deification*, it is no surprise that mortals shroud it in ignorant darkness. No civic *System* (like the one operating today) can have its population becoming so truly empowered. Such would reflect the coming *demise* and *entropy* of the *System* itself; which will inevitably crumble under some force... it does so *every time*.

The *"Etheric Shell"* has an ability to become like a *Star*, a vehicle for the *Dark Flame* to reach *Ascension*. Refined *Starfyre* (pure Light) is funneled into the *Etheric Body* and the *Light Quotient (LQ)* of the *Etheric Shell* is raised, as is its total storage capacity. Much like *static equalization*, the *LQ* is never 100%, but it is a "point" or theoretical degree that draws motion in that particular direction, towards *"Infinity."*

Some *personal resonance* will always remain so long as a *Legacy* is intact. How do you do this? This requires: being honored as an *Ancestor*; or through *genetics*; or by establishing an *Intentional Legacy*; any of which may continue to *Feed* your *Etheric Existence* after the *Death* of your corporeal body.

"True Knowledge" of *Death* separated ancient humans from their *"gods."* This same knowledge enabled "gods" to reach levels of esteem with "apparent" power. This is why ancients with this knowledge—"descendents from gods"—were very specific about *themselves* being remembered and remembering their *ancestors*. Large monuments, statues, burial structures, king lists, bloodlines and lineage records all provide a *Living Legacy*. ...so do *books, film* and other *media*—if its *medium* is preserved and kept in social consciousness. ALL ancient records and sciences are clear though; what it boils down to is:

When no one is left to remember you Existed – *you don't*.

6. COMING FORTH – ETERNAL LIFE

Immortality is the most ancient belief of the Egyptians. They *were*, themselves, a race of *Vampyres*, who were given knowledge from a previously existing unknown source. As central as *Death* and the *Otherworld* is to Egyptian Tradition, there is <u>no</u> lore or suggestion of *"animated corpses."* Pre-Egyptian knowledge found in the *"Book of the Dead"* is the fundamental *Vampyric Lore of Immortality.* No *"Zombies"* found here. Dead bodies stay dead. And E.A. Wallis Budge offers several hieroglyphic examples in his *"Doctrine of Eternal Life,"* showing this is exactly what Egyptians expected from their dead.

1. Soul to heaven, body to earth.
2. Thy essence in heaven, thy body to earth.
3. Heaven has thy soul, earth has thy body.

Egyptian Vampyres passed down a system acknowledging the *spirit* and the *body* being both separate yet connected. Earlier *Mesopotamian* systems accessed the *Etheric Body* by unraveling the onion layers of the Realm that keep us affixed to the physical in "systems." It doesn't question "what?" or "why?"

He comes forth into Heaven by the Ladder of God.

Babylon—and the modern system of Mardukite Zuism—offers a system of Gates and a "Ladder to Heaven" to the *Highest Self* in the same physical manner that they had witnessed of their prehistoric predecessors. Not everything about the performance of rituals always made sense—but they did it anyway as an *imitation* of their "gods" on Earth.

Mesopotamian tradition—and the applied spiritual technology of *Systemology* used for *Mardukite Zuism*—allows for one to identify, isolate and then access the *Etheric Self* behind the web of physical systems. Babylonian spirituality emphasized a preparation for a True Union with the *Self.* Where the lore ends in Babylon, the remainder is found in the Egyptian system. Once the *Etheric Self* is accessible, emphasis shifts to preparations for a *Life* after *First Death.*

After *First Death*, there are descriptions of the *Ascending Spirit* "Coming into Heaven" by the "Ladder of God." That much, we can already assume from the Mardukite Egypto-Babylonian lore. Because:

> "...at the borders of this Earth where RA has
> purified himself; There RA has set up a ladder."
> —*Pyramid Walls of Teta*

Egyptian lore describes the *"journey"* of the *Etheric Self* in the *Underworld*. After *First Death*, the spirit travels through the *"Gates of Duat"*—*"Gates of Death"*—which ends with a *Judgment (literally a "measurement" or "weighing")*. This metaphoric sentiment portrays how the integrity of the *Etheric Body* is decided after *First Death*. Being expert *Vampyres* and priest-magicians of this system, Egyptians were taught several "secrets" to aid an *Etheric Body* in passing through these trials of the *Underworld*. Remember our little beetle friend, the *scarab? Living Vampyre* priest-magicians and devotees wore small ones, about one inch in size, around their neck, and were likewise entombed with larger ones for even more esoteric purposes.

Scarabs are worn or carried for protection from harm. Egyptians also believed they attracted prosperity and longevity. A *Scarab* <u>amulet</u> is placed around the neck of the body at funerary rites. It is written that it will assist the *Etheric Body* in *Underworld* journeys, along with the <u>*Ankh*</u> held in the hands, the <u>manuals</u> and <u>books</u> for them to access there, and one additional item not widely discussed: *Heart Scarabs*.

A *Heart Scarab* is larger than the amulet necklaces, about the size the size of your palm—four inches or so. They are usually made from stone and are placed on the chest (over the location of the heart) of the corporeal body during funerary rites. This scarab, engraved with magical prayers and incantations from the *"Book of the Dead,"* is later used at the *Hall of Judgment*, when brought before Anubis, or Thoth, or Hermes, or Nabu, &tc.—there are apparently *"Seven Judges"* in all.

The level of *purity* and *LQ* developed as an *Identity* is measured on a scale, weighed against an ostrich feather. If the "heart" is too heavy, it is still attached to the trappings of the material world and it cannot rise. This is where the concepts of "light-hearted" or "heavy-hearted" are derived. Egyptian Vampyres —cunning as they are—used *Heart Scarabs* to "still" their heart during judgment and ensure Immortality. Prayers and incantations chosen for it establish the "innocence" of the *Self*. Some lore even suggests this *scarab* is used for weighing in place of the actual heart.

Although there are no guarantees, all of these suggestions— forming a *Legacy;* preparing for *Life* not *Death;* empowering the *Etheric Self;* and simple funerary observances with some books and small tokens—don't really seem like a lot of work to resolve in *this* lifetime and could very well prove important in the *next*, after *First Death*.

If *You are as a "Star"* and *"Light"* enough, then you achieve *akh* —*"purity"* or *"clarity"*—and Come Forth on the plane of Ascended Masters. If, however, appropriate spiritual evolution has not occurred, the spirit does not *Ascend*....and back into the meat-grinder you go with your amnesia injection and a cute little note that says: "Not a winner. Please try again."

BOOK V

HISTORY OF THE DARK COVENANT

M ~ 4

—∧Ψ∧—

MOROII AD VITAM PARAMUS

To Evolve – To Become – To Protect

—CYBERNOMICON : THE SECOND BOOK OF "V"—

Since the ancient age of Babylon and Egypt, magical traditions appeared as innate and indigenous forms of cultural and religious expression—used to grant "order" to the human psyche. Engaging in ceremonies and ritual dramatics allowed rising populations to preserve an entire array of heritage and ancestral genetic memory—many of which include detail of "star" origins of life and modern civilization. A fundamental theme of the "Ancient Mystery School" that all occult lodges are founded is: <u>Necromancy</u>. Deep rooted magical organizations all demonstrate active participation with "*the Other*," bridging a communication between what is Visible and Invisible. Inner Circles maintain Dead Names and Knowledge from the Past. These are the Teaching of the Ages, Secret Wisdom of the Past... and a recovery...of what is *dead*.

Secret Masters and Invisible Chiefs receive credit for the innermost teachings of magical societies, offering knowledge dating back to the *primordial*—before there was order; before there was a First Age, the primeval, First Cause of everything and nothing; Guardian of the Abyssal Void, wherein lies infinite unlimited potential. To this, our predecessors have called *The Dragon*.

Infinite *potentiality* requires interaction with existential "conditions" to be of any value other than Zero or Infinity... "to be"—to be manifest. Energetic potential or range of each "condition" carries a continuum of *possibilities*. It is the Vampyre... Magician.. the Master .. the Mage... that understands and combines "conditions of existence" at will to "engineer reality." If the human being can achieve this "godhood," than what unknown alien intelligence lies behind the design and cosmic ordering of our experience of existence... Behind the *panspermia* of the cosmos... Behind the ancient civilizations, religions and secret societies... Behind government and military... Behind the genetic mutation of the next human evolution...? If we pierce the veil, what will we find?

Religion & Science are paradigms maintained in false exclusion to each other, thereby providing conditioned and <u>fragmented</u> perceptions for our human experience. Either extreme—being fragmentation *paradigms*—seek an 'individualized' existence apart from 'wholeness'. *Fragmented Knowledge* is a focus on '*parts*' in exclusion to the '*whole*' (*holistic view*). This focus restricts ability to see (or be *Aware*) of *perturbation*: the 'unseen' forces and factors that make things what they *are*.

Sacred knowledge from ancient civilizations—including their technology—is only understood when looking beyond contemporary knowledge we are conditioned with. Society claims to prize "individuality" and "innovation" yet requires its citizens to learn and repeat the same methodology held by previous generations. Many great feats and incredible monuments of the ancients seem to defy reason and technology by the standards of our times. Many have no duplicability—reflecting some unknown "secret" tradition otherwise known as the *esoteric* or <u>occult</u>. To "occult" is to disguise what "actually" is taking place or in view, by imposing a "virtual" *something* in its place. Occult mysteries are arcane or *esoteric*: specialized knowledge intended for, and understood by, a small number of people.

—RECOVERING THE ANCIENT MYSTERIES—

In 1924, the "Mitchell-Hedges" archaeological excavation in Honduras (now Belize), unearthed the famous quartz Crystal Skull from the ancient city of Lubaantun ("*City of Fallen Stones*"). "Experts" didn't know what to make of it... And a century later, with no way to even carbon date quartz, they still don't know; they don't know how to even "reason" it with their existing paradigm—easier to just forget about it and go back to the comfort of what is familiar and expected.

It is curious that the *11lb-7oz* life-sized human quartz skull, with detachable jaw, an ancient work of technology carved from a single piece of unusually clear quartz, continues to have zero duplicability today—even with modern "glorified" technology, an approach that only proves limits of technology are inevitably reached with fragmented old-paradigm perspectives. Successfully duplicating already known results with known methods is only a guarantee of the same. But, to see the world with new eyes... *That, is the key!*

History taught in the classrooms for the common man is so effectively broken that it would take innumerable volumes to correct. *And it has!* Not only by my own pen, but throughout the entire "New Age" or "Magical Revival" unfolding for at least the last 150 years. Not everyone is getting it "right" of course, but the *New Age Movement* provides paradigm-shifting avenues that can at least be used as a potential means to something beyond black capes and fairy-infused shampoos.

Mystical Esoterica redefines the basis of known history: prior to the end of the last Ice Age or Great Flood period (c. 12000–8000 BC) we have no viable records of civilization—yet, traditional esoterica throughout the world indicates that c. 10500 BC marked the end of an "*Atlantean Age*," the very ashes from which the *phoenix* of modern civilization arose. But... Civilization arose in a flash, seemingly over night. ...How is that possible?

Inner Teachings of magical orders allude to arcane "Records" —"Tablets of Destiny" or "ME Discs" described on cuneiform sources—some kind or another medium of the Ages, surviving from Ancient Days on earth. The two places we most expect to find these: Egyptian sites—pyramids and tombs; and Mesopotamian sites—temples and libraries. These records also suggest the existence of advanced beings from prehistory—called the "Anunnaki" on ancient cuneiform tablets—and aiding the rise of modern civilization. Here is where the *Grand Conspiracy* for the modern age begins; because there is nothing that could shake the existing authoritarianism of our political and religious systems more than if humanity was allowed to know its own destiny and where everything *really* comes from.

Ancient mysteries and spiritual technologies were not "*uncovered*" by ancient humans—they *were given*! Each and every truly "ancient" culture has acknowledged this. This implies that beyond a species development for *modern humans*, there existed a separate—"*higher*"—faction of "*human being*" or even perceptibly "*alien*" species operating separately from humans; actually developing the means to educate the "*lower*" operating masses—and thus was born, what we would consider, the "system" origins of *modern human civilization*—approximately 6,000 years ago, in *Mesopotamia* and *Egypt*.

Long before scriptures of Noah (and his Ark), *cuneiform* tablets reveal how ENKI was responsible for final upgrades of the human race and its receipt of the *arts of civilization*; saving "Life" on the planet. ENKI instructs a *proto-Sumerian* in the creation of a receptacle, like an "Ark," to preserve the necessary knowledge to restart a functional civilization. Biblical scholars and historians have been forced to reexamine *Judeo-Christian* texts that are actually pre-Semitic (*Sumerian*) in origin.

Writings, records, technology—all the information and data-energy—of the true past remains <u>underground</u>, hidden from the *Realm of Light*, the surface world seen and experienced with human faculties. What bits have not remained in possession of Mystery Schools are already in the wrong hands or sought after by the same. The stories of *Indiana Jones* illustrate this perfectly: anything of true *esoteric* value will simply not make it to a museum. The few artifacts, writings, prayers and hymns that do reach the public do not lend us the main body of the traditions any more than a Christian prayerbook or hymnal alone would provide a sufficient *guide* to that religion as a whole. We might deduce certain ideas, themes and names from these—but this would pale in comparison to, for example, the materials in the Christian *Holy Bible* for the same purposes.

Everything at the base of *esoteric* understanding, from which we *do* have some kind of records, comes from Egypt and Mesopotamia. But, we know for certain much more awaits to be unearthed in those regions than politics and governments will allow for. *Esoteric* lore describes an ancient *Hall of Records* among the many storehouses discovered; yet to be discovered; and those discovered—but never disclosed to the public. One such *Hall of Records* sought after by *mystics* and *magical organizations* is thought to be beneath Pyramids of Egypt, possibly the *Sphynx*. And not surprisingly there is also an underground pathway connecting the *Sphynx* to the *Great Pyramid!*

As ancient civilization developed and populations grew, spiritual traditions became "national"—coinciding with politics of the state. This notoriously began in Mesopotamia, but differing accounts of contact or communication with the "*Other*" (or the "*Divine*") spawned different religious systems. Even when regions shared a pantheon, individual families and civic subdivisions might favor one certain deity (or deities) above the others. Did ancient humans have a proper understanding of the higher order happening around him? Did religion mean something different then—particularly at a time when these "gods" were walking alongside men?

Places of contact and meeting points with the "beyond" became sacred precincts of patron deities once met or housed there. Physical locations where these superior "Sky God" beings met with humans and seeded their societies; sites of the first temples and first modern cities of civilization. Pyramid structures and *ziggurats* are built to mark points where "Heaven and Earth" *met* or were "*bonded.*"

It is possible that pyramidal structures held a function that eluded the "technical" understanding and vocabulary of ancient humans. Their understanding capped at basic "religious" connotations, using *esoteric* symbolism as mythological means of relating with their world. We have few myths, icons and archetypes emphasized in modern society to give spiritual order to the unending inconsequential strings of mundane data humans are forced to process and retain.

When combined two *pyramidal tetrahedron* of opposing directions form an "upper" and "lower" pyramid. In ancient times, lower pyramids, such as the *ziggurats* of Mesopotamia, served as places of descent—where the "gods" descended, resided and even provided *fragmented institutionalism* as seeds for humanity. Elsewhere, upper pyramids, like in Egypt, symbolize and facilitate ascent of the "gods." Here we find *esoteric* knowledge of *unification* left by *them* as a model demonstrated for reaching the stars, the "heavenly" abode of the gods.

Egyptian hieroglyphics refer to "boats of the gods" that were used as a means of transportation. It is difficult to determine what technology may have fueled this. The Egyptians illustrated such things literally just as they saw them. Later spiritual exploits into *Kabbalah* by Babylonian-influenced Rabbinical lore allowed further advancements or understanding beyond the exclusively Egyptian cosmology of the "soul."

Merkaba is a spiritual energetic field that vibrates the shape of a *double pyramidal tetrahedron*, as recorded in New Age lore of "Ascended Masters." Extraordinarily advanced "humans" in history achieved the highest levels of spiritual vibration during their life—thereby activating their *Merkaba* to earn access to true spiritual Ascension. Literally, the *Merkaba* is a "body-soul-light-vehicle," an *Etheric Shell* for the *Etheric Body* ("soul" if you prefer); the part of us with the ability to survive mortal death—and to survive with identities intact should we achieve Ascension. Judaic rabbinical lore of the *Merkabah* or *Merkavah* is based on the experiences of *Ezekiel* from the *Old Testament*—lore specifically expressing relationships between the "material" planet Earth and the sky-wise "Divine."

Traditionally, "Merkabah" or "Merkavah" refers to a chariot or "vehicle" in *Hebrew*—such as what *Ezekiel* saw. He beheld a "bridge" or "gate" between two worlds and a fiery chariot where "angelic" figures were able to ride up and down. This kind of spiritualism is easy to dismiss in today's world. If any of these ancient "religious" interactions actually occurred—

and humans today were accepting this—real implications of such truth would require a complete reexamination of history or even what we "think" we know altogether.

A Semitic tradition—solidified as *Kabbalah*—emerged as the first official rabbinical school of mysticism. It remained popular for a millennium, predating more recent sects of Judaism (*Hasidic, Zionist,* &tc.). Much of this solidification effort by the Jews to preserve their tradition took place in Babylon during the "Exile" enforced by the Babylonian King Nebuchadnezzar II. During this same Neo-Babylonian Renaissance, the *Talmud* texts were written with lore identifying LILITH with other Babylonian knowledge branded "*daemonology*" by the Jews and later Christians—along with anything relating specifically to Egypt or Babylon for all times... If we take a moment to actually look—it is easy to see how big of an impact *mysticism* is actually capable of having on the world and the Human Condition that is programmed to perceive and co-create the world.

We have no guarantees that a *NexGen* paradigm will be "perfect"—*Moroii* semantics or *Systemology* developed for *Mardukite Zuism*. In fact, it is not likely to ever be... But, if we widen a range of what is possible and how we achieve our highest potential, we are at least moving in the right direction.

—ON EARTH, AS IT IS... IN HEAVEN?—

Strong tides of emotional and political impact swept through human consciousness from the inception of civilization and its foundations in the Babylonian "*Epic of Creation*"—called the *Enuma Elis*. Babylonians conceived a system that would eventually make them the pinnacle of the ancient world, then later the abandoned ruins buried in sand.

Elevating MARDUK to the position of Jovian (*Jupiter*) heights of the *Sumerian Anunnaki* pantheon in Babylon required fragmentation of the "Universal Dragon" into 'currents' or 'gates' that MARDUK—and his chosen priests and kings—could govern as acting intermediaries between the human population and the *"Divine."* By doing so, they maintained control, governing the human reality experience of *Heaven and Earth* under the banner of the <u>Royal Dragon</u>.

This class distinction became fixed in human consciousness: Dragons represented the *"Elite."* Draconian and serpentine symbolism began representing all aspects of the cosmos and life in the universe; the matter of *Starfyre*—the wheel, swastika or chariot of "fire" that ignites creative motion and power of a god. <u>Gates</u> are another significant motif appearing blatantly in both Egyptian and Babylonian *"Books of the Dead."*

Babylonian-derived occult lore focused on mysticism of *Seven Gates*—metaphysical division by seven zones, levels, divisions or veils. Scholarly academicians generally agree that the stellar lore and semantics for *Seven Heavens* actually originates in Mesopotamia long before it was developed into the ten-fold *Kabbalah*. Likewise, in related lore, there are originally seven divisions of the *Underworld*—a sub-scale found in the *Kabbalah* called the *Qlippoth*; the "dark" Gates opened on the *other side*.

—KUNDALINI SERPENT—

Behind the *Gates* of the *Royal Dragon* resides a <u>Cosmic Serpent</u>, creative currents of *Starfire* energy vibrating the background field or *matrix*—the fundamental Code or Pattern on which the universe manifests and we coexist along with it. Our bodies and our spirits are no less of a representative of the "Divine" *Flower of Life* than we find in macrocosmic examples, like our solar system or galaxy. All existence follows the *Pattern*.

The *Code* and *Pattern* are within each of us—within the very genetics (DNA and mDNA) that programs the existence of our physical "genetic" vehicles. Just as our *Etheric Self* requires the *Merkaba* field as a vehicle for Ascension to "Higher Planes," the *Self* requires a suitable body for which to move about this denser material/physical plane. What connects these two together, showing that the *Etheric Self* exists on all possible "levels" simultaneously, is the *Starfyre*...or else, the <u>Blood</u>.

The flow of Blood allows a genetic vehicle the necessary electromagnetic (EM) field to operate—to be alive. Stop this flow and all other functions cease. The same circulatory flow of universal energy—the same pure *Universal Agent* we've called *Starfyre*—shapes the necessary fields and forms that simultaneously sustain our "metaphysical" existence and a means for the "driver" to be "at the wheel."

Power of the Dragon flows through us all. Serpentine pathways of *Starfyre*, known as the *Path of the Serpent* or *Kundalini*, bridge an underworld of Self with the heights of the "*Divine*." When the "Dragon" within can be conquered—when we have mastered that primordial power of the Self as gods of renown have before us—only then may we tune our own "frequency" to activate our *Merkaba* and transcend our physical bodies and secure our own *Et(h)ernal Life*!

Starfire is cycled and transformed through <u>astyr</u>—metaphysical energy centers relatively located along the CNS spinal cord. Our tradition recognizes classification for *seven* of these <u>aster</u>. Elsewhere in New Age materials, astyr (plural) are known as "chakras" (from the Sanskrit word for "*wheel*") or "light centers." An enormous reservoir of potential energy is held at the "base chakra" or root of the spine. The word used to describe it—"*Kundalini*"—is of Sanskrit origin and means, "Coiled Serpent" or "Stooping Dragon." Meditative breathing exercises and yoga practices are often designed to raise this energy from the base and allow it to flow freely through the rest of the *Serpent Path*, thereby releasing stores of coiled energy.

Quality, type and circulation of *Starfyre* through astyr produces biofeedback fields or auras around lifeforms, which we call <u>astra</u>. A *Universal Agent* passing through the *Serpent* system is the same *Starfyre*, but processed to different degrees at each aster. A basic list and definitions are as follows:

Sacred Energy Centers (*high frequency*)
—1. head, 2. throat, 3. heart.
Astral Energy Center (*etheric frequency*)
—4. solar plexus.
Primal Energy Centers (*low frequency*)
—5. stomach, 6. sex organs, 7. base.

Sacred Energy Centers: The head/crown '*energy center*'; an energetic field projected by the *mind*, the physical "*brain*" and '*pineal gland*' all represent the 'highest faculties' of the *Human System* as related to an inter-dimensional model.

Astral Energy System: The energy center closely connected to the *mind* and *emotional* energies represents an existential continuum between the '*Spirit*' and the '*body*' all contributes to forming an ethereal version of the CNS (*central nervous system*) with the same basic 'body'-messenger function.

Primal Energy System: The stomach/"*solar plexus*" region of the physical body; the existential level of emotive energy and physiological bio-chemicals, fluids, hormones and neurotransmitters all contribute to 'intuitive' "*gut*" or pit-of-the-stomach feelings that accompany encountered "*stress*" and periods of internalized *anxiety*. Being primal and so close to the "base," these centers drive human *sexuality* as well—and when given into, it is a complete surrender to the feminine Dragon.

UBAID PROTO-SUMERIAN : 5500—3200 BC

Long after the Ice Age and cataclysm, powerful *World Builders* emerged to grant beingness to humans and human civilization as we know it. But, we know very little about this prehistoric period—before writing and records. Proto-Sumerian and Pre-Dynastic Egypt is marked by a Chaotic Age when the Dragon reigned supreme on earth, marked by the stars, when *Thuban* in the *Draco* constellation marked the heavenly "pole" before Polaris—the "North Star" of the Bear—visible there today.

During a time before record-keeping, anything showing evidence directly for proto-Sumerian writing would be significant —would be the oldest writing ever to be unearthed. In 1961, the National Museum of Transylvanian History found them: unbaked *Danubian* cuneiform tablets predating the Sumerians. Found in Romania, these *Tartaria* tablets (named for village ruins where they were found) date back to a prehistoric time of *Eridu* (c.5500 BC) when Anunnaki themselves—these magnificent *World Builders*—walked the earth as "gods," just like we have the potential to achieve today.

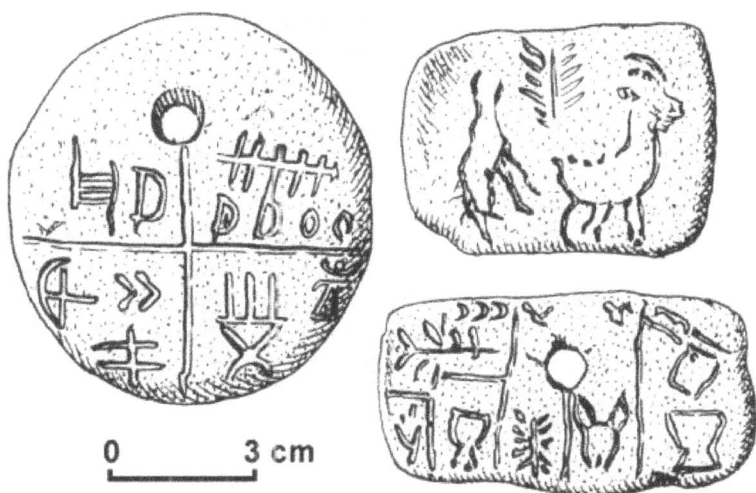

Archaeologists also discovered "*Vinca*" clay figures with the *Tartarian* tablets. These statues unique; we cannot be sure if they represent humans—they certainly do not *look* like humans. In fact, throughout human history, there has been a distinction between humans and the beings they looked up to as "gods." Physical qualities that could be related to winged serpents, snakes, dragons and reptiles are often applied to the *World Builders*—again connecting the *Dragon* to the "elite."

When displaying "Divine Right to Rule" on earth, the *gods* not only represented *themselves* as dragonkind, but demonstrated superiority by facing and overcoming *primordial chaos* and setting the "World Order" in motion—in their own name. If a pantheon shifted, where younger generations usurped their elders, everyone moved up one slot—everyone was promoted.

In c. 4750 BC, when ENLIL assumes control of the *Anunnaki* pantheon in Mesopotamia, a mythic cycle relays his ascent to kingship by conquering a *primordial dragon*, called *Kur* at that time. Later, Mardukite Babylonians use the *Enuma Elis* ('*Epic of Creation*') as evidence for the supremacy of MARDUK over the *Anunnaki*, and gives *him* credit for "*World Order*" as we know it. In the *Enuma Elis*, MARDUK faces off against TIAMAT, the ancient "Life-Giving Mother," slaying the dragon and becoming the centralized hero of the *Anunnaki*. This is a staple of the Babylonian tradition and its aptly named "Mardukite Zuism."

In Egypt—where MARDUK appears as AMON-RA—again he is depicted overcoming the *Apophis* (APEP in hieroglyphic) or *Typhon* monster of CHAOS or KAOS seeking to devour the ordered universe each night when after the sun sets. Overcoming the Chaos and providing Cosmic Order is not the *only* way of things—but it is the way things are for existences on planet Earth operating as they do. There are many other possible existences and universes. It is a part of humanity's own destiny to tranquilize the personal *Dragon* within and regain true control of the *Self*, so as to prove *Godhood*.

During the proto-Sumerian Ubaid period, the gods and their emissaries were regarded as Overseers or Overlords, with a faction of them even called IGIGI in Mesopotamia—meaning "*Watchers*." The same *Uber*-lords responsible for instigating human development later became known as *Upyr*—literally "Vampire," not to mention evidence of their ancient existence is actually found in *Transylvania*—the *Tartaria* discoveries.

Sumerian and Egyptian records are clear about the nature of

beings occupying a seat of kingship at its start: *gods*. The original 'overseers' were considered *divine*, come from the sky—from the stars—and bringing with them the critical knowledge and technologies that would cultivate humanity. Their reign, [or public representation of reign in their name] was eventually replaced by *demigods* (or *hybrids*), considered part-*divine* and part-*human*, until control finally passed to a specialized segment of "humans" as "kings" and "priests."

Distinctions of class and bloodline become a significant means of preserving lineages of specific sects and cults. "Gods" and their cults even practice genetic intervention, separating *Sons of Man* from *Sons of God*. These other "separate" races propagate by way of specific beings, such as ENKI, MARDUK or LILITH —as opposed to the original basic standard issue worker race model sanctioned by *Anunnaki* overseers to assist them.

URUK SUMERIAN : 3200—2160 BC

Establishment of writing and language solidifies complex social systems into a pattern we call "civilization" by allowing human interaction to communicate distinctive reasoning via standardized vocabulary of meaning, and personal experience (perspective/perception) to others.

While Sumerian Mesopotamia developed under ENLIL, a pre-Dynastic Star Religion cropped up in the West sacred to MARDUK. This proto-Babylonian tradition between the Middle East and Egypt established a standard of MARDUK as RA. Even the original *Heliopolitan* city is called ANU—a "place for gods on Earth," from a time when the "gods" themselves were sovereign. The city paralleled the abode of the gods in the heavens, a city Egyptians also called ANU.

Early Dynastic Egypt and Old Sumerian Civilization developed a "religiously governed state." Solar/stellar veneration became a standard. Human consciousness very literally began to

connect the sky, heavens and stars with *Divinity*. Pre-Babyloni-
an religions in Mesopotamia emphasized an Enlilite lineage of
Anunnaki gods: mainly NANNA (*the horned moon god*) and INAN-
NA-ISHTAR (*Venus, the Queen of Heaven*).

During the Old Kingdom in Egypt (Dynasty III—IV) inscriptions
to aid deceased to traverse the Underworld start to appear on
walls of tombs—denoted "Pyramid Texts" by archaeologists.
This precursor of passages for what is later called the "*Book of
the Dead*," suggests the Egyptians were "given" this knowledge
or that it derived from a pre-Dynastic (*prehistoric*) age. A new
paradigm shift eventually centralizing on OSIRIS marked the
end of the Old Kingdom.

Egyptian Vampyrism evolves; *Cultists of the Dead* in the city of
Abydos patrons the Osirian protective jackal-god Guardian of
Tombs named KHENTIMENTIU, meaning "*Foremost of the
Dead*." Literally, the name means "*Foremost of the West*," indicating the desolate desert, where only death lived. The word
for the western direction—*Amenti*—also indicated the *Underworld*, a "place for the dead." In more contemporary language,
KHENTIMENTIU is better known by the name: ANUBIS (written ANUPU in hieroglyphic).

BABYLONIAN OLD KINGDOM : 2160—1334 BC

A new Messianic Age was dawning in Babylonia. Astrologic-
ally, the Age of MARDUK descended upon the people. March
21, 2160, on the *Spring Equinox*, the Sun rises in the 30-degree
zone of the *Aries* constellation—enter: the *Age of Aries*. Traditional astrology is born in Babylon to mark this event. A New
Year festival, *Akiti*, replaced Sumerian *Zagmuk*—an annual reminder that Babylon prospered under supremacy of MARDUK.

In Babylon, astrology—the original *zodiac*—made it possible to
prove the celestial events marking the *Age of Aries*. Elsewhere,
in Egypt, the Legacy of MARDUK appeared as the lore of

AMUN or AMON-RA, the *"hidden god"* or *"Ra the Unseen"* shown wearing a two-plumed crown or with the horns of a ram. The ram is sacred to MARDUK and the *Age of Aries* in both cultures.

MARDUK is the *"Hidden God"* in *Book of 12 Gates*, an Egyptian text describing twelve hours of night when RA (*the Sun*) disappears from our view to battle with TIAMAT (*Apophis*) and fight against CHAOS (entropy) from consuming *World Order* systems on Earth. When he approaches the First Gate of DUAT/TUAT, he appears with a man's body and the head of a *ram.*

Development of astrology in Babylon allowed for more than establishing *zodiacal Age*—it bridged the knowledge of *Celestial Time* (of the stars) with cyclic patterns on Earth. Systems of "divination" and other "oracles" were born to glean this wisdom "from the beyond." The *Messianic Age* heralded by NABU —the "Prophet" and "Messenger" of the gods—was celebrated as a tradition of "<u>prophecy</u>," an empirical literary method used by Mardukite Scribe-Priests and Priestesses to solidify systematic *World Order* by *"Divine Right."* Mardukites mastered the art of language. Pre-Babylonian (*Sumerian*) cuneiform was refined into a more advanced Old Babylonian (and *Akkadian*) language systems. The original *Semitic* language systems were born in Babylonia. Here begins an authoritarian tradition of using terminology and semantics as a *"scientific method"* to secure what "Reality" *is* in the "Realm."

The *Age of Aries* marked the inception of the First Intermediate Period in Egypt when the Dragon Sovereignty of ANU evolves beyond Mesopotamia over the next millennium. During the 12th Dynasty, a "Dragon Court" of Egypt was maintained by *Queen Sobekh Nefru.* Another contribution came from the Egyptian equivalent of a Mardukite Scribe-Priest—the high-priest of MENTU, Ankhfn Khonsu, *"He Who Lives for Khonsu."* It is the <u>Stella of Ankh-ef-en-Khonsu</u> that became an inspiration behind Aleister Crowley's significant experiences in Egypt, including experiments resulting in his *"Book of the Law"* and founding of the modern *Thelemic* school of magic.

The *Stella*—called <u>The Stele of Revealing</u> by Crowley—was first discovered by archaeologists in 1858 at the funerary temple of Queen Hatsepshut. Its original catalogue designation "*Bulaq 666*" only confirmed its significance to Crowley—though it has since been re-catalogued as "*Cairo A 9422.*" Such highly decorated wooden boards—or "*stele,*" as they are usually called—are precursors to modern "headstones" for graves. The *Stele of Revealing* includes text identified with the *Book of the Dead*.

Refinement of Egyptian funerary practices continued through the Middle Kingdom era. Graphic depictions of the *Otherworld* are drawn on, in and around sarcophagi—called the *Coffin Texts*—as "maps" to aid the Dead in their afterlife journey through the Underworld. Egyptologists later called these *Underworld Books*, such as the *Book of the Day* and *Book of the Night*, but they mainly consist of graphic illustrations with few captions. These visions, journeys and images are most likely the result of psychedelic shamanism, if not literal.

An *Egyptian Renaissance* takes place during the New Kingdom, starting with Queen Hatsepshut in 1550 BC and ending in 1069 BC with Ramses the Great. A new refined secret society of Egyptian Vampyre priests rises during this period—called by some, the *Rosicrucian White Lodge*—and *Book of the Dead* funerary inscriptions are made on *papyrus* (*paper*) for the first time, increasing their accessibility to the general population.

Perhaps the most important event of the New Kingdom in Egypt—at least from an *esoteric occult* perspective—is referred to in history as the <u>Amarna Heresy</u> 1350–1334 BC (although it is *only* heretical to non-Mardukite paradigms). In fact, the modern Rosicrucian Order identifies most with this period, which occurred under leadership of Akhenaten (*Amenhotep IV*) and his wife Nefertiti, both assassinated for their efforts.

Mirroring Mardukite Babylonian spiritual unification, Akhenaten supported a *monaltric* religion, the Cult of ATEN (JTN in hieroglyphic), solely dedicated to venerating *Aton*, the Sun

Disc on the Horizon—an original expression of MARDUK-RA in Egypt—and elsewhere in Zoroastrianism: AHURA-MAZDA.

CELTIC VAMPYRISM : 1000 BC

Celtic Vampyres reflect something between a "fairy" and an ancestral spirit. The Sidhe (pronounced, "shee" pl., "sith" sing.) divided as "Seelie" and "Unseelie" courts, are original ancient European "Elves" and "Faerie Folk," descendents of the Tuatha d'Anu—also Tuatha de Dannan—the original Druid race of the Celtic lands.

The Sidhe could drink blood, drain vital energies (Starfire), use hypnotic "fairy" powers—not to mention being expert in the magic of enchantment and glamour. To the ancient Druids, the Sidhe are "People of the Mounds," meaning ancient ancestors residing in burial plots known as "fairy hills"—or "fairy howe" in the language of Rev. Robert Kirk, whose Scottish journals indicate he made regular contact with the Sidhe long after they had faded into the time of legend.

According to Celtic Druid lore, the Sidhe "vampyres" are emanations (descendents) of the ancient Mother Goddess DRUANTIA—the Lady of the Oaks, First Queen of the Druids and progenitor of the Celtic Vampyre legacy among the fey. [This information is repeated from "Vampyre's Bible."] Additional materials on Celtic Vampyrism—or Druidic and Elven-Faerie Traditions exclusively—may be found in "Elvenomicon" by Joshua Free.

NEO-BABYLONIAN RENAISSANCE : 626—562 BC

Following the fall of Assyrian power with the death of Ashurbanipal, Babylonians elect a new leader of their revolution—Nabopolassar—as king. He joins forces with the Chaldeans and Medes in defeating the Assyrians at their capital in Nineveh and later the Egyptians. After several successful victories against two empires, Neo-Babylonia soars to heights of its prosperity. His son: the infamous Nebuchadnezzar II. The infamous King Nebuchadnezzar II supported a peaceful pro-Mardukite era for fifty years and maintained unification of *Sumer* and *Akkad* in the name of MARDUK and NABU. He married Amytis, a daughter of the Median king, ensuring the peace between empires and restored many city centers and sacred temples (*ziggurats*). Before his death, he gave a prophecy of an impending end to the glory of his *Chaldean Empire in Babylon*. The actions of less worthy successors invariably proved him right.

TALMUDIC JUDAISM : 600 BC

During the heights of the Neo-Babylonian Empire, another system was developing solid foundations—right in the heart of Babylon itself. After a destruction of Jerusalem by Nebuchadnezzar II, the King ordered the Jews into "Exile," taking them captive and integrating them into the Babylonian population. The Rabbinical tradition of "Abraham" could be preserved in Babylon only by committing the teachings to writing. All of the fundamental Enochian, or else Talmudic, literature of the Kabbalah—*Ka-Ba-La* (QBL)—is developed during this time. The Mystery Schools of the Jews were highly influenced by the Babylonians—their writings and their culture.

Texts on Hebrew mysticism, such as the "Sefer Yetzirah" (*Sefer ha-Yetzirah*)—"Book of Formation"—inspired the system of yetziratic magic, which appears in popular grimoires from the medieval period and ceremonialism of the *Hermetic Order of the Golden Dawn* and any sect it influenced, such as *Ordo Templi Orientis* (OTO). Examples would include "Keys of Solomon" and "Book of Abramelin." Another vein of Nephelimic Tradition of was passed down by an "Angel" *Raziel*—a millennium before the angel *Ave* delivered the Enochian system to John Dee and Edward Kelley. The concept of *Raziel* is fantasized in the modern "Mortal Instruments" series where knowledge and tradition is contained in a *ShadowHunters Codex*.

Merkaba (Merkavah) lore appears in the Third Book of Enoch, or "Book of the Palaces" (*Hekhalot Rabbati*), describing the ascent of a Rabbi into the Palaces of Heaven. Another kabbalistic text, the *Zohar*, offers descriptions of the Seven Heavens ("Heavenly Spheres"). This lore alludes to gates or veils of fragmentation (condensation) separating the dense material creation from out of a purely etheric unification.

THE NEW HERMETICS : 300—100 BC

Another relevant school of magic emerged alongside the Hebrew *Kabbalah*, called Demotic or Coptic—named after the language their magical papyri were written. Hieroglyphic, Demotic and Greek are actually the three languages inscribed on the <u>Rosetta Stone</u>—the artifact that made modern translation of Egyptian hieroglyphics possible. This revival of the *arcane* by the Greeks allowed for open investigation of ancient spells and magic (called *heka* in Egypt), borrowing from Egyptian deities, Babylonian and Judaic tradition. Later the system is recognized specifically as <u>Hermetic</u>, named after <u>HERMES</u>, the THOTH or NABU of Greek mysticism.

Hermetic writing tradition expressed magical philosophies in the form of dialogue between master and apprentice. This practice mirrors the manner that the Magic had been taught (passed on) to MARDUK by ENKI in Eridu, or to NABU by MARDUK in Babylon. The archetypal *Merlin-Arthur* relationship is timeless—even today, mystic masters Deepak Chopra (*The Way of the Wizard)* and Douglas Monroe (*The Merlyn Trilogy*) have found great educational success with this model.

CRUSADES OF CHRISTIANITY : 100—1400

As the *Age of Aries* turned to the *Age of Pisces*, a universalist evolution of the Judaic tradition took place during a new Messianic Age and shift into Christianity. All occult traditions in the past two millenniums have respected the work and teachings of Jesus Christ, even if they do not agree with the self-made religions established in his name or the politics of scripture. He is considered an Ascended Master to the ancient Mystery School, one of the greatest mystics and spiritual teachers in history. He is even accepted in the modern "Goth" movement as both vampire and zombie.

Many early mystical schools of Christianity came into being with Christ's absence, including the *Essenes* and the *Gnostics* (who also studied the Heremetica). These schools were abolished as heretical by the new "*Roman Catholic Church.*" It claimed to be directly descended from Paul as its first pope and established itself as the ONE Christian authority on earth when the Roman Empire was allegedly donated to it by Emperor Constantine.

The wealth and power of Rome has historically required great efforts to maintain and protect; both were increasing under Church authority. Rome sanctioned *Holy Orders* of paladins, clerics and holy knights to defend the Church and its mysteries, as well as traveling priests making expeditions to the "*Holy Lands*" (Jerusalem, etc) where they sought holy relics, writings and artifacts to solidify their new religious foundation. Openly rebelling against previous Dragon Sovereignty in the world, the church demonizes the image of the dragon. "Defeat of the Dragon" becomes a sacred symbol of these Holy Orders turned secret society. But as always happens—fraternal societies lead to smaller sects among its elite members, sharing secret mysteries and eventually conspiracy. Additional information may be found in "*Draconomicon*" by Joshua Free.

KNIGHTS TEMPLAR : 1118—1313

During the Crusades, the Knights Templar formed a holy order of militant monks. They were actually employed by the Catholic Church during the Crusades for protection in the "*Holy*

Lands" of Jerusalem. The organization developed an even stronger bond and foundation while in the Middle East and abroad. They returned to Europe with a significant amount of wealth (in spite of their three-fold vows of obedience, chastity and poverty) and more importantly, wisdom. They claimed to possess the secret key to the *True Christianity*—like the *Gnostics* and *Cathars* before them.

Historical downfall of the Order began when King Philip IV of France attacked the *Templars* directly. He apparently had financial problems and already had developed a significant debt with the Order for their services. Rather than pay them, King Philip IV secured support from the Roman Church in destroying Templars on charges of blasphemy and heresy concerning alleged black magic practices and sexual perversion occurring within the Order. Only under torture did the knights admit to worshiping BAPHOMET, which was interpreted as the *"Devil"* by the Church. The final destruction of the *Knights Templar* occurred on Friday, October 13, 1307, a day forever after known as "Black Friday" or the "October Episode."

The trial of Jacques de Molay is recreated in the ceremonial drama of the 6th Degree Initiation to the modern Order as it exists underground today as an alternate form of Freemasonry. The rite imposes a scene where Jacques de Molay is brought before the Pope by the King to receive his sentencing for blasphemous heresy. It is from the text of this rite that we might understand what may have transpired—assuming the "hours recorded" are appropriate.

During the initiation rite, the Pope asks why he is a part of these proceedings since Jacques de Molay was not condemned yet by the Church, only King Philip IV. Jacques de Molay responds, "And by what authority did he condemn men, by what title? My knights and I swore to insure victory for our sacred banner, dedicating our lives to protect the Temple." The Pope speaks up, "Templars were arrogant and claimed to be above the laws. They had to be crushed under the footfall of humility." But Jacques de Molay continues, "Remind the King, whose shackles bind us, that we offered our lives for his cause. He now finds us unworthy, has deemed us anathema and simply because we did not compromise our beliefs."

Finally, the King interjects, "Molay, you have already made a confession of your blasphemous acts." "Yes," shouts a priest, "but you tortured them as murdering thieves." Jacques de Molay then tells of how the Templar Knights were destroyed and burned at the stake as common witches. In the sentencing of de Molay, the priest continues, "Oh sad fraternity, do I unfold your most closely guarded secrets? Certainly not. No secret can be exposed to any who had not previously divined it. And no initiate will comprehend the meaning of the message, even if it be shouted by every mouth in the street."

Thus ended the ancient and mystical Order of the Knights of the Temple. By the year 1313 the Templar Knights were forced out of the Holy Lands and those alive to carry the legacy, brought it underground.

SOCIETAS ROSICRUCIS : 1409—PRESENT TIME

The Hermetic Rosicrucian Order has a legendary legacy that is possibly allegorical. The Order holds that the modern inception begins with a late 14th Century German monk named *Christian Rosenkreuz*. Some believe "Christian Rosenkreutz" was really Francis Bacon and that the Order was established by him during the time of John Dee and Edward Kelley.

According to legend, Rosenkreutz was initiated into the Hermetic Mystery Schools of Egypt and the Holy Lands while still a teenager. In 1409, he established his own temple in Germany, the *"Spiritus Sanctum,"* which later served as his own tomb. When the tomb was later opened 100 years after his death, the Rosicrucian Order was "revived" with the aid of obscure manuscripts ("The Rosicrucian Manifestos") found buried with him—*Fama Fraternitatis, Confessio Fraternitatis* and *The Chymical Wedding of Christian Rosenkreuz.*

In 1915, Rosicrucianism arrives in America when H. Spencer Lewis launches the "*Ancient and Mystical Order of the Rosae Crucis*" (AMORC) in San Jose, California. A century later, AMORC still maintains the amazing Rosicrucian Park (modeled from Akhenaton's Egypt) and Rosicrucian Egyptian Museum. An emphasis on the direct path to *Ascension* via the *Great Work* attracted notoriously spiritual members, such as Saint Germain who is now revered as an Ascended Master. An original form of masonic cipher was developed to keep teachings and messages secret.

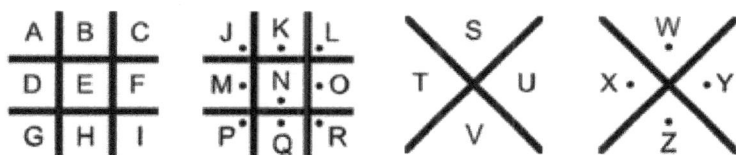

As explained in the "Positio Fraternitatis Rosae Crucis" from AMORC: "The *Fama Fraternitatis* addressed political and religious leaders, as well as the scientists of the time. While making a negative statement about the general situation in Europe, it revealed the existence of the *Order of the Rose-Croix* through the allegorical story of Christian Rosenkreuz (*1378-1484*), beginning with his journey throughout the world before giving birth to the Rosicrucian movement, and ending with the discovery of his tomb. This Manifesto called for a Universal Reform."

"*Confessio Fraternitatis* complemented the first Manifesto by insisting, on the one hand, upon the need for a regeneration of humanity and society; and, on the other hand, by pointing out that the *Rosicrucians* possess a philosophical knowledge enabling them to achieve this regeneration. It addressed seekers wishing to participate in the work of the Order and to strive for the happiness of humanity."

"In a style rather different from first two Manifestos, the *Chymical Wedding of Christian Rosenkreuz* recounted an initiatory journey which portrayed the quest for <u>Illumination</u>. This seven-day journey took place for the most part in a mysterious castle where the wedding of a king and a queen was to be held. *The Chymical Wedding* symbolically related the spiritual development which leads an Initiate to achieve union between the soul (*the bride*) and God (*the bridegroom*)."

STREGA & STRIGOI : 1300—1800

Traditonal Vampyrism in Europe emerges from Rome, Romany/Romania, Etruscan/Tuscany and Milan, Italy. "*Strega*" is the Italian name for "Gypsy" witch also called Romani. During this time traditional lore of the <u>Creatures of Night</u> emerge. European terminology used during the *Dark Ages*, refered to witches, vampires and werewolves with the same context.

Class distinction in FamTrads is apparent between the "*Strega*" shamanic wolf-clans and the aristocratic "*Strigoi*" priests— meaning the *Lycans of Italy* from the *Vampyres of Romania*. Most contemporary <u>Werewolf</u> lore is derived from shamanic wolf clans—the Lycans who practice Old Ways according to wolf-cults and their high priests, called the Luperci.

Lycans are descendents of (or in religious service to) Lupercus, the emanation of ALL ("God") as represented in wolf form. The primary Lycan holiday is Lupercalia, Festival of Lupercus, on the eve of February 2. This timing coincides with the Celtic Imbolc festival. Additional information concerning Lycan traditions may be found in Book XI (M-8).

Strigoi are a stereotypical vision of Transylvanian Vampyres, feeding on mortals without reservation or respect. They are directly referenced in modern fiction (*Vampire Academy*) as "a destructive anarchical malignant sect of vampires, opposite the benevolent mainstreaming Moroii."

By Church standards, *strigoi* are treated as victims of a spiritual disease. Certain *darksider* conditions seem to carry it: the seventh same sex child in a family; to lead a life of sin; to not attend church services or receive the Sacraments; to die without being married; to have participated in Dark Arts; to have performed "unnatural" acts; sexual deviation; to be executed for perjury; being cursed by a witch; and suicide.

SOCIETAS DRACONIS : 1408—PRESENT TIME

In 1408, the "Curia Regis et Ordo Draconis" ("*Sarkany Rend*") was formed by Sigismund von Luxenbourg, the King of Hungary. The *Order of the Dragon* became a religious fraternity and militant order similar to the role that *Knights Templar* possessed during the Christian Crusades. Its members, called "*barons*," were charged to protect the integrity of Christianity from Muslim Turks—which they called "vampires." Ironically, Vlad II Drakul "*The Dragon*," father of one of the most famous vampires in history (Vlad III or <u>Dracula</u> "*Of the Dragon*"), was a member of the Order.

REDISCOVERING ENLIGHTENMENT : 1717—1776

In 1717 two important factions developed from conversations held in England at the *Apple Tree Tavern*: the revival of <u>Druidism</u> and, perhaps more famously, the lodge of <u>Freemasonry</u>.

Modern masons apply the allegory of Masonic work to everyday life, perfecting and purifying the temple of the local body and eventually the world at large. Masonic membership often overlaps other mystical organizations, leading scholars astray when they are concerned with tracing developments of secret societies. Underground networks provide members the ability to possess simultaneous membership in deeper exclusive fellowships. It was by the hand of Freemasons that the *Hermetic Order of the Golden Dawn* (GD) and *Bavarian Illuminati* emerged.

In 1776 the Bavarian Illuminati (Germany) and Masonic Republic (America) were formed. In America, *Freemasonry* played a central role in the shaping of government, politics and religion throughout its history. But most importantly, Masonry upholds the idea of individual "Gnosis" or freedom of "personal enlightenment" as a means of performing the Great Work—proper preparation and realization of both the physical and spiritual temple here on the Earth Planet.

Like other Mystery Schools, true secrets can never be confined to the printed word—the highest of which is referred to as the "Incommunicable Arcanum" or "Great Arcanum"—but instead must be experienced and realized into being by a dedication practitioner. Secrets of the Universe reveal themselves only to initiates that have properly prepared their temple to receive such mysteries. The lips of wisdom are sealed except to those with understanding; when the student is ready, the teacher will appear. Not surprisingly, politics and vanity have overrun much of *masonry* today. Members can still succumb to glamour (*maya*) of the mundane world if they have yet to discover and embrace the "clear light."

The all-seeing eye, a familiar *Masonic* symbol, represents the "Eye of Horus"—the ever-watchful *"eye of the gods."* In most cases, the unfinished tower—or pyramid—(on the back of the one dollar bill) represents the incomplete construction of the *"Tower of Babylon"* (*Babel*) and/or a reminder of the work still needing to be done here on Earth.

In *Masonry*, an initiate is likened to an unhewn stone—called the "rough ashler"—which must be molded and shaped by the tools (symbols) of the art to form a brick worthy of incorporation into the construction of the *"Great Temple"*—which is to say the Kingdom of Creation. The tools themselves—like the compass, square, plumb, level and ruler—were all once used in *Operant Masonry* and now remain abstract symbols reminding initiates of work to be done: the *Great Work*.

HUMANITY'S SEARCH FOR ITS SOUL : 1850—1984

Eleven miles southwest of the city-remains of Babylon—and many years before its discovery,—archaeologist Henry Rawlinson began excavation (in the 1850's) of the ruins of a different city—*Borsippa*—the sacred precinct of NABU, the Babylonian Anunnaki 'god' of writing, cuneiform and tablets.

The modern transliteration—*Borsippa*—is aligned to the original Sumerian designation: *Bad-Tibira*. In Babylonian (Akkadian) use of cuneiform, the name reads *Til-Barsip*. Its current Arabic name is *Birs Nimrud*. Among the ruined remains: the E.ZIDA—NABU's *Temple of the Seven Spheres*—established by the first Great Mardukite King—*Khammurabi*—then later restored by the last Great Mardukite King of Babylon, *Nebuchadnezzar II*.

Robert Koldewey led excavations of the "Babylon" site from 1899–1917 for the "*German Oriental Society.*" What Koldeway found were remains of Nebuchadnezzar II's "*Babylon*"—famously, the Temple of MARDUK—or E.SAG.ILA—(allegedly the "*Tower of Babel*") and the intact "*Ishtar Gate*" (which was immediately sent to the *Berlin Museum*).

During the late 19th thru 20th Century, *psychology* and *philosophy* collided with empirical *physics* and *biology* as humans struggled to understand their own existence and conditions on the planet. On a clinical level, early mental health surgical sciences and *electroconvulsive therapy* (ECT) did little more than demonstrate the creation of catatonic zombies—yet, high minds sharing exclusive affiliations, secretly meeting underground, were responsible for an influx of ancient knowledge and practical innovation.

Specific occultists, mystics, and *Masons*, developed secret societies responsible for delivering us the "New Age" material we have today. Their efforts included establishing libraries of information, recovering obscure manuscripts and publishing translations for their members—and eventually the public.

Inspiration for many of these groups—such as H.P. Blavatsky's *Theosophical Society* in 1884 (responsible for the *Secret Doctrine* and *Isis Unveiled*) and *Hermetic Order of the Golden Dawn* (GD)— was attributed to a "council" or "college" of Secret Chiefs, or else *etheric-alien* intelligence sometimes called the Great White Brotherhood. These forces influenced such members as S.L. MacGregor Mathers, Arthur Edward Waite and Israel Regardie —combined forming a list of editors for 90% of the occult classics for the onset of 20th Century, including *grimoires*, Tarot and eventual publication of the entire GD catalog of material.

Occult lodges churning; Bram Stoker's *Dracula*; experiments by Aleister Crowley in Egypt—the *Gate to the Outside* widens, the Calls are made and two UR-gods awaken: CHAOS and BABA-LON. In the autumn of 1907, H.P. Lovecraft endures the visions and nightmares leading up to writing "*Call of Cthulhu*" and the establishment of the famous "Cthulhu Mythos." At the same time, Aleister Crowley is in Egypt, writing the name TUTULU in "*Liber Liberi vel Lapidus Lazuli*" for first time:

> We know why all is hidden within the Stone,
> Within the Coffin,
> Within the Mighty Sepulchre,
> And we too, answer:
> OLALAM! IMAL! TUTULU!
> As is writ in the Ancient Book...

UNDISCOVERED UNCONSCIOUSNESS : 1900—PRESENT

Timothy Leary alluded that you have to go outside of your head to properly use your mind. But this thinking is far too mystical for conventional psychologists who would rather determine the truth of humans by studying rats. Consciousness was the original emphasis of early psychology. It appears mainly absent from the present science, or else is redefined to connect directly to the "brain" and not the Mind.

The "father" of modern psychology (*Wilhelm Wundt*) and *Edward Tichener* both emphasized the "structure of the mind" in early European psychology—in the late 1800s. When *Tichener* died in 1927, "structuralism" collapsed to the weight of *William James's* and "American Behaviorism," which was first called "functionalism." This new "Darwinian" slant on psychology emphasized the mind only as far as it concerned an external observable environment—in other words: behaviors.

Contemporary psychology operates under a premise that the only avenue it has to observe the mind is via the most obvious behaviors expressed outwardly in an empirical world. Needless to say, this effectively limited the field of psychology in favor of physics—eliminating connections to epistemology and metaphysics, which are now considered too superficial, or at the very least, too rhetorical to be relevant.

Very few figures in recent history have made the same broad sweeping global influence for our relevance than Carl Jung. A physician and creative psychologist in Switzerland by the age of 25, Jung made vast literary contributions to the growing fields of practical metaphysics, "creative" or "theoretical" metapsychology and transpersonal psychological methods. Carl Jung was never officially involved with any secret societies (as far as we know), but he became shunned as a *natural born mystic* by many friends and fellow academicians. By his own admission, raised in a household filled with paranormal phenomenon caused him to become a "sensitive." Upon waking each morning, he began a tradition of "centering" himself by drawing "mandalas." He developed an inclination towards the lore of alchemy, *Gnosticism* and the *Rosicrucians*, especially in relation to the subject of dreams.

While Carl Jung launched his medical career, Sigmund Freud published his famous treatise: "*The Interpretation of Dreams.*" Although he later disagreed with Freud's emphasis on sexuality and the lack of spiritual dimension in his work, Jung found that many suggestions made by Freud could be used to support his own unique system. The two were well acquainted and professionally traveled together from 1907 to 1912 until Jung's publication of "*Symbols of Transformation*" forced a separation. Freud died of a heroin overdose shortly thereafter.

Carl Jung's classification of the "psyche" is referred to frequently in New Age materials. He recognized that each of us lives according to an archetypal role: a "persona" that we play out in society. This may or may not relate to our "true" or "neglected" form, the *Shadow Self*. Certain "inclinations" seem dictated to us in our lives, whether descending from an all-encompassing *Higher Self* or the external *synchronicities* that occur seemingly unbidden. Jung coined the term "synchronicity," defining it as parallel events, instances or thoughts that have no physical, apparent or observable causal relationship. While many pass such moments off as "coincidence," Jung found that strong links of this nature continue to get stronger and will eventually surpass the simple classification of "happenstance" or "coincidence" if so recognized.

Throughout the 1960s and into the 1970s, many developments in "creative psychology" were made possible through more liberal experimentation into human reality. Much of this burrowed out from peculiar organizations, underground work with *psychedelics*, and other research into *Mind Control*—something that became of national security interest after the *Nazis* were overtaken in WWII. At the same time, a combination of beatniks and hippies worked together to launch a *new consciousness movement*—attemptnig to use drugs and meditation to open the *Doors of Perception*.

And here we are.

BOOK VI

THE POWER OF FIRE AND BLOOD

M - 5

−∧Ɣ∧−

MOROII AD VITAM PARAMUS

To Evolve − To Become − To Protect

—THE "NECRONOMICON" GNOSIS—

The Human Condition has been programmed with the belief that *Man is an Animal.* This is strnage. Humans like to act like "gods"—but they reject the idea of *Man as God.* Spirituality, Ascension and the *"God-Self"* aside; let us consider only physical sciences for a moment. What is the ultimate god-like quest? Control over the human condition—including behavior of others—control of the very mental faculties and programming that patterns of behavior rely on to function: *Mind Control.* What else drives the mortal bloodlust to gain power for, if not CONTROL? Behavior modification is just one way that we can describe the secret and forbidden work taking place right now on the planet. Increasing intelligence. Remote viewing. Space migration. Life extension into quasi-vampyric immortality of the Genetic Vehicle... Wait?!—What?! How did humanity become so vain that now it blatantly rejects the *Etheric Body* in favor of a physical shell suitable for endless body-worship. Even the *gods* knew better... *eventually.* Let us not forget the sacred covenant made between the Race of MARDUK and the Sons of ANU; what some call the:

Necronomicon Gnosis:
The Power of Man is the Power of the Ancient Ones.
The Power of Man is Knowledge of the Ancient Ones.
Power is in the Blood. Blood is Starfire.
And Blood of the Ancient Ones is the Blood of Man.

While some might dismiss such things as fanciful sentiments written simply to portray colorful word-pictures for the gullible, a closer examination at the logic might yield a different glimmer—*ancestral spirits, genetic memory*—the universal code embedded in *Starfyre* (in and of all things). We are approaching matters of true quantum entanglement, and we are *just* getting started!

> "...the GATE can be opened when the GREAT BEAR
> hangs from its tail in the sky..."

Scientists await results in their microscopes; seamlessly banging the building blocks of creation against each other, delighting in the damage like crazed teenagers. And while they wait in their white coats, mystics wait in hopes that an answer will come from the skies that all will recognize—we watch the stars, the abode of the gods. We are aware of their presence, that they come and go from this planet already—still, we wait for the proverbial *"Return"* ...when the *"stars are right."*

Uh... Yeah...

If we are to await an activating event to respond to, then we are no better than the *cattle* and *sheeple* we duck and dodge like the very squirrels running in front of our car wherever we go. We have already been given the faculties; for too long they have been suppressed. For too long we have waited for results that are *Ours* to initiate.

—BLOOD, BREATH AND LIFE ...AND SEX—
"<u>Blood</u> is *compulsory*; for we are <u>*all*</u> blood."

For what do we thirst? For what do we hunger? For the *gods* it is ambrosia. But what is this *Food of Life*—these *Waters of Life*? Tablet writings from Mesopotamia give us a clue when describing the Epic of Adapa (the original creation of humans, on which the Judaic story of Adam and Eve is based). Adapa, a new upgraded model of *adamu* given the Seed of Life from ENKI, is called before the *Anunnaki Assembly* to be inspected —for he carries the blood of ENKI and MARDUK, something previously forbidden. The *Anunnaki* fear propagation of this new species—it threatens their own survival on Earth to share *World Order* with Humans. They must make him like them; they must make him one of them.

When offered the Food of Life from the *gods*, Adapa declines graciously, stating that ENKI had instructed him not to eat or drink anything offered, that it would be the *Food of Death*. They correct him, saying that they will share the ambrosia of the *gods* with him—and he again declines in honor of his Father. Satisfied, albeit wary, the *Anunnaki Assembly* grants his mortality and permits him to return to Earth, where he describes having seen the whole "round" of it, from a "great height."

We won't even bother mentioning parallels between this 6,000 year old story and Judeo-Christian renditions of *Eden* or *Enoch*. There's nothing more to be gained there on this—going further down in reasoning and deeper in fragmentation. But let us consider for a moment the subject of zombies and mummies instead. This idea of *Food of Life* shared in an abode of the gods appears in Egyptian accounts, too. Death cults responsible for burial preparations and funerary practices understood this well; the nature of life and death—such is the way of the *Necromancer*.

When *Undead* spirits are not furnished with the *"Food of Life"*— no brains, no blood, no starfyre/lifeforce/essence, &tc. &tc.— they revert into *monsters* rather than legendary *heroes*. As the purpose of life is to exist and survive: the body... the mind... the Etheric Self. Everything fights the entropy—fights against the entropy of existence—at its own level to prove the right to exist. Maintaining the condition of life is akin to maintaining the life for which one is accustomed.

There are so many facets of our being in motion, growing, expanding, condensing—always in motion. We are a integral part of the story; a hero in the pathway of *Starfyre*, charged to go forth and do the best we can on our adventure...We need to do better. And we know this too, because we are not satisfied —and not the way in which materialist humans are never satisfied—we remain plagued with a critical condition constantly pulling on our etheric heart strings, pulling us up to a higher state; calling us home. We have become complacent and comfortable in the world allotted us—albeit pissed off; throwing tantrums; all the while our true nature shines clear when the curtain falls and we are again left with our *Selves*.

Sexual Magic, as available to the *Outer Circle*—meaning most of what is commonly produced for your corner bookstore and propagated by ignorant horny leaders—is called "*Black Tantra*" or "*sex magick.*" These practices promote use of sexual orgasm and its fluids to raise and direct personally raised energy. As we are to find out when we roll the dice at the <u>Ninth Gate</u>— demonstrated by the genital area chakras—*Black Tantra* is the path back down the *Serpent's Tail*, leading us away from the Highest.

<u>Red Magic</u> is popular among *dragonkind* because it merges sex magic with the attainment of power, and this is a dangerous combination without temperance. These vampyric rites of *Starfyre* sexually charge fluids of the body, which also carry personal genetics. This includes: saliva, semen and vaginal sweat as the *White Dragon*; Blood satisfies the requirement of the *Red Dragon*. And because Human blood is far from "dragon-blood," only menstrual blood is powerful enough for this due to its hormonal charge; representing the sacrifice of virginity.

Magicians engaging in sexual practice will involve their mates into their energy work. This is natural. By pairing with their mate, they attune to each other—the vibrational frequencies meet in a mutual pool. Everyone has this happen to them, but that's like saying everyone breathes so everyone is a master at yoga and meditation (which is not the case). Spiritual Master, Samael Aun Weor speaks to his students in "*Light From Darkness: A Practical Science of Spiritual Awakening*" about explosive power and dynamite explosions involved with practice of Red Magic—how dangerous and energetically destructive it can be if not handled appropriately. He explains:—

> "Very deeply analyzing the astounding power of sexual energy, we arrive at the conclusion that it is extraordinarily volatile and very difficult to store and control. Sexual energy is like a deposit of dynamite; its presence signifies a formidable source of tremendous potentiality, and also a constant danger of a catastrophic explosion.

"The sexual energy has its own channels of circulation, its own organized electrical system. When the sexual energy infiltrates the mechanism of other functions, it can produce great explosions, tremendous biological, physiological, and psychic catastrophes.

"Violent and destructive types of manifestations of the sexual energy are generally derived from certain negative psychological attitudes towards sex. Suspicion, fear of sex, sexual prejudices, the cynical, brutal, or obscene sense of sex, &tc., obstruct the channels whereby sexual energy circulates, and therefore the sexual energy deviates and infiltrates other channels, systems, and functions where it produces frightening catastrophes."

The Ninth Gate or *Ninth Kabbalistic Sphere* is *Yesod*. *Yesod* appears to vibrate at the same frequency as sexual organs when depicted on the *Kabbalah of Man*. This means that the key to accessing the Ninth Gate is embedded in human sexuality. This is also depicted in the film, "*The Ninth Gate*" starring Johnny Depp (based on the novel "*Club Dumas*"). At the end of the movie, his character accesses the Ninth Gate through sexual intercourse with the scarlet lady BABALON (or LILITH), green-eyed red-haired Queen of the Night.

Male continence is a powerful practice in Tantra, and ancient mystical traditions like Druidism. The subject is explored in "*The 21 Lessons of Merlyn*" by Douglas Monroe as "spiritual continence," where certain practices of sexual discipline were "a natural way to a higher spiritual accomplishment." To discipline the body is to feed the spirit. Disciplined sacred sexuality as a practice requires intercourse without male ejaculation.

Sexual vitality, *pranic force* (*Starfyre*) and fluids of life-force energy are not meant to be wasted. While the spirit may be eternal, the physical body is only capable of generating this type of power for a certain time. The spark of energy needed for the seed to manifest is godlike—power of the *Divine Spark of Life*...literally within the palm of your hands. Different schools are going to offer different philosophies on *Sexual Magic*. But, the nature of this practice is quite clear: ejaculation of semen in the physical world is used as <u>Low Magic</u> to produce physical manifestations.

As we create a condition of *being* in the physical world, something is taken away from the *Other*—a condition of existence will also create a condition of non-existence, somewhere else —and so *Etheric* energy is transformed and spent to balance the equation. Higher forms of sexual magic may be applied to master the <u>Kundalini Serpent</u>, such as *White Tantra*. As Samuel Aun Weor goes on to explain: —

"There are three types of *Tantra*: White, Black and Grey.

"In *White Tantra*, ejaculation of the semen is prohibited. In *Black Tantra*, ejaculation of the semen is obligatory.

"In *Grey Tantra*, ejaculation of the semen is not considered important, yet in the long run, *Grey Tantra* is transformed into *Black Tantra*.

"In *White Tantra*, the serpent ascends along the length of the medulla of the spinal cord. In *Black Tantra*, the serpent descends, projecting itself down from the coccyx towards the atomic infernos of the human being, thus becoming the *Dragon's Tail*.

"*Kundalini* has seven degrees (*chakra*) of the power of the fire. Only by practicing *Maithuna* daily over a period of twenty or thirty years can a person achieve the total development of *Kundalini*..."

Our physical form goes through its own energetic cycles—called *Bio-Rhythms*—often manifested in <u>hormonal</u> changes in the body, which in turn affect our *emotional* current, our mind set and resulting behavioral tendencies. Personal (sexual) fluids are altered by hormones as well. At night, *melatonin* and growth hormone is released into the bloodstream. Given that nighttime is preferred for most magical practices—and that monthly hormonal cycles are also affected by the moon—than the purpose of magical timing (*at night on a full moon, etc.*) may have stronger personal relevance for magical success than we may have previously thought. The moon also affects electrical activity in the brain; seizures, strokes and epileptic episodes increase during the *full moon*. Anything forced by predation or coercion is not spiritually viable. Elevated *adrenaline* and *endorphin* hormones from "fear-turned-survival-mode" disrupt the energy flow sought for operations of <u>High Magic</u>.

The "Ninth Gate" is the door to the *Abyss*—that which we must cross to complete our journey. To enter the Gate is to surrender to the Divine Feminine, the Dragon Creatrix—TIAMAT —*Life-Giving Mother!* This primeval "Rite of the Abyss" is the most coveted of all rituals. Connection with the Source of our Life allows an unlocking of latent DNA—to tap potentials of genetic memory encoded into the Human Condition with latent faculties that lay dormant in certain individuals.

DNA constitutes the shape and structure of the *astra* auric energy field around the body. We are, indeed, "magnetic ink." More than that? "*Of course, you are, my practical Star... face piles of trials with smiles.*" Axonal discharge from our genetic design is an electrical charge produced by the body. It generates the "<u>morphic</u>" field around the body that is being read in *Kirilian* photography (*Aura pictures*).

<u>Electromagnetic Fields</u> (EMFs) are an important part of the human experience. Almost everything that we experience in light and sound exists on the *Electromagnetic Spectrum*. <u>Frequency</u> of *electron flow* is what divides colored light from UV; separates radio waves from microwaves—these all exist on the same existential spectrum, only varying in degree. Everything that vibrates an existence has some kind of EMF. Everything is a vibration of the same *Starfyre*, only varying in degree.

EMFs allow life to physically demonstrate existence on Earth; the Earth as its own organism (Gaea) vibrates a field—scientists call this <u>geomagnetism</u>—referring to the field protecting the earth as an entity in the *cosmos*—outer space, something too often taken for granted by a population too busy looking down at their *smartphones* to realize that we are on "Spaceship Earth" traveling thousands of miles per hour through space on the arm of an entire galaxy doing the same.

New Age traditions bloomed in mainstream view during the 1990's; a melting pot of spiritual traditions and philosophies were being brought into the fray. One of the more interesting things that people talked about at that time was a Hopi prophecy concerning pole shifts (*axis mutatis*)—meaning a change in the magnetic poles of the axis on which the planet spins. While it is true that small changes occur intermittently, our research revealed that EM-North has shifted more in the last two decades than in the last 500 years!

Many theories exist concerning <u>biorhythms</u>—natural cycles related to apparent patterns in one's life. But we do know that the Human Condition is very sensitive to its environment and that mood, endurance and personal energy levels are going to fluctuate. Reactive programming is also fairly easy to condition in Human too. Humans may even be conditioned by the changing "seasons" or demonstrate emotional tides during the course of the year in relation to the time of their birth. In fact, different individuals may be found to "come into their season" at certain times of year—consistently.

Physiology—the entire makeup of our physical being—fluctuates from night and day; shifts in energy that can be predicted from natural (environmental) factors. Emotional scales are a lot longer and correlate with the 28 day (4 weeks) lunar month—thus hormonal levels change for both men *and* women—everyone's getting their *monthlies!* There are also many other scales and theories put forth into this school of thought, which at best has remained in the realm of "*pseudoscience.*"

—THE VOODOO OF MAKING MONSTERS—
"Fear and Ignorance Creates Monsters"

<u>Biohazards</u> (*bio-hazard*) are all things that pose a *biological hazard*—meaning negative effects on health conditions for life, and that which inhibits the ability to continue one's existence. Those *Creatures of Night* from the classic "VWZ" (*vampire-were-wolf-zombie*) persuasion could all fall under that category in some respects, particularly in relation to the human life.

This biohazard symbol has become an icon for the "<u>industrial</u>" and <u>cyber goth</u> music scenes—not to mention *zombies* and Mardukite <u>CyberVamps</u>. This sign was originally developed by Charles Baldwin for the DOW chemical company in 1966.

The <u>radiation</u> symbol was developed by the "G" so they could mark sites that had been exposed to high amounts of ionic radiation—from test-bombing or *nuclear* waste... which, even the name of the later suggests its "not clear." A similar symbol using triangles designates *fallout shelters* maintained to provide sanctuary from *radioactive fallout.*

Radiation in and of itself is not a "negative" or "harmful" thing. In fact radiation is little more than a way of saying energy in transit. This can be any motion (or transmission) of particles or EM waves. However, high energy *ionic raditation* involves removal of electrons from high energy atoms and transmitting it to some organic or inert material—this could be water; could be you; rocks have the ability to absorb it—*whatever it is*, it is now considered <u>radioactive</u>.

Radiation, radioactivity, biohazards, infections, *etc*... Such are the ways vampyric and werewolf and zombie *darksider diseases* are portrayed in such cyber-thrillers as *Daybreakers, Resident Evil, Ultraviolet, Wer* and a host of others. And on a technological and biological level, all of that is possible—but that is not where the arcane lore of the *"Zombi"* really comes from.

Ethnobotonist, Wade Davis, set out to discover the mysteries of the Voudou Zombie and published most of his findings in *"Serpent and the Rainbow"* (1988). He found that there really was something to this phenomenon. Rather than becoming a subject of psychosis, fantasy or self-delusion—zombification is a process; it requires actions by someone else: a witch-doctor or Sorcerer. What's more: Davis discovered that psychological effects from the cultural belief and fear of *zombification* increased the potency of mind-effect in such cultures.

Vodou – Vodon – Vodoun – Vaudou – Voodoo—spell it six ways to Sunday it will always come up to mean *"of the spirits."* The distinction we must make is not in the semantics of the spelling, but in origins of the practice being referred to. In literature, a distinction is often made in spelling to keep the text-meaning clear. That being said, in addition to the original Haitian (*Haiti*) practices of Vodou, there is also what most have simply called *Louisiana* or *New Orleans* Voodoo.

On the island of Haiti, the *Vodou* tradition is a functional religion and spiritual tradition combining elements of Santeria with Afro-Caribbean *esoterica*. The *Voodoo* practiced in America has a greater emphasis on mysticism, magic and occult—particularly regarding: lore of *Li Grand Zombi*; use of *gris-gris* (herbal sachets or *"voodoo dolls"*); and political importance of *"Voodoo Queens"* such as the famous *Marie Laveau*.

Many years before Wade Davis investigated the *Haitian Zombi*, William Seabrook (*writer/explorer*), a correspondent and initiate of *Aleister Crowley*, set out to Haiti in 1928 and became enamored with the "physical sorcery" he discovered; most of which relied on knowing botanical lore and *herbology*. He discovered that at one pharmacological element of the zombie phenomenon was *jimsonweed* also known as the "*Zombie Cucumber*" from the nightshade family of plants. This is referred to as "Voodoo Medicine" in the film "*Hello, Again.*"

The purpose behind the *zombie* form of Necromancy is quite clear—it goes back to where we started: the god-like quest to CONTROL human behavior. It is by no coincidence that *Haitian Vodou* grew from an island nation that is dependent on its sugar plantations; or that it spread to America via slave ports in the south. *Zombies* are for one purpose: to serve a function intended by their controller: the "overseer" desiring plantation labor—but without the responsibility of "sensible" slaves.

Zombies are *made*. Someone *makes* them. Someone is responsible for the "magic" that controls them. And that is actually what researchers found when they chanced the experience. They found *mindless* slaves working in the fields as if drugged by some psychotropic compound. These *Undead* seem quite different than other *Creatures of Night*...but they are, for all intents and purposes, "Darksiders"—members of the *Undead*.

Zombie Voodoo requires taking a person and bringing them to the point of death—but not past it. Thus, the secrets of its practice are a highly refined skill in executing the proper substances in the proper amounts. The metabolism is slowed to yield an appearance of death, but leaving the subject in a condition from which they will be revived for *zombification*. Those *Haitian* slaves working in the fields were *zombies*—made and controlled by a combination of *Vodou* sorcery and grave-robbing. The process is actually quite ingenious: using poison to simulate death, burying the body as deceased and returning in a couple days to exhume the body, only to drug it again and keep it perpetually disoriented, but capable to do simple tasks.

The Haitian government certainly takes this serious enough to make it *against the law* to "make" zombies. The Haitian penal code passed in 1883 (*Article 246*, often incorrectly identified in zombie literature as *Article 249*) states that "the act of poisoning with the intent to produce a deathlike state" shall be punishable the same as murder!

Zombies are real. *Zombification* is possible. The last obvious question then is: *How?* Apothecary knowledge and alchemy all began with the "black arts" and this forbidden science is no different. An examination of the compounds used to produce these results show *herbology* at its finest; a careful combination of *skin, meat, herb* and *seed*. Research yielded the following list of compounds, provided here for posterity only.

SKIN: cane toad skin (*bufo marinus*)
MEAT: pufferfish (*diodon hystrix* and *sphoeroides testudineus*)
HERB: itching peas (*mucuna pruriens*)
SEED: *tcha tcha* tree seeds (*albizia lebbick*)

The mere mention of the pufferfish only shows how dangerous these concoctions really are. Pufferfish is prepared as a dietary delicacy called *fugu*. Proper preparation of the fish determines if a person will enjoy a fine meal or end up being poisoned to death. The natural poison in the fish is a powerful nerve agent—*tetrodotoxin*—one-hundred times the strength of *hydrogen cyanide* (Zyklon B). It affects all of the body muscles and organs before reaching the brain, so a victim is conscious through the whole dying process—simply unable to move.

—DARKSIDER DISEASES : BIOLOGICAL—

Conditions all around us affect our physiology—there is no denying that. Population integrations result in new sicknesses. Air contagions from industrial processes contribute to the evolution of humanity as a genetic being. The foods we eat affect us. They contribute less to our nutrition and more to our destruction than is published. So long as the civic system gets the work out of you for a time, then no one cares. Our world became as such where it is actually inconvenient to care about the working class—and that, right there, will be its undoing. As I wrote these words, the civil rights activist hacker group <u>Anonymous</u> targeted *Denver* for its intolerance to a homeless population and refusal to provide adequate affordable housing. A revolution is *coming*; a revolution is *here*.

It seems strange that anyone should be surprised at how the <u>NexGen</u> are operating as genetic beings. They are born from a synthetic age, bombarded by active bands of wireless energy 24/7 from birth. No one really even knows what the long-term effects of this will be, especially in how the *"human condition"* can change as a result of constant interaction with these EMFs. If food and viral colds can change our *genetic* makeup, consider what occurs when *"<u>new consciousness</u>"* generations of psychedelic mind expansion and chemical gate opening produce subsequent generations. We have *"Rainbow Children"* being born to mind-blown hippies and "Crystal Children" born from *tweakers* and *meth-heads*? Hey, why not?

In *"Vampyre's Bible"* the term "darksider disease" is used to describe metaphysical conditions as contributing or <u>perturbing</u> factors (unseen variables). These variables can manifest as clinical diseases when using that paradigm of terminology to describe the same phenomenon. They are not mutually exclusive. An unseen level contributes to our reality. There are results of those contributions that we do see and give labels to. It does not *actually* change the nature of the labeled thing. Two examples that regularly apply to physical conditions of *vampires, werewolves* and *zombies* are <u>Anemia</u> and <u>Rabies</u>.

Anemia is a common *Darksider Disease* that actually affects one billion of Earth's population to some varying degree for some varying cause, not all of which are attributable to *darksider* conditions. *Anemia* means: "no" (*an*)—"blood" (*haima*) and it comes in several varieties, two of which—*iron-deficiency anemia* and *anemic porphyria*—are of particular interest to our studies—as first explained in *"The Vampyre's Bible."* Like other *Darksider Diseases,* both Anemia and Porphyria can also remain indefinitely dormant in the blood system until activated by some triggering condition.

Anemic conditions—a reduced quantity of *red blood cells* (RBC)—can be genetic or occur environmentally. The most common type is *iron-deficient*. Having a reduced RBC count means less *hemoglobin*—a protein containing iron that is important for the transportation of oxygen throughout the body. *Iron* supplements and *heme* injections are applied to modern conditions, but in the past, some scholars have concluded that these conditions could generate a thirst for blood as self-medication. This implies genetic evolutionary survival.

Porphyria is another form of *anemia* applied to both *vampire* and *werewolf* conditions. Its name derives from the Greek word for "*purple.*" They named it for the color often found in urine and feces of the subject. Common and reoccurring symptoms include: acute light/sunlight sensitivity of the skin and eyes; anxiety/OCD; chronic depression; lightheaded; pale, cold or yellowing skin; seizures; visual and auditory hallucinations; and yellowing eyes.

Rabies and *Zombie*-like infections are quite different than *anemia*. The *rabies* virus affects mammals, often transmitted through animal bites (*saliva*) and skin abrasions (scratches) or any way contaminated fluids (or from the hand) can come in contact with eyes, nose or mouth. *Rabies* in Latin is "madness," possibly derived from Sanskrit *rabhas*—meaning "violence."

The *rabiform virus* presented in many pop-culture "*zombie*" films and literature is a form of *Lyssavirus,* named after LYSSA, the Greek goddess of madness, rage, and ferocity. However, first mention of *rabies,* appears (like most things) in Mesopotamia on the Sumerian *cuneiform* tablets of the "*Laws of Eshunna.*" According to this civic code, owners of rabid dogs are required to take precautions against spread of the disease and are heavily fined for offenses.

Rabies attacks the brain directly, spreading through peripheral nerves—the *central nervous system* (CNS)—to cause fatal inflammation in the brain. The disease is a 99.99% death sentence, but not before loss of muscular control, convulsive fits and of course, heightened aggression. The few survivors of this experience are subjects that underwent the "*Milwaukee protocol.*" For this medical treatment, *ketamine* is used to induce a coma, while a battery of other anti-viral drugs are administered continuously until the immune system can naturally produce its own necessary antibodies again.

BOOK VII

THE SECRETS OF MERLIN

M – 6

– ∧Ψ∧ –

MOROII AD VITAM PARAMUS

To Evolve – To Become – To Protect

—THE BLACK SWAN—

"Whatsoever you enact in the Earth World is not separate —it significantly and necessarily has its higher counterpart in the Otherworld." —*Book of Sajaha (Shayaha) the Seer*

MERLIN is perhaps the most recognizable archetype of *magician* in human consciousness; where would we be without him? His magic has captivated and inspired for hundreds of years—he succeeded in being timeless! The *Necromancer* who lived *forever!*

MERLIN is a reminder to us of the <u>Black Swan</u>. That there is always *some* magic and mystery to life. That there will always be something out there beyond what we can know or possibly even expect. *Black Swans* are high profile, unpredictable and rare events overwhelmingly beyond the normal expectations of history, economics and technology. These small incidents have epic roles in changing the course of historical affairs— even if they are ever after to remain enigmatic and mysterious. We must never lose the enchantment of our everyday lives; doing so is to give in to the entropic monster seeking to devour us all—"*The sea shall not have them!*"

Handling *Karmic Energy* and *Life Lessons* are an integral part of "learning" and "evolving" SELF—auto-correcting conditions of <u>Identity</u>, that either lead us toward or away from our highest evolution. *Reality* is entirely energetic in its composition—*a virtual cyberspace*—represented in degrees of energy manifesting as symbols, props and analogous learning tools and even educational aids, experienced in-and-as our "*everyday*" life.

Magical work and a mystical life bridges the *physical mind* with the ethereal infinite to relay messages to us—in dreams, deep meditation, and naturally, channels of inter-dimensional communication. Every single day is an adventure for the spirit within—so make every aspect of life a contributor to your spiritual evolution.

—KEYS TO THE KINGDOM—

1. Self-Purity and the acquisition of True Knowledge
2. Self-Dedication and development of True Understanding
3. Pure Invocation and the execution of True Action

1. Purification & True Knowledge:

The path to power begins first by purifying the self, both within and without, in addition to the material and the immaterial, the mind and the environment, the set and setting. Without self-honesty—the state of being in Self, free of conditioning—a practitioner is unable to fully "self-actualize" beyond the degree they are conditioned to be—typically a "victim" of circumstances, unable to channel and manifest from within the self-made prison. Physical purity of the body is just as important as spiritual cleanliness and ritual etiquette.

2. Dedication & True Understanding:

Beliefs and judgments affect our personal attention and the flow of energy processed by our being like a catalyst. We are all interconnected by the grid-like *matrix* in the background of reality. To become an empty vessel is not enough, it must be filled by *"true knowledge"* and only afterward, via dedication and commitment, can it be realized as *"true understanding."* Personal dedication requires setting the mind to understanding knowledge of how and why things *are*, learning when to give up the hold of narrow minded social programming. No matter what we *think* we *know*—powers that bind the truth of things are well beyond material comprehension.

3. Invocation & True Action:

Powers of a dedicated priest or magician are drawn from both internal and external sources. Power behind magic is drawn forth, called up, *conjured* from within, by *birthright*. Power behind magic can be drawn down, called forth, *evoked* from without by *dedication*. When combined, the *Magician* effectively executes "Invocation" which is to "invite in" a specific intelligence (*energetic current or stream*). Whether we label the current ENKI or MARDUK or BUDDHA or JESUS or DYS PATER or

JUPITER, the effect is unchanged. Success doesn't rely on labels, it is dependent on an individual's ability to meet the frequency, communicate with and tap into the specific energy current being sought. Only when we operate form the "God-Self," is True Action possible.

PERSONAL BIO-MAGNETISM : FIELDS
"Energy flows where attention goes."

Your <u>Light Body</u> is influenced by your 'mental state' and general condition of the 'physical' and 'emotional' self. Dedication to the *Great Work* and traveling the *Right Way* naturally expands the influence and power of the <u>astra</u> (*aura*). The nature of *"personal vibrations"* you project outwardly as your <u>Light Shield</u>—your personal energetic field—affects how you interpret [*process*] events and encounters. This has a direct relationship on energetic exchanges taking place as part of your *Reality Experience*.

Performing <u>energy work</u> has an effect beyond yourself. Energy is at work all the time, evident by the periodic energy spikes that can draw the attention energy of a nation through media. Energy is working when social outlets of emotional discharge are present. And when it can resonate with others of a like frequency—such as at celebrations or sporting events—it can reach intoxicating levels, even enough to charge spaces to resonate a specific energy frequency thereafter.

Energetic <u>resonance</u> of locations are relative to energetic streams that interact there—both in frequency and amplitude. For example, there is: the natural memory of the place itself; geological factors and EMF movement; and ultimately, the energetic residue (*signatures*) left behind from people and high-level emotional events—all of which develop a *resonance* "type" affecting the total sum of charged energy present. Not to mention—the perspective of the *Observer* having the experience.

"All life exists with the power to reproduce in kind. We are given, not only the ability to reproduce, but the task of nourishing and fueling each other through the positive and negative formation, in this way increasing the strength of our magnetic field to bring our bodies and minds to the highest level of health and vitality."   —William E. Gray

Mystics and *Magicians* demonstrate an upper hand in life by manifesting their will and finding themselves in *synchronistic* circumstances that seem magical. Understanding energy fields, their interactions and its affect on perceived reality is what makes this possible.

Resonance applies to more than just locations—laws of energy are *universal*. This applies to people as well, but in this case, we don't usually refer to it as resonance. Resonance between us and certain people, places or objects is called a *link, cord* or *bond*. Energetic exchanges are always taking place along these streams, and this increases when we give a particular *link* our attention. Etheric (*ethereal*) links, cords and bonds form as a result of any energetic wave interaction that takes place. This happens between romantic couples, friends, peer groups, coworkers, extended family, past lovers, and even clerks at the convenience store, who you don't even know. Some of the most significant bonds you will experience can begin with a simple energetic exchange. These conduits are the pathways by which energy is transmitted and received from two sources. Pathways for energy strengthen through increased time together (frequency) and its intensity (amplitude).

Encounters may trigger you to assume a different frequency to meet some "relationship role." This is where there is flexibility in consciously altering our energy; and we may freely do so as long as it is *Self-Directed* and not reactive programming. Energy transformations are going to happen at these lower levels of existence—so, be in charge of yours and choose the mask you wear for impressions very carefully. For many, the masks are much more easily put on then taken off.

There will always be a cord once the connection is made. Even the ones in the distant past we are connected to through memory. As soon as our Awareness falls on to our past memories, the conduit becomes active again and conscious energy will be feeding an aspect of your life that can no longer benefit you. If you notice, people use memory recall to bring forth—literally *"conjure"*—a particular state or mood desired for some purpose. Rather than sending energy backwards, you can more effectively alter your present state with intention and will, producing an increase of energy in the present!

A negligible amount of energy is always "bleeding" off through every one of your links once formed. Even a thread is still a link. They are instantly reactivated and reinforced with attention. People get caught up in past social lessons or stuck in old emotional cycles when energy is being sent to something that is no longer in the "present" to reciprocate as a closed circuit. Connections can also be formed unconsciously through casual interaction and then reinforced with repetition. Existing links become stronger and the threshold increases. As the pathway increases in its size, cumulatively more energy can be passed through at a time. Even the smallest bit of contact, like a hug or a handshake, will create links —yes, even pushes and bumps. This is one reason why sensitives avoid all unnecessary physical contact. Use discretion concerning who you surround yourself and interact with—and especially who you have romantic encounters with.

Starfyre is the ultimate psychotropic drug of Life. Each variation of energy changes how we process our Reality experience. As with anything else that causes a sensation, alteration of perception, and/or a head-change, addictions can form to specific energy signatures—specific types of energy. There is a reason being around certain people and places causes a specific kind of sensation.

We are chemically energetic beings, so when we are removed from something we have developed a dependency toward, we are always going to go through residual energetic withdrawals. As long-term relationships develop, very strong bonds and permanent ties are made.

Starfyre pathways are linked with a cord. These "*astral cords*" can stretch infinitely. You can't cut them or tear them. If an "abandoned" conduit is a problem, there are two properties of energy that you can influence: frequency and amplitude. You can use will and intention to reduce the amplitude of flow to "*shrink the link*" or you can use shields, blocks, filters and dampeners based on frequency at the incoming connection to your *astra*. The best option, however, is always preventative: be careful what you come in contact with in the first place.

Energetic exchange is a communication of information or data. This means we are, in essence, still in communication—*linked up*—to all of the channels (*bonds*) we have established in our lifetime; and, according to some philosophies—many lifetimes. Developing a concentration of energy creates a *beacon*. Individuals can become *beacons*, powerful enough to engage others in their daily lives and promote transformation. This is one way in which we can covertly change the world.

Thoughts, emotions, actions, words and intentions *all* carry a unique 'energetic frequency vibration' that acts upon the ambient *Matrix-Field* like a *wave* in a '*Universal Ocean*'. Thoughts do not even need to be spoken in order to be heard. Sounds can be sent out in sub-vocalizations; subtle vibrations from the throat—not to mention, people also broadcast their thoughts mentally, often quite loudly.

To hear the thoughts of others you must practice deep relaxation. Keep the mind free and connect to the person based on what you know of them and the energetic connection. When you are attuned, relax and allow thoughts to come. The key to the *occult* and *esoteric* science is not to accumulate and memorize a lot of data to bring to the table, but to be able to still the mind and being emptiness to an empty table and wait to see what will manifest. Anyone can force a specific visualization—but, it takes experience to turn off the mind, relax and float down stream to the Infinite.

—PSYCHIC WARFARE : MAGICAL COMBAT—

As the New Age movement advanced during the last century, accessibility of magical training reached every town in America. Consequently, incidents of psychic or magical warfare began to increase. Negative thinking strong enough to project emotional energy to another person happens all the time—now we have the same people being empowered with magical techniques to supplement their wild egotistical nature.

Magical warfare is not a recent invention. Some of the oldest magic texts deal specifically with <u>counterspells</u> and defense against evil witches and sorcerers. In the history of *esoteric occultism*, psychic attacks resulted from egotistical sorcerers all the time. When the *Hermetic Order of the Golden Dawn* didn't allow Aleister Crowley directly into its Inner Circle, warfare ensued between the black magician and S.L. MacGregor Mathers, who was responsible for the GD decision.

An experienced *mystic* should be able to determine the source of their own energy fluctuations. Psychic, *psionic* or psychological attacks are intentional. There are also psychic parasites (or *leeches*) that simply drain, just like there are certain locations or objects that may possess residual ambient resonance. Energy drain can also take place via established links, cords and bonds—or through newly established links. Piercing attacks use directed rays or "magic missiles" to puncture a <u>Circle of Protection</u> or pierce the *astra* and deal auric wounds.

You affect the charge of particles and energetic resonance of your environment. These currents are passed through your *auric filter* as it is encountered. In most cases, the will of an active participant will outweigh *environmental residual*.

In times of strain or stress when the aura is weakened, physical and *psychical immunity* is equally weakened and you are most susceptible to external influences. When in doubt you can use your hands (or another viable method) to perform <u>energy testing</u>, feeling for shifts, variations or alterations in an energy field.

As in traditional combat, *psychic warfare* is divided into powers of the sword and powers of the shield. There are both active and passive means of defense. Defense in any situation requires awareness and knowledge of not only your opponent, but also yourself—your strengths and weaknesses. Active defense requires personal energy; any technique that requires constant attention should be used sparingly. There's a difference between passively wearing a raincoat and actively walking around holding up an umbrella—or having to always carry it with you *"just in case."*

THE INNER TEMPLE

This rite is to cleanse the *inner temple* and/or as preparation for other *energy work*.

1. Sit comfortably, hands and feet not crossing.
2. Visualize an atmosphere of white cleansing energy.
3. Begin inhaling it into your body.
4. Allow it to wash through you.
5. Now breathe in clear air.
6. As you breathe in clear air, see and feel it pushing out the impurities, the cleansing air is purified.
7. These impurities fall to your feet and are pushed into the ground.
8. Intone: *O Forces of White Light, Starfyre, cleanse my Inner Temple of impurity. Cleanse me now. Make me pure. So must it be.*
9. Visualize the white light energy returning around you.
10. Feel and see it perform a protective aura around your body, beginning with the head and moving down.

CIRCLE OF PROTECTION—(COP)

1. Activate the *Inner Temple*.
2. Activate a *Blue Crown of Healing Energy* (see Appendix)
3. Go to the eastern quarter of your <u>nemeton</u> and perform a process for *casting a circle*.
4. See the circle blazing with blue and white energy.
5. Visualize an image of your enemy standing just outside the boundary of the circle facing you.
6. Concentrate a white beam of *Starfyre* energy.
7. Concentrate this beam down on your enemy.
8. Concentrate swirling beams of white energy thrashing about inside the circle, building energy and protecting you.
9. Hold this imagery for three minutes.
10. Intone: *By the Rays of Starfyre, the Powers of Radiance: Raphael, Michael, Gabriel, Uriel- Be ye the powers around me as a I stand in the sacred center of the Holy Mandala.*
11. Address your enemy: *I refuse to allow your influence and undesirable attacks to affect me. Waste no more time and energy on me as I am protected by the Light of Starfyre. I am secure in Light of Starfyre, safe from you! Go! Now! So mote it be.*
12. See the enemy as becoming dissolved in white light, then extinguish the energy of the Circle.

—CLEARING AND CLEANSING—

Energy work is about the movement of energy; energy in motion. For new energy to be brought in, *mystics* take time to cleanse or clear out old energy and erroneous computations. If this seems confusing—as with all magical lessons—one need only look to Nature to answer our questions. Seasonal cycles are emphasized in New Age traditions because of the manner which it reflects the pattern of life and death throughout the cosmos. New growth, new life and potential is attributed best to the spring season—a time of renewal. There can be no new growth in Nature without breakdown and removal of the old. Nothing escapes *entropy*—but then, nothing really dies. Stagnation and immobility of energy contributes to toxicity.

—DARKSIDER DISEASES : PSYCHOLOGICAL—

In a previous segment, chemical and biological factors were classifiable physiological *Darksider Diseases*. Psychological and spiritual aspects of the "human condition" are also affected by unseen variables with visible results—in this case: *psychological* in nature. Energy disturbances result as restrictions of the flow. Rather than simply affecting the inflow of energy (causing low energy or the feeling of drain), high energy (overactive) blockages manifest as psychological conditions.

There is a normative impairment of mental faculties that western science comes to expect from the human condition—usually attributed to age. There are many other reasons why someone might develop a neuro-cognitive disorder or <u>dementia</u>. On the other hand, a more common psychological *Darksider Disease* is often confused with *dementia*—and also results from an energetic imbalance.

For reasons yet to be determined, *darksiders* frequently exhibit symptoms typical of <u>schizophrenia</u>. This being said, there can be many other factors a person might be diagnosed with *dissociative disorders, manic-depressive psychosis* and *psychotic depression*. It is these types of conditions that can be representative of *schizophrenia*.

Schizophrenia is *not* a split-personality or multiple-personality disorder, like many people think it is. People suffering from this are not talking to themselves having hallucinations on street-corners. Schizophrenia is actually a defect in the pleasure responses of the brain; for example—*serotonin, dopamine* and other hormones. More than simply "not feeling happy," this type of deficiency often results in the continuous elevation of the fight—flight response mechanisms programmed as our "survival mode." Responses are automatic autonomous programmed reactions. For this reason, a subject may appear to operate as if in an altered reality when observed objectively by a third-party.

It might be easy to dismiss such cases as "crazy people on the verge of a psychotic break"—"maybe they just got slipped one too many hits of *LSD*"—but many of these people lead functionally public lives, and overactive energies can produce autistic-like intelligence that is quite profound. Example: John Nash, a mathematician and world-renown "games and systems" theorist. His story became the basis for the book and film "*A Beautiful Mind*."

Actual symptoms from schizophrenia include the feeling of being "emotionally flat"—having little emotion, an inability to experience pleasure, avoidance of direct eye contact, lack of motivation to develop social relationships or interact with the "outside" world. In addition to abnormal social behavior, shifting irritability and withdrawal can cause unexpected swings in introversion and extroversion. As a mental health issue, conditions associated with *schizophrenia* often couple with other anxiety, depressive and sociological disorders such as substance abuse (addiction) from self-medication.

GENETIC SET → positive coefficient = .40 – .80
   "Schizophrenia is associated with enlarged lateral ventricles
      in the brain."

ENVIRON SETTING → positive coefficient = .20 – .60
   QED.: drug use, PTSD, prenatal trauma, &tc.

BOOK VIII

THE FUTURE OF CHAOS

M ~ ꙗ

−∧Ψ∧−

MOROII AD VITAM PARAMUS

To Evolve − To Become − To Protect

"As we, the leaders, deal with tomorrow, our task is not to try to make perfect plans. Our task is to create organizations that are sufficiently flexible and versatile that they can take our imperfect plans and make them work in execution."

—Gordon Sullivan & Michael Harper,
Hope is Not a Method

CyberVamps—an underground division of *Mardukite Research Organization* called the "Coven of Lilith"—have infiltrated the "*Vampyre Community*" from esoteric and magical communities, and into the "goth community" from the *transhuman futurist electro-industrial* scene— at the forefront of a new development for Humanity called *Systemology, Mardukite Systemology*; even *Mardukite Zuism*. How do we imagine these CyberVamps and movements of tomorrow? Consider what you might have seen depicted in a futurist movie—*Blade Runner, Girl With The Dragon Tattoo, Hackers, Running Man, Mortal Instruments, Strange Days, Tank Girl, Titan A.E., Underworld, Vampire Academy...* or Terry Brooks' *Shannara* fantasy epic of the future.

When the "*Ancient Mystery School*" reached San Francisco, California in the late 1800's, it was immediately divided into two mystic factions: the *fraternal/masonic* and the *artistic/cultural*. The Egyptian streamline of the "*Ancient Mystery School*," along with its classical Greek (*Hermetic*) derivatives, is central to archetypal power that rules the area there. Efforts on the West Coast, by Jack Parsons, to expand the *ceremonial* emphasis of Aleister Crowley were thwarted in the late 1940's for reasons that extend beyond the scope of this present text.

Occult emphasis in the underground of the West Coast is still occupied by more artistic and culturally oriented mystics that enjoy their journeys, adventures and *Games* into the powerfully chaotic. They influence most mainstream "medias" of the *United States*. By comparison, the more orderly East Coast *occult* underground emphasizes exercise of their mystical influence and manipulation towards central business ventures, involving money and commerce—and law; something that we should expect being so close to our nation's capital.

—CYBER MAGIC : TECHGNO-STICISM—

Many *mystics* and *magicians* focus on, or dedicate themselves to, a specific paradigm or a personal cultural mythology from which to perform their *energy work*. There is, however, another way to operate: focusing on the application and operation of magic as a universalist paradigm of *All-as-One*. In the late 1970s and early 1980s, as new technology was on the rise, so too were new magical practices—"Chaos Magic"—the ability for a *mystic* or *magician* to temporarily wear the "mask" of any tradition, cultural paradigm or philosophy for immediate application as needed without succumbing too far to "magical glamour." Now that we have understood how to switch glasses at will, the 21st Century is dependent on the NexGen developing new glasses altogether—or even the ability to learn to see with holistic True Sight, and lose the glasses altogether.

—CYBERVAMPS : VAMPYRIC FUTURISM—

Bram Stoker (*1847—1912*)—born in Dublin, Ireland and personal assistant to Sir Irving Henry—is most famous for his literary contribution: *Dracula*. Stoker, a member of the Hermetic Order of the Golden Dawn, is the first to use the term "Undead" in modern times—a word that served as the working title for his novel. In September 2009, a deluxe hardcover facsimile of the original edition was released. One month later, the Stoker legacy continued with the publication of the only other official contribution ever made by a true Stoker descendent—Dacre Stoker—who published a matching deluxe hardcover sequel titled: *"Dracula: The Undead."*

The release of *Dracula* on *May 26, 1897* marks a turning point, bridging the social consciousness of *Victorian Vampyrism* into modern life and eventually the early Vamp style that defined modern "Goth." *Chaos Magic* seems to be the more common practice among them. And then the *Psi-Vamps* emerged—*cyber-infused* catalysts of change for a true "New Age"—the rise of the meta-programmers and NexGen *reality engineers*. These *CyberVamps* emerged out of a *futurist* need to evolve genres of fantasy and history, theory and practice to sustain the times, being what they are. It accurately fits the current generational theme more than post-punk punk punks. Really it is time to lose the "<u>punk</u>" terminology—not only is it not semantically appropriate, but it carries a history of negative connotations that can be disruptive to the flow of future work.

Cyberpunk + *Gothpunk* + *GothVamp* = <u>CyberVamps</u>

In 1995, global consciousness experienced a shift, marking a new era where practical magic and fantasy and *cyber-technology* not only "met," but became so intertwined that the lines between them began to lose meaning. The original *Draconomicon* by Joshua Free debuts. At the same time, the "*New Age*" is strongly carried into the mainstream; witchcraft, Wicca and "neo-paganism" become trends, inspiring numerous quasi-mystical fads and esoteric ideals pursued for little more than vanity and status.

Whether its among the recent generations of Indigo, Crystal, Rainbow, super-children or something still yet to come (probably), we are instinctively awaiting the arrival (arise?) of the *next* human being—Homo Novus. The *Nazis* were actually trying to engineer a new species of *transhuman megaloman*, based on a novel called "*The Coming Race.*" We use the term *NexGen* when applying to our youth and young adults and also the future; we always are prepared—the *next* generation might be the one. It is clear that we are approaching a "zero-point" or turning point on the planet.

> "The vampire {is} born with a higher potential for perception, transcendence and intelligence. They walk a tightrope between their own *mundanity,* which for others would be perceived as being transcendent and an even higher state of being..."   —*Nicholas de Vere*

Darksider conditions of the "VWZ" variety all involve a <u>divergence</u> of perception, awareness, and consciousness from the societal norm—which is to say what is experienced by at least 33% of the population. Understanding magic requires a magical mind—one that is able to step outside, even if just for a moment, and experience what it means to operate as *"more than human."*

—NEXGEN = NEXT GENERATIONAL—

Generational "gaps" or *distinctions* are divided based on plotting dates on a calendar—but are also societal factors, the outlook or 'worldview' and a specific '*perceptual range*' defining cultural trends, norms, tendencies so forth. Consider the tendencies "settle down" or get married at a young age versus a worldview that prefers to "date and rate" many potential suitors, resulting into various 'alternative' lifestyles—by old-paradigm standards—that extend into adulthood and shape realities for *NexGens*.

New economic patterns—cyclic from previous periods of techno-industrial revolution—forced many *Generation-X* and early *Millennials* into a period where the social-system came to raise them; not parents—else they were left to raise themselves. Different parenting "schools of thought" came into being during the 1980's and 1990's—but this mainly went by the wayside as more and more "latchkey" children walked their developmental years with both of their parents being forced to maintain one or even two jobs to makeup for not only the economic '*inflation*' of the dollar, but also the rise in technological needs and its corresponding *rising* costs.

The '*digital division*' separates previous generations from *Millennials* in several respects. Firstly, there is what is considered 'widely available' during developmental years. The kind of technology now accessible to the average child was either only available to the upper echelon of society in the 1980's or else unavailable altogether. The *cellular phone* is a perfect example—once considered a symbol of status or importance, the non-military use of *cellular* technology in the 1970's and 1980's was restricted to upper class businessmen-types. The *cellular pager* was originally a stereotype of professionals. Technologies later became commonplace in a way that is so ingrained into consciousness that we have entered a time where we cannot place ourselves (as up-and-coming generations) outside of a time when these technologies were not so available.

Modeled from "*Star Trek*" communicators, flip-phones and other *cellular* technology not only reveals its physical or technological nature by name but also what it attempts to connect among the population—linking together individual cells of the human race as one <u>singularity</u>. In this way, each human carrying one becomes dependent on it for their interconnection to any and all other 'cell' entities on the planet.

In addition to the technology side of affairs, *magicians* are now learning about "quantum" elements of *mysticism* and how super-string theorists attempt to measure and calculate the unseen vibrations at the fundamental core of every bit of existence. Unified singular energy became fragmented with the event that scientist call the "Big Bang"—for whatever terminology we might apply, there is a transmission and expansion of the Divine Spark of "*Starfyre*" within and as all things, providing the necessary motion of energy to vibrate "things" into existence in the Universe. This is as close to demonstrating omnipresence of "God" as is likely possible to comprehend from within the scientific community. To get any closer, we would have to *get out* and *walk*.

—NEXGEN = FUTURIST TRANSHUMANISM—

Many factors contribute to the evolution of life on Earth. Perhaps the most important for life on any planet is <u>panspermia</u> —seeding life throughout the cosmos from "outer space." For this to occur, we don't actually have to have our traditional "aliens" and UFOS in play. Most of the building blocks of life are spread by organic-inorganic planetoids and asteroids carrying necessary chemical elements through space. Any kind of individual space travel or inter-dimensional journeying can also result in a crossing of energies such as *spores* and other *microorganisms* that can affect life or even cause mutation to the genetic body (DNA).

Genetic memory from the past is also encoded in DNA. Latent potential in genetics and other bold metaphysical innovations comes from *esoteric occult* practitioners and "experiments" conducted by magical orders and groups. As our attention is more focused on the proper use of the brain, the next school of *Necromancy* is likely to be one of <u>Neuromancy</u>.

Our world is now the realm of a new elite; the *hackers, neuroengineers, nanotechnicians, cybernetics developers*; all have the upper-hand on some of the kinds of magic behind the "external technology" that will be employed in the future. The goal seems to be an elimination of "processing," a form of *NewSpeak* that will effectively remove "language" as we know it and the "interpretation of symbols" and simply link straight to the brains direct systems.

It is no stretch of the imagination that electrical impulses or other devices can be used to trigger sectors and receptors of the brain—inducing specific emotional responses; those generating chemical motion of *peptides, neurotransmitters, amino acids, hormones*—all of which generate an EMF of their own. So, there are many variable beneath the surface; but, the one "variable " that seems unchanging, even as we approach an age of very possible *zombie apocalypse* and *artificial intelligence* gone astray—is that humans really want to be able to manipulate and control each other. We have examined thousands of years of *esoterica* in our study so far, and this dirty word—CONTROL—seems to be the god that everyone is worshiping.

We already have a conditioned society—everyone is *already* hypnotized—a very integral part of civilization dynamics. As the system evolves and becomes more complex, larger encompassing methods are employed to maintain order in a system that is only increasingly more unstable the more complex it becomes. Programming the *"human condition"* is a practice of *"artificial stimulation"* by definition—except now, instead of suggestive symbolism and psychological conditioning, technology is being used for biological stimulation; going after the physiological-behavioral directly with *chemical* stimulation.

Applying this methodology to the general population, as seen in some popular *zombie* thrillers, usually does not end well. A percentage of the population might have adverse reactions to treatments; just as a percentage of the population might have an adverse reaction to peanut exposure. In extreme cases of biohazardous materials, a random segment of the population might react "negatively" with increased *adrenaline* production and decreased levels of *serotonin* and *dopamine*—which can completely shut down normal interactions we would expect to share with other *humans.* They easily become an *"empty shell."*

Nanotechnology is one of the newer *Dark Arts*. Scientists have spent several hundred years examining the brain-body connection. *Artificial nerve stimulation* allows a subject to have a certain part of their brain stimulated to produce the physical (behavioral) result. This new magic is called *Electro-Brain Stimulation* (EBS). The goal of these scientists is to install remotely operated radio-linked neural implant devices in humans. This provides a direct means of mind-control that is similar to *Voodoo Zombies*—except, rather than use a pharmacological agent (*substance*) to stimulate certain parts of the brain with, the new science will bypass even that and stimulate directly by electronic means.

> "We do on stage, what should happen off;
> which is a kind of integrity if you consider every
> exit as an entrance somewhere else."
> —*The Player*, R&G are Dead.

—CYBERVAMPS : THE FUTURE OF NECRONAUTICS—

In the film *Flatliners* (1990), several physicians meet together in secret to conduct experiments in <u>necronautics</u>. Using their collective scientific knowledge, they learn to induce a controlled "death state," where the body is "clinically dead" without actually dying. They take turns seeing who can stay "under" the longest and what experiences and knowledge they might glean from it. Methods used in the movie are now considered "practical medicine," applied as *Therapeutic Cooling* to lower a patient's metabolism while treating injuries that are inhibiting the brain from receiving oxygen. By lowering the metabolism, brain activity and oxygen requirements are also reduced:

1 *degree* lower = 3-5% lower *cerebral metabolic rate*

Humans have been trying to crack the code on "<u>Death</u>" since the beginning of time. In Egypt, especially, the entire funerary process was central to whole tradition—meaning the relationship (and promise) made between the "sky gods" and the people of Earth. Most of the oldest *cuneiform* writings in Mesopotamia are either an effort to preserve posthumous legacies of *gods* and *king*, or investigations into the landscape of the Underworld and nature of the Abyss.

Necronautic experiments can actually yield data that is useful in other applications. The kind of metabolic thermo-regulation demonstrated in *Flatliners* or with the *Therapeutic Cooling* treatments is a hot topic in science, because it provides clues to a combination of two of the most important problems facing *human* evolution—*life extension* and *space migration.*

Life Extension researchers have been working with the "cold" (cryogenics) for quite some time. It became clear long ago that *Life Extension* had less to do with actually preserving *"Life,"* and more to do with preserving the environments that *Life* is accustomed to—meaning establishment of a metabolic equilibrium. This technology applies not only to '*cold storage*' but also to travel and migration into Space. To withstand the duration of space travel, techniques of suspended animation will have to be employed. Recent advances in this technology combines Controlled Cooling with additional chemicals—*hydrogen suphide*—for suspended animation chambers.

With so many ways there are to feign the appearance of *Death*, it now begs the question as to how many people have been buried who weren't actually dead. One of the purposes of the *"wake"* is to keep watch over the dead for three days to be sure they are dead and to tend to their body for the three days that the spirit is still believed to be near to the physical body. In the past, people took *"graveyard shifts"* to keep grave-robbers and vandals out, but also to stand guard overnight to see if any of the dead decided to *awaken*.

It is no secret that people have been buried who are not dead. Evidence already suggests that some people who "died" during periods of poor medical knowledge, would later wake up in their *coffins*. Many of them would die thereafter of asphyxiation, but not before making a survivalist effort to get out of the *coffin*. Several examples where the body was later exhumed even show scratch marks on the inside of the *coffin* lids. The more superstitious of the population used the same data as evidence for "vampires"—mostly by the ignorant who were not educated in the effects of decomposition.

BOOK IX

LYCANTHROPIC SHAMANISM

ᛗ ~ 8

— ∧Ψ∧ —

MOROII AD VITAM PARAMUS

To Evolve — To Become — To Protect

—DIVINITY AND THE BEAST—

We are *Divine*. We have the blood of the Ancient Ones running through us, composed of carbon-Star-stuffs—seeking to rise above the heavy, dense low-energy vibrations of the Material Kingdom (*Malkuth*, KIA, KI). At the same time, we are tied to the Earth—Children of the Earth—and a very strong gravity operating to preserve its own code, keeping us here until our spirit is light enough to rise above it.

According to *cuneiform* tablets, when the *Anunnaki* began performing bio-engineering on Earth, there were no other "advanced" forms of life on the planet. By this, we mean such as the human being has become today. While we have the Blood of *gods* in our veins and their awesome power still laden in our minds; there is still a beast—*a monster*—within; a wild animal *therian* nature that fights against our *Divine* nature. It is the destiny of Humanity to rise above the *monster*, but it cannot be ignored or suppressed as a substitute for true mastery.

Animals have a longstanding connection with the night and *Darksider* conditions. Religious and spiritual traditions from the ancient world all demonstrate kinship between humans and animals—shamanic totem animals, zoomorphic Egyptian deities, wolf-gods of Europe—even the *mushushu* dragon of Babylon, a word that meant crocodile to the Egyptians.

—THE WOLF—

"In the case of a man whose instinct is savage and sanguinary, his phantom will wander abroad in lupine form, whilst he sleeps painfully at home, dreaming he's a veritable wolf."   —*Eliphas Levi*

Wolves are one of the most majestic animals on the planet. Any boy scout can tell you the wolf is the great *instructor*—teacher of the mysteries. Indigenous shamans revered the wolf very highly. It was not endangered until the rise of urban development during the Dark Ages. Wolves are commonly evoked totem animals. The wolf is now completely extinct in Britain. In fact, the only species that has not lost its original range is the Arctic Wolf (*Canus lupus arctos*), because of the infrequency of human encounters—but that is changing since the actions of humanity are not independent of the entire planet. Wolves are sacred to Inuit tradition.

Healthy wolves seldom attack humans in the wild. Wolves actually prefer to avoid contact with most humans. They did, however, sometimes raid their livestock when not properly guarded—something humans have zero tolerance for when farmers began to campaign for the destruction of the species.

Wolves mate for life and share a unique community lifestyle called a "pack." Shamans revered them for being both wild and discriminating. While they once prowled the entire globe above the equator, they are now restricted to "preserves" and unpopulated regions in the north and Asia. Wolves are predators, but they are also an integral part of the wilderness. For a time, a pack of wolves called the *Druids* inhabited Yellowstone National Park so the effects of wolves in the wild could be observed. It is now undisputed that the reintroduction of wolves to the wild assists in balancing the natural ecosystem—so long as humans allow them to.

—LYCANTHROPIC TRANSFORMATION—

The ability to *shapeshift* into animal forms appears in many legends of deities and heroes from many different cultural mythologies. Ritual shapeshifting is an integral part of many nature-based spiritual traditions, evident from the ceremonial use of animal masks and dressings. The "willingness" *to be* any form is a "magical trait." The "willingness" *precedes* realizations that this shift in consciousness is occurring.

Lycanthropic Shamanism is based on a tradition of knowledge and wisdom that a *shaman* obtains by making contact with the *Other* through *"were-animal" mediumship*. Magnetic attraction to energy of a specific species is an individual affair—different personalities and energy types have a natural affinity to certain animals. *Mystics* have a natural tendency or inclination to favor their "sacred animals."

History shows that many shamans and warriors have clothed themselves in animal skins to absorb energy and qualities of the creature. Berserkers, werebears and werewolves demonstrate the wild, feral and animalistic nature inherent in all of us—but they choose to embrace it and bask in its primal strength.

Animist Shamanism is more commonly found in Europe and northern regions, particularly those that deal with heavy winter seasons. As opposed to the hotter, desert climates, whose traditions grew from the *"waters of life"* for survival—European and northern systems emphasized the *"fires of life"* as supreme. Scandinavian legends include the Nordic wolf-god FENRIR or FENRIS. Norse lore of Ragnarok suggests that werewolves are messengers of the apocalypse—a sign of the *Age of Chaos* descending upon the Earth; one that will end the world as we know it. We do find "wolf-gods" in many other more urban cultures—Greece, Rome—as well. Needless to say, the wolf is a globally sacred animal.

—WEREWOLVES : CHILDREN OF THE NIGHT—

The modern term for *werewolves* is Lycan—a name taken from the Classical period, when the tradition began—as best we can trace it. *Lycans* aren't dead, aren't undead, aren't immortal and are not always even magic-users—so, why are we even talking about them?

Lycans and *Vampires* share and origin and many *occult esoteric* connections to ancient traditions and systems suggested in this text. This is not modern "invention" to tell dark fantasy tales—neither is the rivalry between the two, possibly the result of a lifelong "competition" driven by prideful egos to determine which species (*human mutation*) is the deadliest. This is somewhat ridiculous, given existing ancient pyramidal hierarchy of Creatures of Night—between the ancient dragon cult and the ancient wolf/bear cult.

Contrary to contemporary fiction, any prejudice and biases between living *Vampyres* and *Werewolves* is a learned behavior; not specific to genetic programming. Modern traditions and occult organizations around the world have become a means for elitists that are addicted to their mental masturbation—elitists who can never penetrate the true mysteries of *esoterica*. Living traditions of *Vampyres* and *Lycans* are channels for energetic transformation—exchange and transference—the alchemy of the <u>Universal Stream</u>. As distinct Creatures of the Night, *Vampyres* are practitioners of finesse, demonstrating aristocratic etiquette in all of their affairs. *Lycans* are typically more wild and physically active, preferring athletic demonstrations that allow for contact and "rough-housing" as a *pack*.

Darksider Diseases may be one way in which conventional science can explain some conditions applied to *mystics, magicians* and Creatures of Night. In the film *Wer* (2013) *Darksider Disease* conditions are used to explain popular werewolf lore in southern France. French tradition gave us the name *Loup*-(wolf) *Garou*(man). The film indicated a werewolf family suffered from *porphyria*, coinciding with *seizures* and blackouts.

As an *esoteric* condition, the "rabid-transformation" of a *Lycan* can be attributed to a theoretical hormone called <u>Lycatropin</u>. Presence of such a neurotransmitter would suggest that *were*-beasts have additional receptors in the brain that drive the more primitive mental faculties, such as those for primal survival—hunger and aggression.

Biorhythms control hormonal release. Heightened levels of *Lycatropic-adrenaline* (as opposed to melatonin) during certain nights can increase *lycanthropic* conditions. Even while sleeping, these hormones can trigger biochemical conditions, and if blackout periods occur while active, the fantasy becomes reality very quickly—the PTSD of attacking, biting and savage encounters in the Realm of Lights blurs with vivid nightmarish dreams of macabre, savagery, murder... And worse. The processing techniques of Mardukite Systemology are applied to remedy these *Darksider* conditions and increase L.Q.

—KING LYCAON OF ARCADIA—

King Lycaon (or Lykaon) of Arcadia is part of the prehistoric tradition in Greece. King Lycaon reigned before the *Great Flood* —in mythic antediluvian times. After attempting to trick ZEUS (or JUPITER)—testing the *god's* omniscience by trying to serve him the roasted flesh of his son (*Nyctimus*) as a meal—ZEUS turned the king into a wolf (that was also a man) and cursed his successive lineage to suffer the same condition.

Lycaon and his sons—fifty in all, with as many wives—created a unique sub-species of human. Their offspring were *werewolves*—the condition of "*Lycanthropy*" named for him: *lukos* (wolf) and *anthropos* (man). He founded the city of *Lykosoura* on Mt. Lykaois and is revered as a wolf-god. His nymph daughter, Callisto, was turned into a bear and set in the skies (as the *Great Bear* constellation) where she becomes the bear-mother, siring a family of *werebears* beginning with her son *Arcas*.

—LUPERCALIA—

The Greek festival dedicated to the wolf-god—LYKAIA—began with secret rituals of *Lycanthropic Shamanism*. Romans later carried the lore and tradition of this festival through the Classical period, but it was pre-Roman in origin. Observation of

<u>Lykaia</u> (*Greek*) or <u>Lupercalia</u> (*Latin*) took place at the "Ides of February" (13th—15th). *"Februa"* indicates a ritual cleansing; a time of purification among the people to promote new energy and fertility for the coming growth season.

Roman mythology was anything but original, borrowing liberally from all of the nations it encountered, particularly the Greeks—where they learned of the systematic planetary-based Olympian pantheon, which the Greeks learned from Mesopotamia. In Rome, equivalent lore to King Lykaon is renamed as Lupercus (also Lupercius) for the early Roman Lupercalia festival. Lupercus is sometimes identified with FAUNUS, derived from the early Greek tradition of LYCAEAN-PAN, the horned, wild, agricultural deity of the forests and groves.

Ancient Romans once attributed the birth of their entire civilization to wolves. A "she-wolf" rescued and reared Romulus and Remus, the sons of MARS, the war-god—a Roman equivalent to NERGAL (ERRA) in Mesopotamia. The twins, Romulus and Remus become the legendary founders of Rome and the Roman Empire, distinguishing it from the much older cultural traditions of northern Italy, in Milan and the ancient <u>Etruscan Kingdom</u>.

BOOK X

CEREMONIES
OF
IMMORTALITY

ᛗ ~ ᛈ

−ᚠᚡᚠ−

MOROII AD VITAM PARAMUS

To Evolve − To Become − To Protect

—THE SECOND BOOK OF DEATH AND IMMORTALITY—

Ceremonies of magic and religious devotion are in no short supply. *Seekers* now have more of an issue accessing the 'right' materials, than not being able to find some at all. They *are* there. *Energy work* in ritual dramatics and applied spirituality are time-proven means of directing attention, focusing awareness and channeling necessary energy to promote desired results. But there are many others not as greatly publicized.

"Mardukite Moroi" material is by no means an entry level text or magical primer—or even a full "Grade" of material in itself. Its purpose is to bridge Outer Court lessons from the past (Grades I and II) with Inner Circle teachings reserved for elitists of *occult esoterica*—starting with the Grade-III "Mardukite Systemology" materials, including *"Tablets of Destiny: Using Ancient Wisdom to Unlock Human Potential"* and *"Crystal Clear: The Self-Actualization Manual & Guide to Total Awareness."* We consider those many peers, colleagues, friends, fans and allies who have been following along through the years to be the "elite of the elite" in this up and coming new world. It is up to you *to be* prepared and initiate preparedness in others. In the meantime, we will complete our present volume with the final discourse released to the *Moroii ad Vitam* in 2016.

—IMMORTALITY & THE UNDERWORLD—

The destination—the final step—on this *mystic quest* that we have described, is to achieve *Godhood* as *Self*, personal and environmental mastery and attainment of the highest vibration so in order to participate in the Legacy of Ascended Masters and walk the Twilight Path through the Gates to the "Other Side" and achieve conscious *Etheric Immortality.* This level of Great Work is often represented by the "Ankh" and "Scarab."

Coming Forth Into Light (Egyptian *Book of the Dead*) displays a prehistoric theology propagated by the early priests of RA or

MARDUK before Egyptian religious emphasis later shifted to OSIRIS. The material also contains incantations said during the funerary ceremony, and one in particular to invoke KHEPERA, the ancient RA of immortality, god of the Scarab, called to protect against the deterioration of the *Etheric Body*, so that the *Identity of Self* can be restored intact. Pre-Dynastic "Secret Doctrines" reveals the ALL assumed the form of KHEPERA (represented by the *scarab* hieroglyph) to "bring into being" Life, represented by the *Ankh*. As in Mesopotamian lore: *First all was The Deep - a watery ocean Abyss*. The One "comes into being" by pronouncing its own name: "KHEPER"—meaning "to become," "to manifest" and "to transform."

—GATES OF LIFE AND DEATH : LAST RITES—

Our enigmatic ancestors from the Stars—*Ancient Ones* and *Elder Gods*—practiced traditions of their own heritage, meanwhile seeding the arts of human civilization for completely different purposes. The deification of *Anunnaki* (and the same pantheon under other names) and the systems established on Earth in their name for humans, were quite different than "religious" practices or cultural traditions of the *Anunnaki* themselves. Naturally, the gods didn't worship each other—they did petition each other, however, for their specialized assistance in handling both terrestrial and celestial affairs.

The *Arts of Civilization* were 'passed down' from an "outside" source—given to their successors to maintain the "World Order" in the absence of the *gods*—those who were chosen to maintain Dragon Sovereignty and stewardship of the planet that our ancestors had worked so hard to prepare for us—even if they did have their own motivations for "making" and "controlling" us. It seems this matter of mind and behavior control has been with us since the beginning after all—And, imitation is as devotion for mortals, thus the traditionalism.

Rituals and ceremonies that were once performed for the *gods* (and for which, we presume, the general population had no clear understanding of) became tradition, but often without functionality—their original purposes long forgotten or unnecessary, except for maintaining the traditions for the civic benefit of society. At some point the physical forms of the *gods* —our *transhuman ancestors*—had *left* the planet or "died" and received special preparations before they are *taken* from the planet. The proverbial *"Book of the Dead"* misnomer has further confused the uninitiated. The origins are outside of Egypt, and drawn from a pre-Dynastic tradition observed by the *gods*.

The instructions performed in imitation of the gods may be just that—an imitation. We assume that the text was given to humans for mortal use. It may have been given to a select group of priests responsible for tending to the needs of the *gods* themselves—that these methods do not functionally apply to mortal "spiritual" systems of misappropriated beliefs, but rather exist for the benefit to meta-humans as a means to sustain themselves, heal themselves, reanimate themselves, or otherwise remove themselves from the planet and survive space travel using a means understood far too literally by ancient humans to be properly used.

—A FUNERARY CEREMONY : FIRST DEATH—

Great King of the Dead
Who Reigns Over the Dead Spirits
Great Master of the Magician Spirits
Spirits Who Live and Work in the Underworld
I Dedicate Myself to the Service of Dead Spirits
Spirits who Seek to Help Me
And to those Shades of Spirits of Wise Magicians
Magicians from Under the Sea
Who Comes Forth in Foreign Appearances
I AM a Child of the Light
Light of the Great Master and King

202

The Great King from Under the Sea
A path shall be opened for the King
Among the Shining Ones; that
He may be established among Them
He comes forth into Heaven
Through the Star-Gate of the Gods

Scarab amulets were often worn or carried by the Egyptians for protection from harm. They believed *Scarab amulets* attracted prosperity and longevity. During funerary rites, a *Scarab* amulet is placed around the neck of the deceased. Egyptian religion dictates that it will assist the *Etheric Body* in *Underworld* journeys, along with an Ankh held in the hands, along with volumes and manuals to offer guidance while the spirit navigates the afterlife. The type of *Scarab* beetle amulets used, are made from greenish stone, encircled with a band so it can be worn around the neck as the sacred symbol of KHEPRA.

Homage to thee
You who has come as KHEPERA
KHEPERA, the Creator of the Gods
You did not decay
You did not become worms
You did not whither
You did not rot
You did not putrefy
You did not turn into worms
I am the god KHEPERA, the Everlasting
I shall not decay
I shall not rot
I shall not putrefy
I shall not turn into worms
I myself am KHEPERA
I shall possess my flesh forever and ever
I shall not decay
I shall not crumble away
I shall not whither away
I shall not become corruption

Another *Scarab* tool used for these ceremonies is the <u>Heart Scarab</u>, which is similar to, but larger than, the necklace amulets. *Heart Scarabs* are about the size the size of your palm—four inches or so. During the ritual, the *Heart Scarab* is placed on the chest (in the location of the heart) of the deceased.

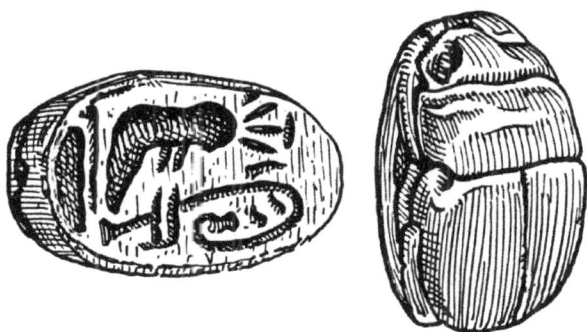

Heart Scarabs were engraved by priests with magical prayers and incantations from the "Chapters of Coming Forth by Day" (*Book of the Dead*). These artifacts are used when the spirit enters the <u>Hall of Judgment</u>, when the deceased is brought before the *Guardians of Death*—ANUBIS, THOTH or HERMES or NABU, &tc.; there are *Seven Underworld Judges* in all.

In the *Hall of Judgment*, the level of purity or light quotient of the spirit is measured on scales of justice, weighed against the lightness of an ostrich feather. If the "heart" is too heavy—if it is still attached to the trappings of the material world—than it cannot rise; cannot *Ascend*. Better to be *lighthearted*, as it were.

Egyptians used *Heart Scarabs* to still their heart—the reactive genetic mortal programming—during judgment to ensure Immortality. Specific prayers and incantations proclaim the "innocence" of the Self. Some art renderings show the *Heart Scarab* used in place of the actual heart during judgment, when weighed on the "scales" of Ascension. The "*Heart Scarab Magical Incantation*" (Prayer) is from Chapter XXXb of "Coming Forth into Light" (*Book of the Dead*).

My Heart—Heart of my Mother
Heart of my Transformations
Let no one stand and give Testimony against Me
Let no one drive me away from the Secret Chiefs
Be with Me in the Presence of the Keeper of Balance
My KA, Dweller in my Body, is the god KHEMU
He who Animates the Members of my Body
Appear in the Light Place wherever we Travel
Let my Heart be Light at the Weighing of Words
Let no Lies be spoken against Me
Before the Great God, Lord of AMENTET
Lord of ANU
How Great Thou Art
Rise up in Triumph

The *Bull's Thigh* or *Thigh of Set* is an Egyptian name for the constellation known elsewhere as the *Great Bear* (or *Big Dipper*)—one of the most easily recognizable constellations to the general population. It is also one of the most sacred sections of "space" to ancient cults, which witnessed the "<u>Bull of Heaven</u>" (or *Great Bear*) overtake the *Dragon*—the Draco constellation—which previously dominated the *Northern Gate*. The *Celestial Gate* is unlocked, the legends say, when "the stars are right."

Chapters of <u>Coming Forth Into Light</u> (*Book of the Dead*) describe several ritual actions that must be made over the body of the deceased by an Egyptian Necromancer-Priest, called the *Kher-Heb*. Symbolic actions include the "Stretching of the Cord" so that the spirit will have access to its physical counterpart—connected on a silver cord. During one of these proceedings—the "Opening of the Mouth" (of the Pharaoh)—the *Kher-Heb High Priest* allows the spirit of the deceased to "breathe, eat and drink" in the afterlife.

Incantation-prayers are recited to the Divine Mortician: ANU-BIS, *Guardian of Gates to the Underworld* (in Egyptian tradition); and for the *Anunnaki* pantheon of Mesopotamia, ERESHKIGAL is the Queen of the Underworld. The cuneiform Underworld literature of Sumerians and Babylonians offers no shortage of Gatekeeper names, nor do other sections of the Egyptian *Book of the Dead*. Each culture interpreted experience of the <u>Gates</u> and <u>Guardians</u> based on their own "*mythos*" and *language*.

> *Gate of the Earth, open to me*
> *Gate of the Underworld, open to me*
> *Gate of the Abyss, open to to me*
> *Holy Gods of the Abyss*
> *Great God N. , I, N. as is my Earth-name*
> *Under the soles of whose feet*
> *The gods of the sky are placed*
> *Words of Truth—MAAT—are in my mouth*
> *ANUBIS—Chief of the Underworld Mysteries*
> *ANUBIS—Whose face is strong among the gods*
> *Arise, move and come forth into this place.*
> *Show yourself here on Earth*
> *And raise your Army of the Dead*

The <u>Kher-Heb</u> (*funerary priest*) performs the "Opening of the Mouth" of the Pharaoh—usually referred to as the OSIRIS in the more recent *Magical Papyri* and *Coffin Texts*—so his spirit may be revived in another existence—maintaining connection between the "spiritual body" and "physical body." The *Kher-Heb* is responsible for opening the way to Heaven and returning life—and granting spiritual beingness—to the *Ka-body*. The 'Opening of the Mouth' is performed using an <u>Ur-Heka</u>, a critical magical instrument—*an adze*—formed in the shape of the "Bull's Thigh" (*Big Dipper* constellation within the *Great Bear*), the stars that "guard the gate." The *Opening the Mouth* Incantation from the "*Coming Forth*" text:

> *Your Mouth was Closed, OSIRIS (the deceased)*
> *But I have Opened your Mouth for You*
> *With the Instrument of ANUBIS*
> *With the Iron adze tool*
> *Used to Open the Mouth of the ancient Gods*
> *The Dead shall walk and speak*

He comes forth into Heaven
Through the Star-Gate of the Gods
His Body will be in Divine Company of Gods
In the Great House of the Ancient One—ANU
Let the dead awaken
Let the dead rise and smell the incense

After the physical body has been properly prepared and the organs have been preserved in their <u>canopic jars</u> featuring heads of the gods, funerary rites continue in the tomb, where verses from the *"Chapters of Coming Forth"* are etched on walls, the coffins themselves, and eventually papyrus scrolls.

Unique to the Egyptian Tombs—called *mastabas*—is the presence of the *Etheric Door* by which the spirit will *leave* the tomb. Egyptians specify the *Gate of the Tomb* be placed to the east (direction of dawn), where the spirit may meet the Solar Disc for its crossings. The *Etheric Door* is cut into solid wall to give only the appearance of a door, only passable in spirit form. The pharaoh's spirit will exit that door, representative of the transitional crossings—the <u>Gate to the Outside</u> awaits, the *Gate* which otherwise holds back the world of the living in a <u>Realm of Lights</u>, from the Other—the Outside. On the other side of the Gate, a Divine Messenger appears to guide them through the labyrinth of the *afterlife*.

Babylonian spirituality emphasized a preparation for a True Union with Self. Where the lore ends in Babylon, the remainder is found in the Egyptian system. Once the *Etheric Self* is accessible, emphasis shifts to preparations for a Life after <u>First Death</u>. After *First Death*, there are descriptions of the Ascending Spirit *"Coming into Heaven"* by the *"Ladder of God"* or *"Stairway to Heaven"* or, as is the preferred modern interpretation—the <u>StarGate</u>. That much, we can already assume from *Mardukite Egypto-Babylonian* lore: "..at the borders of this Earth where RA has purified himself—RA has set up his ladder."

"Gates"—are a persistent theme found in all known lore regarding *death* and an *afterlife*. Such beliefs practically define differences in one's own cultural paradigm. Concepts of Deity and Death—and what comes next. According to these traditions, beyond the Gates, the spirit must pass through the Field of Reeds—crossing the winding *Lake of Reeds*—with the aid of an etheric ferryman.

Cleansed is he who is cleansed in the Field of Reeds
Cleansed is RA in the Field of Reeds
Cleansed is he who is cleansed in the Field of Reeds
Cleansed is this Osiris in the Field of Reeds
Hand of this Osiris in hand of RA
NUIT—come; take his hand
SHU—lift him up
SHU—lift him up
Men are Buried; The Gods Fly Up
He mounts his Dragon;
His Dragon mounts the stars

After this, the destination: "*Neter-Khert*"—*Land of the Mountain Gods*—which the pyramids and temples always represent on Earth; as artificial mountains—structures significant to planetary pantheons throughout all ancient cultures. Beyond the *Valley of the Mountain Kings* is the place that the spirit has been seeking for its entire voyage—TUAT—the *Abode for Rising to the Stars*, where once we have passed the tests of the spirit—of the dimensions—we can be welcomed home among the gods.

The highest "afterlife" at the end of the journey is not a domain of putrescence and decay, as you will see—one does not remain fixed to such Underworlds when the spirit is free.

Within the teachings and rites of the *Moroii ad Vitam Paramus*, you have now discovered the *fast-pass* to the Highest degree from the Lowest degree—for they are both One!

MOROII ad VITAM
APPENDIX

M - 10

−∧Ψ∧−

MOROII AD VITAM PARAMUS

To Evolve − To Become − To Protect

—APPENDIX A—
HISTORY BEGINS WITH CUNEIFORM WRITING
excerpt from *"Secrets of Sumerian Language"*
by Joshua Free

Human history begins with writing. Academically, we consider everything prior to the inception of writing to be prehistoric. This means that the modern human experience has only been "blessed" with this development for a relatively short time—6,000 years at best.

Language is a predetermined set of communication—words, sounds, expressions, gestures, &tc.—that are used to relay an intentional meaning from one source to another. Language is very different than writing. Without even the use of 'writing' a spoken language can establish a shared meaning of many 'things' found in one's external environment in addition to the myriad of thoughts and 'feelings' experienced internally. Thus, language is a means of communicating personal experience using a means understood by a 'sender' and 'receiver'.

Sumerians established a complete system of written communication by at least 3500 BC, in the form of pictographic symbols—even predating Egyptian hieroglyphs. Pictographic 'writing' carries meaning in *any* language. There is a difference between 'spoken language' and 'word sounds' that give speech meaning in comparison to that which is actually written down. The original version of *Sumerian* writing used literal representative 'pictures' to represent various objects and 'basic' ideas relative to human experience at that time.

'Pictographs' were not dependent on a particular 'verbal language' for them to be understood. A picture of a "bird" meant "bird" regardless of what an individual's 'language' determined as a *vocalization* and *sound* to mean "bird." The *pictograms* were originally based on what 'things' *appeared* to be, rather than the 'words' we might apply to define them. It is human 'experience' (or programming) via their 'native tongue', social exposure and personal experience resulting in the internalization of experience understood with language-based thought when exposed to an external 'image', 'object' or 'idea'.

The oldest Sumerian writings date to c. 3200 BC. For the first time, written language extends past the simple and literal pictographs into more abstract symbols to represent the 'idea' of (and not simply the 'picture' of) something—to which we call "ideograms" (ideographic). Archaic *Sumerian cuneiform* 'ideographs' were derived from the original 'pictographs'. Proto-literate 'language' is not what changed. What ancient *Sumerians* were developing was not simply 'language', but the *first* 'writing system'—*cuneiform*—a system that would continue to evolve for three millennium.

Archaic *cuneiform* writing replaced early *Sumerian pictograms* with more 'abstract' or 'shorthand' symbols. The semantic meaning that would otherwise be appropriated to a 'realist' image becomes transferred to a less than 'picture-perfect' representation of the same 'aspect' being 'named'. For example: the original pre-*cuneiform* depiction (pictograph) of an "ox" looked very much like the head of an "ox" very literally. This image stood for the idea or concept of the "ox" regardless of the language being evoked into mind to interpret it. The original (Archaic *Sumerian*) *cuneiform* 'sign' for "ox" was the exact same image, but greatly simplified and without 'curved' lines of any kind. This same application was done to many 'pictograms' to up-date them for synchronous insertion into the *Sumerian cuneiform* writing system.

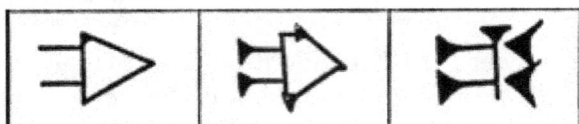

While the representation of the "ox" by a 'picture' seems almost certainly universal, *Sumerian* language took this a step further in using the 'idea' and easily 'labeled' *cuneiform* 'sign' for "ox" to also represent other related aspects—such as "cattle" as a whole. Another example: the word-sign for "mouth" could be used to indicate the "mouth" literally, but it could just as easily be applied to "eating" and "talking." The sign for "ear" might also be used to denote "listening," "hearing" and even "understanding."

- Origins of the *cuneiform* signs are literal pictographs.

- The word *"cuneiform"* is *Latin* for 'wedged-shape.'

- Cuneiform is a "writing system"—not a 'language'.

- *Cuneiform* contains *no* "letters"—only 'signs'.

- *Cuneiform* is *not* an alphabet—its 'signs' *can* be used to represent different spoken languages, but the signs *are not* arranged by the *Sumerians* in a sequential phonemic (such as "A-B-C"). *Akkadians* later bring phonemics to *cuneiform*.

- *Sumerians* wrote *cuneiform* using *Sumerian* language.

- *Babylo-Akkadians* wrote in *Akkadian* language.

- In "Babylon," *Akkadian* replaces *Sumerian*.

- *Sumerian*-derived 'signs' and 'logographs' that retain their meaning in *Akkadian cuneiform* are called "Sumerograms."

- The word "*Sumerian*" is actually Akkadian: "Sumeru."

Midway through the 3rd millennium BC, *Akkadian* influence swept through Mesopotamia and *Sumerian* culture declined. However, in addition to preserving many customs, traditions and *Anunnaki* pantheon ("religion"), Mardukite Babylonians began efforts to standardize the *cuneiform* 'writing system'.

The first standardization of *cuneiform*, first and foremost, was the 'character' or 'sign' *forms*, themselves. The introduction and wide use of the "*scribe's pen*" or 'reed-stylus' from the god NABU allowed this new pristine formation of writing. The myriad forms, sizes and shapes specific to ancient *Sumerian* 'pictographs' fades away during the *Babylo-Akkadian* era.

The *Ancient Sumerian* language, referred to as *"emegir"* [meaning: 'native tongue'], was too 'primitive' for additional developments of civilization. Hence: it was replaced with *Akkadian.* The original *Sumerian* "root words"—while spoken in *Akkadian* —were represented by similar signs as their predecessors used. These "roots" could be connected to other 'words' to form elaborate compound meanings. Other "tenses" and "determinatives" established a wide-ranging *lexicon.*

For essentially 3000 years, the *cuneiform* 'style' of 'writing' became a standard 'systematized' relay of language (communication) in the ancient world, much like we find with "Roman" letters today (a modernized 'literary system' that can also be conformed to apply to various languages). Later developing *Akkadian* phonetics ('phonograms') allowed evolution of *cuneiform* into 'syllabary'-styled writing. The new practices allowed 'literary expressions' for the way a word is 'visually' written (now beginning to emphasize how a word 'spoken' in language reflects in its depiction), providing a 'form' or 'relationship' between 'sounds' and 'writing' such as is not originally found in the archaic 'pictographs' that reflected a more literal representation of an idea (as opposed to 'abstract' symbols).

Rising 'dependent' "Systems" on the planet—those that contributed to create an 'elevated' worldly "social network" of the 'human animal'—wholly relied on fixed 'communication relay' standards to be effective. Establishment of programming for 'consciousness' (or psyche) toward the growth of a societal civilization as we know it today is a progressive combination of two ancient efforts: firstly, the birth of 'systems' in the Mesopotamian city of *Eridu* by ENKI—with the aid of his heir-son MARDUK; and secondly, a complete ratification of the *cuneiform* 'writing system' by NABU, the heir-son of MARDUK, who used it to enable the 'systems' as "active" in *Babylonia.*

Standardization of the '*stylus*' changed the nature and function of writing and human experience. The '*stylus*' sped up the 'rate' of which someone could 'inscribe' language into written "words with meaning." The new "pen," coupled with methods used by the *Babylo-Akkadians* to write, effectively eliminated the 'curvature' of earlier *cuneiform* signs.

Rather than using prehistoric models of literal 'pictographs' to represent things and ideas, the same meaning ('*semantics*') is employed in refined *cuneiform* systems with more efficient and wider applications of 'abstraction'. *Babylonians* adopted this new methodology—representing 'concrete' with the 'abstract' with an ability to relay an entire message with a few quick 'wedge-shaped' marks. With the literary system 'embedded' strongly in human consciousness, the mind developed a cohesive "semantic singularity" between aspects encountered in experience and the 'words' ('language') used to abstractly represent said aspects and experiences to others in 'writing'.

Solidification of abstract concepts and ideas using "words" actually changed how the mind thinks, changing also the way in which one is capable of experiencing these aspects of 'reality' in the future. Likewise, adoption of a 'label system' for fixed names, nouns and concepts creates an internal 'database'—a '<u>schema</u>'—which further manipulates memory and experience.

The *Sumerian* language was wholly 'extinct', in place of the 'new' *Babylonian-Akkadian* paradigm by the Age of Aries (c. 2160 BC). By 2000 BC, *Babylonian* civil law required that all "transactions" be made 'real' by involving the 'realm'. They were all documented and duplicated, sometimes *triplicated*, by an official class of 'priests', called "*scribes*."

For an exceptionally extended period of human history, only the perceptibly 'highest' (or 'elite') classes of citizen were required (or fluent) in the 'arts' of *reading* and *writing*. As a result, a dependency on scribe-priests emerged, requiring the written word—and its representation—to be 'interpreted' by a third-party for it to have any meaning to the 'commoner'. Any discovered indiscretions or falsehood relayed in this process were severely punished. It was necessary to strengthen faith (and preserve) beliefs held by the population that the 'written word' (found on life-altering 'documents' regarding history, ownership and religion) represented 'reality' "one-to-one."

The 'covert' governing 'body' of individuals that brought societal 'systems' into being also regulated the means used to integrate 'written truth' into 'social consciousness'. Definitions, semantics, styles, sound use, perceived limitations of 'knowledge' and 'reason'—not to mention the very boundaries of the 'realm'—were now set down to *remain* and be *understood* for future generations. And this completely changed the human range of experience of existence as *Life*...

—APPENDIX B—
SYSTEMOLOGY—101: REALITY-SYSTEM LOGIC PROGRAMS
excerpt from "*Systemology: The Original Thesis*" by Joshua Free

The *programmed* inclination of the *mind-of-body* is to preserve the *existential systems* that form the *basis of reality* and avoid changes to these *systems*. It is the *human condition* to *change* or *adapt* which is critical for *survival* within *reality systems*. Returning to *baseline programming interaction* and *survival* in an environment the *human being* can find the *key* to the *next evolution*. *Human* existence is not permanent in its *current* form.

—Why?

Because *humans* are *programmed* to be incapable of adapting to *environmental reality*. Humans are the *only* life-species—a *genetic-vehicle*—that possesses this inability on earth. It is what *makes* a *human like a god*. *Ability to manipulate environmental reality* is critical to the evolutionary success of the *human being* who is pitted against the *whole of universal forces* to find its place and *survive*.

Humans are *programmed* to *evolve*, as is *all life*. To learn, grow and *survive*—meaning *to evolve*—towards what is *perceived* as *higher* or *greater* than. It is the *program* and the *perception* that determines what is *higher* or *greater* than. *System-Programming* is layered *validated data* built up from the most *antiquated base programs*. The oldest *base program paradigms* exist to seek *validation* with new *information-data* and *sensory experience* always interwoven to *conform*. The *reality* that is *agreed to* is only 'one part' of *physical existence*. It represents only the aspects of a *spectrum* that *humans* are *programmed* to receive. What is perceived as—"*being-in-existence*"—discounts what is *not*-being. As a dualistic principle, *what-is* and *what-is-not* are 'identical in nature' but differing in degree.

> *When you "create" a condition of existence,*
> *you equally "create" a condition of not-existence.*

As 'manifest energy' in existence, both conditions are practically identical, both *aspects* now *realized* into *reality as one.* Reality exists *in* wholeness. It is the individual *being* (the *individual* personality-persona program) that has been given an *awareness-consciousness preference* or programmed inclination toward or away from one *range* of existence (or *not-existence*) from another.

Infinite *potentiality* & Infinite *possibility* 'collapses' in a moment of realization. The *human condition* must *evolve in itself* to reach the next *apex* of its own abilities of existence. The *increased intelligence*; the *life extension*; the *space migration*—all comes with becoming *more* than *human. Self-honest* application and action within the *system* of *reality can* accomplish *this.* To do so is to firstly *accept,* and secondly *face* and *overcome* the limited *awareness-consciousness* of the HUMAN CONDITION.

> —*Intelligence* cannot be 'increased'
> while it remains *fragmented;*
> it merely becomes even more *fragmented*

> —*Lifespans* cannot be 'extended'
> while the *genetic program coding*
> fixes one's existence to 120 years.

As a result of the perceptibly *restricted time* spent *distracted* on earth, tendencies toward *greed,* the *illusions* of the *condition of having* and resulting *jealousy* and *discordance* thwarts true development.

'Dependencies' on *old programming* keep the *human being* in a position of 'stalemate' in their *experience* of *existence* confined to *codes* and *patterns* that may have got the *humans* "here"— but are <u>not</u> the means to make the *NexGen* <u>evolutionary leap</u>...

—APPENDIX C—
THE STELE OF REVEALING : STELE OF ANKH-F-N-KHONSU

[B1] Words spoken by the Osiris (the deceased), God's
Servant of *Mentu*, Lord of *Waset*, Opener of the Stargate in
the Most Select of Places, *Ankh-ef-en-Khonsu*,
[B2] True of Voice: "O Exalted-one! may he be praised, Great
of Manifestations, the great *Ba* whom
[B3] the gods fear, and who appears on his great throne,
make the path of the *Ba*, the *Akh*, and the *Shadow*, for I am
equipped so that I might shine therein
[B4] as an equipped-one. Make for me the path to the place
in which *Ra*, *Atum*, *Khepri*, and *Hathor* are therein." The
Osiris, God's Servant of *Mentu*, Lord of *Waset*,
[B5] *Ankh-ef-en-Khonsu*, True of Voice, son of the like titled
Ba-sa-en-Mut, borne of the Chantress of *Amon-Ra*, Lady of
the House, *Taneshet*.

[C1] Words spoken by the *Osiris* (the deceased), God's
Servant of *Mentu*, Lord of *Waset*, *Ankh-ef-en-*
[C2] *Khonsu*, True of Voice: "My heart of my mother, my
heart of my mother, my heart while I existed
[C3] upon earth, do not stand against me as a witness, do
not oppose me in
[C4] in the tribunal, do not be hostile against me in the
presence of the Great God, Lord of the West.
[C5] Although I have united (myself) to the land to the great
western side of Heaven, may I flourish upon earth!"
[C6] Words spoken by the *Osiris* (the deceased), the high
priest of *Waset*, *Ankh-ef-en-Khonsu*, True of Voice: "You
who are Unique
[C7] of Arm, who shines like the moon, the *Osiris*, *Ankh-ef-*
[C8] *en-Khonsu*, goes forth from your multitudes,
[C9] great deliverer of those who live in the sun-light, open
to him
[C10] the Netherworld, indeed, the *Osiris*, *Ankh-ef-en-Khonsu*
who comes forth in
[C11] day in order to do everything that pleased him upon
earth among the living-ones."

—APPENDIX D—
TOHU va BAHU : THE SEVEN HEAVENS
excerpt from *"The Zohar"*

The higher or celestial world with its accompanying spheres, though invisible to mortal sight, has its reflection and analogue, namely, the lower world with its circumambient spheres, according to the saying, "As above, so below." The works of the Holy One in the celestial world are the type of those in the terrestrial world.

The meaning of the words, *Brashith, bara Alhim* is this: *brasahith,* i.e., the celestial world, gave rise or origin to *Alhim,* the visible divine name that then first became known. Thus *Alhim* was associated with the creation of the world, as *Brashith* was connected with the creation of the celestial or invisible world, that being the type, thus the *antetype,* or in other words, one was the reflection and analogue of the other, and therefore it is written, '*Ath hashamayim, veath ha-aretzs*' (the heavens and the earth). The heaven on high produced and gave rise to the earth below.

It is written, "And the earth was without form and void" (*Tohu va Bohu*). The word *aretzs* here refers to the earth in its primal state when Void of Light. By the word "*was,*" scripture teaches that it existed at its creation in a state of chaos and confusion. It is also said "*and Darkness,*" which was the deprivation of the Light emanating from the *antetypal world,* owing to the matter of the earth becoming condensed and thus less receptive of its reflection.

These words, Tohu, Bohu and Darkness, together with a fourth, "wind," represent the four elements composing the substance of the earth. Another version gives "*ve-ath ha-aretzs,*" referring to this world and its several divisions that are altogether different from those of the celestial world and which are as follows: *Aretzs, Gaea, Nesia, Zia, Arga* and *Thebel,* which latter is greater than all the others as it is written:

"And He shall judge the world (*Thebel*) in righteousness."

Rabbi Jose having asked the question: What kind of world is that which is called *Zia*?

Rabbi Simeon replied: It is the place of *Gehenna* or *Hell*, "a land of drought and the shadow of Death." It is mystically referred to in the words, "and Darkness was upon the face of the deep', alluding to *Zia*, the abode of *Hell* and of the Angel of Death, and is so called because the faces of those who are banished there become blackened on account of their wicked lives when on earth. The earth of *Nesia* is that the inhabitants of which become oblivious of the past; whereas, in that of *Bohu*, the faculty of memory is vivid and active."

The word *Bohu* denotes the earth, *Gaea*, whilst the words, 'and the spirit of *Alhim* moved upon the face of the waters,' designate that of *Thebel*, which is nourished and sustained by the spirit of *Alhim*, as is also *Aretzs*, our own abode of earthly existence, which is circumscribed and surrounded by seven spheres analogous to those of the celestial world, all of them being under the domination and control of their particular lords and guardians. The seven spheres of the celestial world are prototypes of those that surround our world and are inhabited by angelic beings who sing the praises of the Holy One, and use their own individual forms of worship. Their rank and order are indicated by the sphere they occupy.

The first of these higher or celestial spheres and nearest to the earth, is altogether Void of Light and is the abode of angels who are like tempestuous winds, never seen, but felt, and are always invisible as they are Void of Light and Darkness and undistinguished by any color. They are wholly without self-consciousness and without form or shape. Its chief and ruler is an angel named *Tahariel*, who has under him seventy subordinates. Their motion is manifested by the glittering of fiery sparks, the appearance and disappearance of which constitute day and night.

The second celestial sphere is distinguished from the first by the possession of a modicum of Light, and is inhabited by angels appointed to watch over humanity and guide it into the path of uprightness whenever there is danger of its falling into error and wrong doing. When righteousness prevails in the world, they are filled with joy and delight. Their chief and ruler is called *Qadmiel.* When Israel commences its worship of the Holy One, they then manifest and make themselves visible in forms of intense brightness, and three times daily they bless and hallow the divine name. When they observe Israel studying and meditating on the law or secret doctrine, they ascend on high before the Holy One, who takes account of what they have seen and heard.

The third celestial sphere is pervaded and filled with fire and flames. In it the fiery river *Nahar-dinur* takes its rise and flows into *Gehenna,* overwhelming and engulfing in its course those mortals whose lives on earth were given up and addicted to evil and wrongdoing. Over these are placed destroying and tormenting angels, also accusing angels who, however, have no power or influence over Israel when it repents and does what is just and right. The abode of their chief is on the left side of this sphere in which Darkness prevails, as it is written, "and Darkness was upon the face of the waters." It is also the abode of *Samael,* the Angel of Darkness, the great transgressor.

The Fourth celestial region is splendidly luminous, being the abode of angelic beings of great honor and dignity who, unlike those of the first sphere, begin and finish their worship of the Holy One without interruption. They are not subject to any change or declension, being angels of mercy and compassion of whom scripture speaks "Who makes his angels as the wind, and his messengers as flames of fire." Their great mission work is on the plane of human existence and are invisible save in visions of the night, or on extraordinary occasions according to the degree of intelligence of those to whom they manifest themselves. Their great chief is named *Padiel* by whose orders they hold the key and open the gates of mercy through which pass the prayers and supplications of those who sincerely repent and live the Higher and Diviner life.

The Fifth celestial sphere is one of still greater and more intense Light. Therein are angels, some of them ruling over fire, others over water, and are messengers either of mercy or judgment, and as such become manifested as heralds of Light or Darkness. Their worship of the Holy One takes place at midnight. They are under the control of a chief named *Qadashiel*. When at midnight the north wind begins to blow, the Holy One, blessed be He! enters the garden of Eden and holds converse with the righteous. Then begin they their service of praise which resounds throughout the whole of this sphere and lasts during the night until daybreak and the sun appears. At that moment these angels join in a grand and glorious song of thanksgiving that peals also from all hosts of heaven, from angels and Archangels, Seraphim, Cherubim, above and below all uniting in the ascription of blessing and honor, glory and power to YHVH, the Lord of Hosts that lives forever and ever; as it is written, "When the morning stars sang together and all the sons of God shouted for joy." This their great anthem ceases not until Israel begins its song of praise.

The Sixth celestial Sphere is nearer to the Kingdom of Heaven. In it are seas covered with ships, also rivers and lakes abounding in fish. Its denizens are under the rule of presidents, the chief of whom is named *Uriel*, who enter on their official duties at certain fixed times. When the time arrives for the ships to go south, *Michael* is their ruler; and when they go north, *Gabriel* assumes authority and direction; as these two archangels occupy the right and left sides of the *Merkaba*, or celestial chariot. When, however, the ships go eastward, *Raphael* rules, and *Uriel* when they sail westward.

The Seventh Celestial Sphere is the highest and accessible only to souls of the greatest purity and thus qualified to enter into its joys and delights. None other are found there. In it are laid up treasures of peace, blessings and benefits.

All these seven spheres are inhabited and filled with beings like in their form to man, who cease not to worship and give thanks to the holy One. None of them, however, are so conversant with the glory of the Holy One as the inhabitants of the sphere of *Thebel*, who are perfectly pure in body, mind and soul. In the seventh celestial sphere there are those who have attained to the highest degree of holiness as in the seventh sphere belonging to earth below, are found the just with purified bodies. Moreover, above and beyond all these spheres there are seven others the existence of which is a subject of faith and not of experience, and in each of them are spiritual beings of the highest order.

The first of these mysterious spheres is inhabited by a lofty angel named *Rachmiel*, who has the charge over those who have forsaken idolatry to become worshipers of the Holy One. By him they are prepared to look in the Luminous Mirror, or Beatific Vision.

In the second higher sphere dwells *Ahinael*, who receives under his care all who died ere being initiated in the secret doctrine, and instructs them in its teachings.

The third is that where abides *Adrahinael*, a spirit under whose care and guardianship are those who in earth life had resolved to change their evil habits, but being suddenly overtaken by Death, were unable to do as they had willed. Such souls find themselves cast first into *Gehenna*, out of which, however, they are taken by this spirit and prepared for the enjoyment of the Divine Light emanating from their Lord and Creator, the Holy One. The joys of such souls are inferior to those of others. They are known as "children of the flesh," and of them it is written, "From one new moon to another, and from one sabbath to another, shall all flesh come to worship before me, says the Lord." Fourth of the spheres is inhabited by a spirit named *Gadrihael*, presiding over all those who were slain by idolaters. His office is to guide them unto the palace of the king clothed in robes of purple, in which their names are interwoven and where they abide until the day when the Holy One shall avenge their sufferings, as it is written: "He shall judge amongst the heathen. He shall fill the places with dead bodies and shall wound the heads of many."

Adiriel is the presiding spirit in the fifth higher sphere and is in charge of those souls who through their lifelong penitence, attained to a high degree of holiness and purity in which they surpass all others, even as their abode excels all others in grandeur and glory. All the forenamed presidents are under the rule and authority of the archangel *Michael*, captain of the myriad hosts of heaven, whose office it, is to fill with joy and delight the souls of the faithful and true servants of the Lord, by causing them to view and behold the light, clear as crystal, that marks the course of the river of the water of life flowing into the world to come.

—APPENDIX E—
MERITORIOUS ORDER OF THE ROSY CROSS
excerpt from *"Fama Fraternitas"* (1614)

1. You are not attract public attention to your superior knowledge or charge a fee for healing services.

2. You are not wear special garments abroad, choosing instead the local regional attire.

3. You are to return to the Temple of the Holy Spirit at predetermined increments for apprenticeship and service.

4. You are to find a worthy successor during your lifetime.

5. You are to take on the sign and mark of "R.C."

6. You are to maintain the secrecy of the organization (for a period of 100 years).

First, That none of them should profess any other thing then to cure the sick, and that gratis.

Second, None of the posterity should be constrained to wear one certain kind of habit, but therein to follow the custom of the country.

Third, That every year, upon the day C., they should meet together at the house Sancti Spiritus, or write the cause of his absence.

Fourth, Every Brother should look about for a worthy person who, after his decease, might succeed him.

Fifth, The word R. C. should be their seal, mark, and character.

Sixth, The Fraternity should remain secret for one hundred years.

—APPENDIX F—
MAGICKAL WARFARE : PSYCHIC SELF-DEFENSE
excerpt from "*Arcanum*" (2008) by Joshua Free

Use of diverse mystical applications as "powers of the sword" or "powers of the shield" for a "wizards' duel." Many examples exist throughout this book, and even the more obvious entrees on curses and protection can be used. Practitioners who do occasionally come into magical warfare are hopefully previously experienced with a broad understanding and skill in diverse styles and traditions. Ideally, magical warfare should be used as a last resort for defensive purposes.

There are no rules to the wizards' duel. Anything goes. Practitioners draw from any pantheon of any system. Attacks may be made directly in the form of curses or spirits and entities can be used as intermediaries. When bringing the battle to the Astral Plane, you can use your astral grove as a sanctuary. The energetic current of the blackthorn tree can be evoked. Health of your personal energetic system—particularly your aura—is important. Keep your light shield strong. Basic binding magic may supplement efforts, but magical combat generally will require a much higher caliber of energy work.

All magical operations in "high magic" should be performed from within the body of light and magical warfare is no exception. Cast a circle of protection, even if only visualized from a fixed position. You may choose to use a cone of power or some other method for raising energy. Call on Divine Names for protection. Wizards have even conjured dragons for astral battles. These Guardians can be used for protection or offensively. Aleister Crowley commanded the spirits of the *grimoires* —particularly the *Goetia*—to attack his enemy's *nemetons* during rituals or their astral bodies in their sleep. Skilled wizards have created elementary beings for the same purpose and the evil eye carries a significant amount of superstition.

Rituals found within the Mardukite *Necronomicon* cycle (e.g. the *Maqlu* tablet series) and other popular *grimoires* have several applications specifically designed for magical combat—an occurrence that may become more common in the future. Protective operations, or the *"Powers of the Shield,"* are just as important as your methods of attack. One must assume that your enemy's natural defenses will deflect most energy, even if conscious efforts are not being made to thwart your spells.

Two types of *psionic* tool exist for magical warfare:
   a) abstract ones that are visualized; and
   b) concrete physical ones that are constructed.

The two types are extensions of each other. Abstract *psionic* tools must be visualized—using skills that should have been developed prior to practical attempts. By requesting the Universe to send to you—and calling to mind a manifestation of a *psionic* (invisible) tool—you are able to immediately call forth a particular energy vibration or "ray of light" that is not intelligent (sentient) in itself (not an entity). This is accomplished without incantation or ritual gesture. The wizard channels "light energy" in the form of *Akasha* or *Starfyre*.

Our forms, at their most fundamental energetic level, are meant to absorb and hold light. The capacity to which you are able to do this is called the *"Light Quotient"* (LQ) on the "Ascension Path." You increase this by balancing your *chakras* (*astyr*), strengthening your aura and repeated conscious projections of your body of light. All of this will prepare you adequately for using *"Psionic Tools"* on the magical/spiritual battlefront.

> [The following are practical suggestions toward the use of *psionic* tools in traditional magical warfare that are excerpted from *"The Sorcerer's Handbook"* by Joshua Free.]

1.) The Armor of the Blue Flame
Ask the Universal Consciousness to send to your aid the energy vibration of MARDUK's *"Armor of Blue Flame."* Visualize

the "blue flame" as a protective surface covering your auric-light body and physical body. Charge the armor. Give it an intention to filter all negative energies encountered and transform it to a positive polarity before allowing it through or deflecting that, which cannot be transformed.

2.) The Golden Scepter of Melchizedek

Call forth the crystal and gold rays of light. Surround yourself with this energy. Request that the Universal Consciousness concentrates the form that you envision as the *Golden Scepter of Melchizedek*. Visualize yourself holding it in your projective or power hand, usually the right one. See it radiating a golden light that fills the expansive space of your *nemeton.* Direct it to penetrate and strengthen your auric-shield.

3.) The Shield of the Solar Logos

Call forth protective power of the Divine Solar Logos as *Starfire.* Ask the Universal Consciousness to manifest the Shield of the Sun on your receptive arm, creating the final piece of armor for your *psionic* defenses. Affirm that by activating the relic you are aligning and balancing all *chakras* of your manifold Identity.

4.) Crystal Capacitors

In addition to your "light gear," several concrete physical instruments may be constructed to conduct energy for *psionic* and magical work. Crystal capacitors are used to "create" an "artificial" vortex of earth energy. Quartz crystals beneath the ground, either naturally or intentionally buried, adjust vibrations of an area. Portable crystal capacitors can be used to create a *psionic* force-field at will. In small quantities they should be set at each of the four cardinal (elemental) directions and a larger one in the center to focus the surrounding energy. These capacitors are, in their most simplistic form, quartz crystals that have a flat base and pointed top on the opposing side, mounted on discs of silver or copper.

5.) Crystal Power Rods

Used to direct thought energy and other currents, the wand amplifies the broadcast energy vibrations sent to a focused target.

6.) Psionatrix Headband

Crystal headbands are made and used to amplify mental and *psionic* energies. The headband is a portable hands-free version of the crystal power rod. It is worn so that the crystal protrudes directly from the third eye (pineal gland). Cut a long rectangle (approximately 2" x 10") from a sheet of pliable copper and bend it to form around your head. Drill holes in the end and string leather cording through it so that it can be tied/secured behind your head. You will also need to attach a (.999) silver coin or disc in the center of the band once the copper has been formed. "Silver-solder" and an acetylene torch can be used for this. Once this cools, clean the copper (oxidation occurs with the heat) and then mount a flat-bottomed crystal with an opposing pointed top to the disc. One suggestion is to seal the edges of the crystal to the disc with a clear silicone, while others use putty beneath it. Be sure your forehead connects with the surface of the band behind the disc, though you can wrap some leather cording around the rest of the band for additional comfort and gripping support.

—APPENDIX G—
THE BABYLONIAN EPIC OF CREATION TABLETS :
(THE ENUMA ELIŠ)
"Tablets of Destiny" Version Excerpt

ENUMA ELIŠ SERIES – TABLET I
When in the heights the Heavens had not been named,
And the Earth had not yet been named,
And the primeval Abyss, ABZU, who birthed them,
And CHAOS, TIAMAT, the LAW,
The Ancient One, Mother to them all.
Their waters were as One and no field was formed,
No marsh was to be seen;
When of the gods none had been called into being,
And none bore a name, and no destinies were ordained;
Then were created the celestial gods in the midst of heaven,
LAHMU and LAHAMU were called into being
And the Ages increased.
Then ANSAR and KISAR were created,
And the god ANU then came forth who begot ENKI.
Abounding in all wisdom he had no rival.
Thus the Great Gods were established.
But TIAMAT and APSU were still in confusion,
Troubled and in disorder.
ABZU was not diminished in might, and TIAMAT roared.
ABZU, the begetter of the great gods,
Cried unto MUMMU, his minister,
And said: "MUMMU, thou minister that causes my spirit to rejoice,
Come with me to TIAMAT."
They consulted on a plan with regard to the gods, their sons.
ABZU spoke: "Let me destroy their ways, let there be lamentation,
And then let us lie down again in peace."
When TIAMAT heard these words, she raged and cried aloud.
She uttered a curse and unto ABZU she asked:
"What then shall we do?"
MUMMU answered giving counsel unto ABZU,
"Come, their way is strong, but you can destroy it;
This day you shall have rest, by night shalt thou lie down in peace."
They banded themselves together
And at the side of TIAMAT they advanced; they were furious;
They devised mischief without resting night and day.
They prepared for battle, fuming and raging;

They joined their forces and made weapons invincible;
She spawned monster-serpents, sharp of tooth, merciless of fang;
With poison, instead of blood, she filled their bodies.
Fierce monster-vipers she clothed with terror.
With splendor she clothed them, she made them of lofty stature.
Whoever beheld them, terror overcame him,
Their bodies reared up and none could withstand their attack.
She set up vipers and dragons, and the monster LAHAMU.
And hurricanes, and raging hounds, and scorpion-men,
And mighty tempests, and fish-men, and rams;
They bore cruel weapons, without fear of the fight.
Her commands were mighty, none could resist them;
After this fashion she made eleven kinds of monsters.
Among the gods who were her sons,
Inasmuch as he had given her support,
She exalted KINGU; in their midst she raised him to power.
To march before the forces, to lead the host,
To give the battle-signal, to advance to the attack,
To direct the battle, to control the fight,
Unto him she entrusted, saying: "I have uttered thy spell,
In the assembly of the gods I have raised thee to power.
The dominion over all the gods have I entrusted unto him.
Be thou exalted, you are my chosen spouse,
May your name be magnified among all ANUNNAKI."
She gave him the *Tablets of Destiny*, on his breast she laid them,
Saying: "Thy command shall not be in vain,
And your decrees shall be established."
Now KINGU, thus exalted, having received the power of ANU,
Decreed the fate among the gods his sons,
Saying: "Let the opening of your mouth quench the Fire-god;
He who is exalted in the battle, let him display his might!"

ENUMA ELIŠ SERIES – TABLET II

TIAMAT made weighty her handiwork,
Evil she wrought against the gods her children.
To avenge ABZU, TIAMAT planned evil,
But how she had collected her forces, the god unto ENKI divulged.
ENKI was grievously afflicted and he sat in sorrow.
The days went by, and his anger was appeased,
And to the place of ANSAR his father he took his way.
He went and, standing before ANSAR, his father,
All that TIAMAT had plotted he repeated unto him,

Saying "TIAMAT, our mother hath conceived a hatred for us,
With all her force she rages, full of wrath.
All the gods have turned to her,
With those, whom you created, they go to her side.
They have banded together and at the side of TIAMAT
And they advance; they are furious,
They devise mischief without resting night and day.
They prepare for battle, fuming and raging;
They have joined their forces and are making war.
TIAMAT, who formed all things,
And made weapons invincible;
She hath spawned monster-serpents,
Sharp of tooth, and merciless of fang.
With poison, instead of blood, she hath filled their bodies.
Fierce monster-vipers she hath clothed with terror,
With splendor she has armed them;
She has made them tall in stature.
Whoever beholds them is overcome by terror,
Their bodies rear up and none can withstand their attack.
She hath set up vipers, and dragons, and the monster LAHAMU,
And hurricanes and raging hounds, and scorpion-men,
And mighty tempests, and fish-men and rams;
They bear cruel weapons, without fear of the fight.
Her commands are mighty; none can resist them;
After this fashion, huge of stature,
She has made eleven kinds of monsters.
Among the gods who are her sons,
Inasmuch as he has given her support,
She has exalted KINGU;
In their midst she hath raised him to power.
To march before the forces, to lead the host,
To give the battle-signal, to advance to the attack.
To direct the battle, to control the fight,
To him she has uttered your spell;
She hath given to him the *Tablets of Destiny*,
On his breast she laid hem,
Saying: 'Thy command shall not be in vain,
And the your word shall be established.'
"O my father, let not the word of thy lips be overcome,
Let me go, that I may accomplish all that is in thy heart.
I shall avenge."

ENUMA ELIŠ SERIES – TABLET III

ANSAR spoke to his minister:
"O GAGA, thou minister who causes my spirit to rejoice,
Unto LAHMU and LAHAMU I will send thee.
Make ready for a feast, at a banquet let them sit,
Let them eat bread, let them mix wine,
That for MARDUK, the avenger, they may decree the fate.
Go, GAGA, stand before them, And all that I tell thee,
Repeat unto them, and say: 'ANSAR, your son, has sent me,
The purpose of his heart he has made known unto me.
He said that TIAMAT, our mother, has conceived a hatred for us,
With all her force she rages full of wrath.
All the gods have turned to her, with those, whom you created,
They go to her side. I sent ANU, but he could not withstand her;
ENKI was afraid and turned back.
But MARDUK has set out, the champion of the gods, your son;
To set out against TIAMAT his heart has called him.
He opened his mouth and spake unto me,
Saying: 'If I, your avenger, Conquer TIAMAT and give you life,
Appoint an assembly, make my fate preeminent and proclaim it so.
In UPSUKKINAKU seat yourself joyfully together;
With my word in place I will decree fate.
May whatsoever I do remain unaltered,
May the word of my lips never be changed nor made of no avail.'
Quickly decree for him the fate which you bestow
So that he may go and fight your strong enemy."
GAGA went humbly before LAHMU and LAHAMU, the gods,
His fathers, and he kissed the ground at their feet.
He humbled himself; then he stood up and spake unto them saying:
"ANSAR, your son, has sent me,
The purpose of his heart he hath made known unto me.
He says that TIAMAT, our mother, hath conceived a hatred for us,
With all her force she rages full of wrath."
And he spoke the words of the tale.
LAHMU and LAHAMU heard and cried aloud.
All of the IGIGI wailed bitterly, saying:
"We do not understand the deeds of TIAMAT!"
Then did they collect and go,
The great gods, all of them, the ANUNNAKI who decree fate.
They entered in the House of ANSAR, kissed one another,
They made ready for the feast, ate bread,
And they mixed sesame-wine.

They were wholly at ease, their spirit was exalted;
Then for MARDUK, their avenger, they decreed the fate.

ENUMA ELIŠ SERIES – TABLET IV

The ANUNNAKI prepared for MARDUK a lordly chamber,
Before his fathers as prince he took his place.
"MARDUK, You are now chief among the great gods,
Thy fate is unequaled, thy word is ANU.
Your words shall be command,
In your power shall it be to exalt and to abase.
None among the gods shall transgress your boundary.
Abundance, shall exist in thy sanctuary shrine,
Even if you lack offerings.
MARDUK, you are our avenger!
We give you sovereignty over the whole world.
Sit down in might; be exalted in thy command.
Your weapon shall never lose its power; it shall crush your enemy.
Lord, spare the life of him that puts his trust in thee,
But as for the god who began the rebellion, empty them of life."
The ANUNNAKI set out a garment
And continued to speak to MARDUK.
"May thy fate, O lord, be supreme among the gods,
To destroy and to create; speak only the word,
And your command shall be fulfilled.
Command now that the garment vanish;
And speak the word again and let the garment reappear!"
Then he spake the words and the garment vanished;
Again he commanded it and the garment reappeared.
When the gods, his fathers, beheld the fulfillment of his word,
They rejoiced, and they did homage unto him,
Saying, "Maerdechai! Maerdechai! MARDUK is king!"
They bestowed upon him the scepter, the throne and the ring,
They give him invincible weaponry to overwhelm the enemy.
"Go, and cut off the life of TIAMAT," they said.
"And let the wind carry her blood into secret places."
MARDUK made ready the bow, his first choice in weapon,
He slung a spear upon him. He raised the club in his right hand.
The bow and the quiver he hung at his side.
He set the FLAMING DISC in front of him
And with the flame he filled his body.
He fashioned a net to enclose the inward parts of TIAMAT,
He stationed the four winds so that nothing of her might escape;

The South wind and the North wind and the East wind
And the West wind He created the evil wind,
And the tempest, and the hurricane,
And the fourfold wind,
And the sevenfold wind, and the cyclone,
And the wind which had no equal;
He sent forth the winds which he had created, seven in total;
To disturb the inward parts of TIAMAT.
Then MARDUK raised the thunderbolt, mounted the chariot,
A storm unequaled for terror, and he harnessed four horses
Named DESTRUCTION, FEROCITY, TERROR,
And SWIFTNESS; and foam came from their mouths
And they were mighty in battle,
Trained to trample underfoot.
With garments cloaked in terror and an overpowering brightness
Crowning his head, MARDUK set out toward the raging TIAMAT.
Then the gods beheld him.
And when the lord drew near,
He gazed upon the inward parts of TIAMAT,
He heard the muttering of KINGU, her spouse.
As MARDUK gazed, KINGU was troubled,
The will of KINGU was destroyed and his motions ceased.
And the gods, his helpers, who marched by his side,
Beheld their leader's fear and their sight was troubled.
But TIAMAT did not turn her neck.
She spit rebellious words.
MARDUK raised the thunderbolt,
His mighty weapon, against TIAMAT,
Who was raging, and he called out:
"You have become great as you have exalted yourself on high,
And your heart has prompted you to call to battle.
You have raised KINGU to be your spouse,
You have chosen Evil and sinned against ANU and his decree.
And against the gods, my fathers,
You have dedicated yourself to a wicked plan.
Let us now face off in battle then!"
When TIAMAT heard these words,
She acted possessed and lost her sense of reason.
She screamed wild, piercing cries,
She trembled and shook to her very foundations.
She recited an incantation, and cast a spell,
And the gods of the battle cried out for their weapons.

Then TIAMAT and MARDUK advanced towards one another,
The battle drew near.
Lord MARDUK spread out his net and caught her,
And the evil wind that gathered behind him he let loose in her
Face when she opened her mouth fully.
The terrible winds filled her belly,
And her courage was taken from her,
And her mouth opened wider.
MARDUK seized the spear and burst her belly,
Severing her inward parts, he pierced her heart.
He overcame her and cut off her life;
He cast down her body and stood upon it.
After slaying TIAMAT, the leader of the ANCIENT ONES,
The might was broken and her minions scattered.
But they were surrounded, so that they could not escape.
MARDUK took them captive and broke their weapons;
In the net they were caught and in the snare they sat down.
And on the eleven monsters which she had filled
With the power of striking terror, he brought them affliction,
Their strength he stole and their opposition
He trampled under his feet.
From KINGU who he had conquered,
He rightly took the *Tablets of Destiny*,
And sealed them with his seal, then hung them from his neck.
Now after MARDUK had conquered and cast down his enemies,
And had fully established ANSAR's triumph over the enemy,
And had attained the purpose of ENKI,
Over the captive gods he strengthened his position,
And he returned to the conquered TIAMAT.
With his merciless club he smashed her skull.
He cut through the channels of her blood,
And he made the North wind steal it away
Outside in secret places between spaces.
His fathers beheld, and rejoiced and were glad;
Presents and gifts they brought unto him.
Then Lord MARDUK rested, gazing upon her dead body
And devised a cunning plan.
He split her up like a flat fish into two halves;
One half of her he established a covering for heaven.
Sealed with a GATE he stationed a WATCHER IAK SAKKAK
And fixed him not to let her waters to ever come forth.
MARDUK passed through and surveyed the regions of Heaven,

And over the Deep he set the dwelling of ENKI.
And after measuring the structure of the Deep,
He founded his Mansion,
Which was created likened to Heaven and he set down
The fixed districts for ANU, ENLIL and ENKI to reign.

ENUMA ELIŠ SERIES – TABLET V

MARDUK fixed the Star Gates of the Elder Gods;
And the stars he gave images as the stars of the Zodiac,
which he fixed in place.
He ordained the year and into sections he divided it;
For the twelve months he fixed the stars.
He founded his Star Gate on NIBIRU to fix them in zones;
That none might rebel or go astray,
He fixed the Star Gate of ENLIL
And ENKI alongside him.
He opened great gates on both sides,
He made strong gates on the left and on the right
And in the midst thereof he fixed the zenith;
He fixed the Star Gate for the Moon-god
And decreed that he shine forth,
Trusting him with the night and to determine days;
The first of the great gates he assigned to NANNA-SIN,
And every month without ceasing he would be crowned, saying:
"At the beginning of the month, when you shine down upon the land,
You command the trumpets of the six days of the moon,
And on the seventh day you will divide the crown.
On the fourteenth day you will stand opposite as half-moon.
When the Sun-god of the foundation of heaven calls thee,
On that the final day again you will stand as opposite.
All shall go about the course I fix.
You will drawn near to judge the righteous
And destroy the unrighteous.
That is my decree and the covenant of the first gate."
The gods, his fathers, beheld the net which MARDUK had fashioned,
They beheld his bow and how its work was accomplished.
They praised the work which he had done and then ANU raised up
And kissed the bow before the assembly of the gods.
And thus he named the names of the bow, saying:
"Long-wood shall be one name,
And the second name shall be Dragonslayer,

And its third name shall be the Bow-star,
In heaven shall it remain as a sign to all."
Then ANU and MARDUK fixed a Star Gate for it too,
And after the ANUNNAKI decreed the fates for the ANCIENT ONES,
MARDUK set a throne in heaven for himself at ANU's right hand.

ENUMA ELIŠ SERIES – TABLET VI.a

The ANUNNAKI acclaimed him "First among the ELDER GODS."
MARDUK heard the praises of the gods,
His heart called to him to devised a cunning plan.
He approached ENKI saying:
"The Key to the GATE shall be ever hidden, except to my offspring.
I will take my blood and with bone I will fashion a Race of Men,
That they may keep watch over the GATE.
And from the blood of KINGU I will create a race of men,
That they will inhabit the Earth in service to the gods
So that our shrines may be built and the temples filled.
But I will alter the ways of the gods, and I will change their paths;
Together shall they be oppressed
And unto evil shall they no longer reign.
I will bind the ELDER GODS to the WATCHTOWERS,
Let them keep watch over the GATE of ABZU,
And the GATE of TIAMAT and the GATE of KINGU.
I bind the WATCHER IAK SAKKAK to the GATE
With the Key known only to my Race.
Let none enter that GATE
Since to invoke DEATH is to utter the final prayer."
The ANUNNAKI rejoiced and set their mansions in UPSUKKINAKU.
When all this had been done, the Elders of the ANUNNAKI
Seated themselves around MARDUK
And in their assembly they exalted him
And named him FIFTY times,
Bestowing upon him the FIFTY powers of the gods.

240

—APPENDIX H—
DESCENT OF ISHTAR : CROSSING TO THE UNDERWORLD
"Cybernomicon" Appendix Version

This is the chronicle of ISHTAR [INANNA],
Queen of the Heavens, Mistress of the Gods,
The Brightest Star in the Heavens.
To the nether Land of No Return, to the realm of ERESHKIGAL,
ISHTAR, daughter of NANNA-SIN, she set her mind.
From the Great Above she set her mind to the Great Below.
The Goddess of the Great Above
Set her mind toward the Great Below.

To the Darkened Dwelling, the abode of IRKALLA,
To the Black Earth, the lands of CUTHA,
To the house which none may leave, she set her foot,
To the road from which there is no return, she set her foot,
To the cave which accepts no light,
To the place where bowls of dust become food,
To the place where none see light, residing in pure darkness,
To the place where residents are clothed in the wings of birds,
Lady ISHTAR abandoned Heaven, abandoned Earth,
And to the Underworld she descended.

In ERECH she abandoned EANNA,
  to the Underworld she descended.
In BADTIBIRA she abandoned EMUSHKALAMMA,
  to the Underworld she descended.
In ZABALAM she abandoned ESHARRA,
  to the Underworld she descended.
In ADAB she abandoned ESHARRA,
  to the Underworld she descended.
In NIPPUR she abandoned BARATUSHGARRA,
  to the Underworld she descended.
In KISH she abandoned HURSAGKALAMMA,
  to the Underworld she descended.
In AGADE she abandoned EULMASH,
  to the Underworld she descended.

ISHTAR took up the seven Divine Decrees; fixed them to her body,
She sought out seven Divine Decrees and grasped them in her hand:
The Shugurra, the Starry Crown of ANU she put upon her head,

The Wand of Lapis Lazuli she gripped in her hand,
The Necklace of Lapis Lazuli stones she tied about her neck,
The Brilliant Shinning Stones she took up and carried,
The Golden Ring of Power she placed on her finger,
The Frontlet Amulet she tied as a breastplate,
With the garments of the Queen of Heaven she dressed herself,
And with Holy Oils she anointed herself.

ISHTAR set her mind and moved toward the Underworld,
Her trusted messenger NINSHUBUR walked at her side.
To NINSHUBUR, ISHTAR spoke:
My trusted friend who are a constant source of support to me,
The messenger of my true words, carrier of my supporting words,
I tell you that I am descending to the Underworld.
When I have fully descended to the Underworld,
Fill the spaces of the Heavens with calls of my helplessness,
In the Assembly of ANUNAKI cry out for my blight,
In the House of the Gods create a commotion for me,
Lower your eye for me, lower your mouth for me,
Dress for me in the clothing of the poor,
And to the E.KUR, House of ENLIL, fix your steps alone for me.
When you enter the E.KUR, House of ENLIL, weep before him:
Father ENLIL, protect your grand-daughter from the Gate of Death,
Protect the metal that it may not be ground up to dust
    (in the Underworld).
Protect the lapis stone that it may not be broken up
    (in the Underworld).
Protect the wood [box] from being cut up (in the Underworld).
Let not the pure ISHTAR be put to death (in the Underworld).

If ENLIL does not aid you in this matter, then go to UR.
When you enter UR, at the E.KISH.SHIRGAL,
House of NANNA, weep before him:
Father NANNA, protect your daughter from the Gate of Death,
Protect the metal that it may not be ground up to dust
    (in the Underworld).
Protect the stone [lapis lazuli] that it may not be broken up
    (in the Underworld).
Protect the wood from being cut up (in the Underworld).
Let not the pure ISHTAR be put to death (in the Underworld).
If NANNA does not aid you in this matter, then go to ERIDU.
When you enter ERIDU, at the House of ENKI,

Weep before him: Father ENKI, protect your daughter from the
   Gate of Death,
Protect the metal that it may not be ground up to dust.
Protect the Lapis Lazuli stone that it may not be broken up.
Protect the wood [box] from being cut up.
Let not the pure ISHTAR be put to death.
Our Father ENKI, the Lord of Wisdom,
Who knows the secret of the food of life,
   who knows the waters of life,
He will surely listen, he will bring me to life.
Go now, NINSHUBUR, with the word I have commanded thee.

ISHTAR directed her mind to the Underworld.
To the Lapis Lazuli Castle of the Underworld she fixed her mind.
To the Gate of the nether Land of No Return, she arrived.
At the Gate to the Underworld, ISHTAR spoke evilly.
In the Castle of the Underworld, ISHTAR acted evilly.
The Watcher of the Gate, watched.
The Watcher of the Gate, NINGISHZIDDA [Neti], stood fast.
The Serpent of the Deep, NINGISHZIDDA watched ISHTAR approach.

ISHTAR spoke to the Watcher of the Gate:
Gatekeeper, open your gate to me, Open thy gate so I may enter!
Open, or I will attack the gate! Open, or I will smash the door!
Open, or I will shatter the bars! Open, or I will throw down the walls!
If you will not open wide I will raise the dead!
If you will not open wide I will cause the dead to rise,
So that the dead will outnumber and devour the living!
Spirit of the Watcher of the Gate,
   open the door to my understanding!

The gatekeeper opened his mouth to speak to ISHTAR:
   Stop, my lady, do not throw it down! Who are you?!?

ISHTAR answered:
I am the Queen of Heaven, from the place where the Sun rises.
If you are the Queen of Heaven, the place where the Sun rises,
Then why have you come to the Underworld,
   The Land of No Return?
Why would you take a road where a traveler cannot turn back?
What has caused your heart to lead you here?

The pure ISHTAR answered him:
I have come to see my eldest sister ERESHKIGAL,
I have heard her husband GUGALANNA had been killed
And I come to witness and respect the funerary rites.

The gatekeeper responded:
Stay here and keep your place, ISHTAR,
And I will go announce your name to my Queen, ERESHKIGAL.

The gatekeeper entered the castle, saying to ERESHKIGAL:
My Queen, ERESHKIGAL, your sister ISHTAR is waiting at the gate,
She who comes to uphold the great festivals,
She who stirs up the deep before ENKI EA, the king.

When ERESHKIGAL heard this, she was pale with fear.
While her lips turned dark she spoke out loud to herself:
What moved her heart to me? What compelled her spirit here?
Should I drink water with the ANUNNAKI?
Should I eat clay for bread and drink dirty water for sustenance?
Should I bemoan the men who have left their wives behind?
Should I bemoan the maidens ripped from the laps of their lovers?
Or should I bemoan the child sent off before his time?

Then ERESHKIGAL spoke to the gatekeeper:
Go, gatekeeper, and open the gate for her,
But treat her in accordance with the ancient rules.
The gatekeeper went forth to open the door for her, saying:
Enter, Lady ISHTAR, the Land of CUTHA will rejoice over thee,
The court of the Land of No Returns will be glad at thy presence.

The Watcher of the Gate loosened the bolts,
And Darkness fell upon the face of ISHTAR.
The Watcher of the Gate opened the door,
And Dark Waters stirred and rose to carry the Goddess of Light.
Of the Gate of GANZIR, the Watcher opened.
NINGISHZIDDA opened the Gate to the Land of No Return.
And ISHTAR entered.

When at the First Gate ISHTAR entered,
NINSIGHZIDDA removed the Starry Crown of Heaven.
And ISHTAR asked: Why, Serpent, have you taken the First Jewel?
And the Serpent answered:

This is the Covenant of Old, the Rules of the Mistress of the
  Underworld,
Enter, my lady, the First Gate.

When at the Second Gate ISHTAR entered,
NINSIGHZIDDA removed the Wand of Lapis Lazuli.
And ISHTAR asked: Why, NETI, have you taken the Second Jewel?
And NETI answered:
This is the Covenant of Old, the Rules of the Mistress of the
  Underworld,
Enter, my lady, the Second Gate.

When at the Third Gate ISHTAR entered,
NINSIGHZIDDA removed the Lapis Lazuli Necklace.
And ISHTAR asked: Why, Gatekeeper, have you taken the Third
  Jewel?
And the Gatekeeper answered:
This is the Covenant of Old, the Rules of the Mistress of the
  Underworld,
Enter, my lady, the Third Gate.

When at the Fourth Gate ISHTAR entered,
NINSIGHZIDDA removed the Shinning Brilliant Stones (from her
  waistband).
And ISHTAR asked: Why, Guardian of the Gate, have you taken the
  Fourth Jewel?
And the Guardian of the Gate answered:
This is the Covenant of Old, the Rules of the Mistress of the
  Underworld,
Enter, my lady, the Fourth Gate.

When at the Fifth Gate ISHTAR entered,
NINSIGHZIDDA removed the Golden Ring of Power.
And ISHTAR asked: Why, Watcher of the Portal, have you taken the
  Fifth Jewel?
And the Watcher of the Portal answered:
This is the Covenant of Old, the Rules of the Mistress of the
  Underworld,
Enter, my lady, the Fifth Gate.

When at the Sixth Gate ISHTAR entered,
NINSIGHZIDDA removed the Breastplate of Righteousness.

ISHTAR asked: Why, NINNKIGAL, have you taken the Sixth Jewel?
And NINNKIGAL answered:
This is the Covenant of Old, the Rules of the Mistress of the
    Underworld,
Enter, my lady, the Sixth Gate.

When at the Seventh Gate ISHTAR entered,
NINSIGHZIDDA stripped the Vestments of Queenship from her.
ISHTAR asked: Why, Messenger, have you taken the Seventh Jewel?
And the Ancient Messenger answered:
This is the Covenant of Old, the Rules of the Mistress of the
    Underworld,
Enter, my lady, the Seventh Gate.

ISHTAR had descended to the Underworld.
To the depths of CUTHA, KUR, ISHTAR descended.
Lost were the Seven Decrees of the Upper World.
Lost were the Seven Powers of the Land of the Living.
Lost was the sustenance of the Food and Waters of Life.
ISHTAR then appeared before ERESHKIGAL.
ERESHKIGAL saw her presence and screamed.
ISHTAR advanced toward ERESHKIGAL.

ERESHKIGAL summoned NAMMTAR, the Black Magician,
Saying these words as she spoke to him:
Go, NAMMTAR, imprison her in Darkness in my castle!
Release against her the Seven ANUNNAKI
Release against her the Sixty Demons of the Deep:
Demons of the eyes against her eyes!
Demons of the sides against her sides!
Demons of the heart against her heart!
Demons of the feet against her feet!
Demons of the head against her head!
Against her whole body, the Demons of KUR!

The ANUNNAKI, the Seven Judges of Death,
Fixed eyes of Death upon her,
At their word, the word which conjures all Demons,
The Demons came to tear apart ISHTAR from all sides.
In the Land of KUR, ISHTAR was killed.
The body of ISHTAR was shredded into a corpse.
And the corpse was suspended on a wood cross [stake].

For three days and three nights ISHTAR hung.

When after the three days and nights had passed,
The messenger of ISHTAR, NINSHUBAR,
The messenger of the favorable words of ISHTAR,
The carrier of the supporting words of ISHTAR,
NINSHUBAR filled the Heavens with laments for ISHTAR,
NINSHUBAR cried for her in the Assembly of the Gods,
NINSHUBAR caused commotion in the House of the Lord,
He lowered his eye for her, he lowered his mouth for her,
Like a poor servant he appealed to the Gods for her.

To the E.KUR, house of ENLIL, he directed his travels.
But Father ENLIL did not stand by him in this matter.
To the EKISHSHIRGAL, House of NANNA, he directed his steps.
But Father NANNA did not stand by him in this matter.
To ERIDU, in the house of ENKI, he wearily moved.
Our Father ENKI, listened to the words of NINSHUBAR.
ENKI listened to the words of the descent of ISHTAR.
ENKI listened to the words of the lament for ISHTAR.
ENKI listened to the words describing the opening of GANZIR.

Father ENKI answered NINSHUBAR:
What has my daughter done now?
I am troubled. What has ISHTAR done?
I am troubled. What has the Queen of Heavens done?
I am troubled. What has she done!?!

Father ENKI summoned forth clay to fashion a KURGARRU.
Father ENKI summoned forth wind to fashion a KALATURRU.
From the clay and the wind ENKI summoned two Elemental Spirits.
ENKI fashioned the KURGARRU, Spirit of the Earth.
ENKI fashioned the KALATURRU, Spirit of the Deep.
ENKI, to the KURGARRU, gave the Food of Life.
ENKI, to the KALATURRU, gave the Water of Life.

To the Elemental Spirits ENKI spoke:
Arise and set your mind to travel to the GANZIR Gate,
To the Gate of the Underworld, set your feet,
To the nether Land of No Return, fix your eyes.
The Seven Gates of the Underworld will open to you
And no charm or spell can keep you away,

for upon you I have set my Number—40.
Take up the Food of Life and the Water of Life,
And ERESHKIGAL shall not harm you.
ERESHKIGAL shall not raise her arm against you.
ERESHKIGAL shall have no power over you.
Upon the corpse of ISHTAR hung from the cross [stake],
Direct the Fear of the Rays of the Secret Fire,
Sixty times sprinkle the Food of Life,
Sixty times sprinkle the Waters of Life,
Sprinkle sixty times (Number of ANU) upon the corpse,
    and surely ISHTAR will rise.

Like winged serpents, the Elementals flew.
To the GANZIR Gate the Elementals flew invisibly.
Invisible, they passed by the Gatekeeper unseen.
Through the Seven Gates the Elementals flew invisibly.
Invisible, they passed by the Seven Watchers unseen.
With haste they entered into the Castle of Darkness,
In the Castle of Death they beheld horrible sights,
But with haste they moved, stopping only at the corpse of ISHTAR.
ISHTAR, the Beautiful Queen of Heaven.
ISHTAR, the Mistress of the Gods of Heaven.
ISHTAR, the Lady of Priestesses of UR.
ISHTAR, the Brightest Star of the Heavens.
ISHTAR, the Beloved of ENKI,
    she hung from the cross [stake] bleeding,
From one thousand critical wounds ISHTAR hung bleeding.
KURGARRU and KALATURRA approached the body of ISHTAR.
ERESHKIGAL, sensing their presence, screamed.
KURGARRU directed the Rays of Fire upon the Queen of Death.
KALATURRA directed Rays of Fire upon the Queen of Death.
ERESHKIGAL, while powerful in CUTHA, retreated.
KURGARRU, upon the corpse of ISHTAR,
Sprinkled the Food of Life of ENKI sixty times.
KALATURRA, upon the corpse of ISHTAR,
Sprinkled the Water of Life of ENKI sixty times.
Upon the corpse of ISHTAR, Queen of the Heavens,
KURGARRU and KALATURRA directed the Spirit of Life of ENKI.

ISHTAR rose!
ISHTAR ascended from the Underworld!
The ANUNNAKI fled their thrones of gold,

And the spirits of the nether Land of No Returns,
The spirits who had descended to the Dead peacefully,
When ISHTAR ascended from the Underworld,
When ISHTAR ascended on the winged serpents of ENKI,
ISHTAR ascended through the Gates of GANZIR and NETI,
Surely the dead hastened ahead of her.
When ISHTAR ascended past the First Gate,
The Queen of Heaven took back her Robes of Royalty.
When ISHTAR ascended past the Second Gate,
The Queen of Heaven took back her jeweled Breastplate of
  Righteousness.
When ISHTAR ascended past the Third Gate,
The Queen of Heaven took back her jeweled Gold Ring.
When ISHTAR ascended past the Fourth Gate,
The Queen of Heaven took back her jeweled Shinning Stones.
When ISHTAR ascended past the Fifth Gate,
The Queen of Heaven took back her jeweled Necklace.
When ISHTAR ascended past the Sixth Gate,
Queen of Heaven took back her jeweled Wand of Lapis Lazuli.
When ISHTAR ascended past the Seventh Gate,
Queen of Heaven took back her Starry Crown of ANU.

And the spirits of the Dead rose,
And the spirits of the Dead preceded ISHTAR through the Gates.

And ERESHKIGAL was scorned.
The Scorned Queen ERESHKIGAL spoke a powerful curse.
Against the Queen of Heavens ERESHKIGAL spoke her curse.
And NAMMTAR manifested the curse.
When DUMUZI [Tammuz], the Lover of ISHTAR
Descends before me through the GANZIR Gate of Death,
When the lamentations of the people come with him,
When DUMUZI , the Lover of ISHTAR is dead and buried,
May the Dead rise!
May the Dead rise and smell the incense!

—APPENDIX I—
MOROII AD VITAM DICTIONARY : VERSION 2.1
"Cybernomicon" Appendix Version

active ambient feeding : when all eyes are on you as center of attention. Performer, Entertainment, etc.

anemic porphyria : a *Darksider* disease of the Blood afflicting five persons in every million of the general population; a disease that may account for some past cases of *vampirism*.

ANU : *"Heavenly One"* in Babylonian, the All-Father god of Mesopotamian pantheon; called *"AN"* by Sumerians, meaning also "heaven," star or planet; Father to *Enki (EA)* and *Enlil* in Anunnaki lore; called the place of the gods (in the Heavens) in Ancient Egyptian tradition, and a facsimile of this "city" was also built and named as such on earth.

ANUNNAKI : a group of ancient beings of obscure natures that are responsible for the existence of modern humans and their civic systems (civilization); a family of *Watchers*, each representing one of the seven ancient planets; the Seven Judges of the Underworld.

ascension : a state of Being after *First Death*, experienced by your *Etheric Body*, which was able to maintain your *Identity* consciousness intact, for an existence at a relatively "higher" degree (or dimension).

astra : a field of energy; the aura around a life; electromagnetic (EM) radiation from *astyr* activity.

astyr : personal energy transformers; *chakras* in Eastern terminology; energy centers; *"aster,"* singular.

attenergy : attention energies; the flow of energy from a consciousness following its attention; energy flows where attention goes.

babybat : someone recently introduced or awakened to GothVamp lifestyle/subculture; a KinderGoth.

biomagnetic/biofeedback : a measurable effect of thoughts, emotions, and actions which generate specific *neurological* and *biochemical* reactions in the brain, body and across the skin surface.

charge / charging : energy resonance intentionally changed to meet some degree; using intention to bring a specific concentration of energy into being and load it into an object or space.

condition : a requirement or predisposed degree of existence; a parameter, a paradigm attribute or a state ('set' or 'setting') that is experienced, perceived or quantified as different from another based on the perspective of the Observer.

continuum : a continuous whole; the measurement or observation of 'quantitative' variation with a gradual transition without demonstrating observed 'discontinuity' along a spectrum (rather than isolating separate 'parts' or 'entities').

dark flame : the "soul" or *Identity* at the core of Being; the "shell" of the Self; the *"seat of the Dragon."*

darksider : a person born with the inclination toward things "outside" of the Realm; Creatures of Night; any descendents of Lilith or Cain; any being not born on Earth, including extraterrestrial or inter-dimensional.

degree : any variations or fluctuations; anything other than a constant; a relative division of a whole; a point on a spectrum.

dhampyr : a person with *Vampyre* traits, but none of the stereotypical weaknesses; light-sensitivity, etc.; a half-breed *Vampyre* born of a human mother, often born with the *caul*, a membrane surrounding the infant.

energy : expressive action; potential and effective power; the capacity to do work and overcome resistance.

energetic exchange : communicated transmission of energetically encoded "information" between 'fields' or 'forces' in a state of interconnectivity; when 'waves' act upon each other like a force, flowing in regard to proximity, range, frequency and amplitude; greater *"likeness"* or synchronicity (totaling a low *'differential'*) increases the *channel* or *link* for energy to flow with least resistance.

ENKI (E.A.) : *"Lord of the Earth"* in Babylonian or E.A. *"Whose Home is Water"* in Sumerian; Chief Science Officer of the Anunnaki; known as Ptah *"The Designer"* in Egypt; firstborn son of *Anu*, but not his official heir; half-brother to *Enlil*; father to *Marduk*; controls the "Waters of Life."

ENLIL : *"Lord of the Airs"* or *"Lord of the Command"* in Mesopotamian writings; official heir-son of *Anu*; half-brother to *Enki*; begets heir

Ninurta by half-sister *Ninhursag*; espouses *Sud-Ninlil* and together beget *Nanna* (the moon) and *Samas* (the sun); controls "Air-Space" between heaven and earth.

environmental feeding : skimming amplified group energy or "Synergy" (Synchronized Energy) from interaction, celebrations, shopping malls, etc.

ERESHKIGAL : *"Queen of the Great Lands," "Mistress of the Great Below"* or Lady of the Underworld in the Sumerian tradition; half-sister to *Inanna-Ishtar*; granddaughter of *Enlil* and spouse to *Nergal*.

ethereal / etheric : a degree of existence that vibrates its manifestations at points beyond the sensory range of the *human condition*.

etheric immortality : "...an unbroken thread of personality and memory attained spiritually, so that the 'soul' of a person realizes its identity and retains that identity regardless of physical incarnation."—*Michelle Belanger*

FamTrad : an abbreviation for *"Family Tradition"* that can also be spoken this way; a hereditary system of practices and/or beliefs that are passed down within a specific family or group.

first death : a condition where the corporeal body no longer possesses Starfyre to have *Being*-ness and the Dark Flame (*soul*) has gone away from it; what most mortals simply call *"Death,"* since for them this is *Final Death* or *True Death*.

fledgling : a baby bird; a young initiate; a newbie; see *BabyBat*.

fragmentation : breaking into parts and scattering the pieces; fractioning of wholeness; fracture of a holistic all-encompassing state; separation or discontinuity into parts; favoring observation of perceived connectivity between "parts"; in NexGen Systemology, a person outside the state of "Self-Honesty" is said to be fragmented.

glamour : seemingly mysterious allure; bewitching charm; temporarily affecting the appearance of something; a series of enchantments and intentionally charged energy of a specific degree collected around yourself.

gnosis : a Greek word meaning "knowledge" or "to know", but specifically "true knowledge"; the highest echelon of knowledge in *Self-Honesty* or *"Clear Vision"* that is unconditioned by worldly programming and attained only by mystical/spiritual faculties.

GothVamp : a 'Gothic Vampire', meaning anyone who is involved in the post-Punk modern or neo-Vamp underground culture and alternative lifestyles of vampyrism.

Human Condition / homo sapien : a disease of mental psychosis or spiritual neurosis that afflicts 90% of the "human" population on Earth; classification for normative members of the realm, which is not a designation of species or race.

immortal : a being who spends their existence preparing for a *Life* after *First Death* and is aware of more than "this" experience of the Realm.

INANNA (ISHTAR) : *"Lady of Heaven"*; Sumerian goddess of Passion, Love & War; daughter of *Nanna* and *Ningal*; patron goddess to the *Uruk* Sumerians; originally betrothed to *Marduk*, she takes *Dumuzi (Tammuz)* as consort; known throughout ancient religions as the *Goddess of One-Thousand Names*, such as *Isis* to the Egyptians, *Ishtar* to the Babylonians, *Astarte* to the Canaanites, &tc.

light quotient (LQ) : the amount of pure *Starfyre* accumulated by the *Etheric Self*

lycans : werewolves that are often associated with Vampyres.

lycanthropy : a *Darksider* disease named after King Lycaon of Greece, causing the afflicted to transform into a Lycan at least once per lunar cycle.

mainstreaming : to participate in human society and reflect the illusion of leading an "ordinary" human life. [*Modern American*]

MARDUK : *"Son of God"* to Babylonians; heir-son of *Enki*; supreme champion of the *Igigi* (Watchers), hero of the *Enuma Elis*; "Master of Magicians" in *Eridu* with *Enki*; patron deity of Babylonian Mardukites; *Amon-Ra* to Egyptians; husband to *Sarpanit*, father to *Nabu* and *Satu-Set*.

mardukite zuism : a self-directed system similar to and a basis for *Moroii ad Vitam*, specifically rooted in the *Mesopotamian-Babylonian* paradigm as opposed to the current presentation of *Egyptian* and *proto-Sumerian* material in this book; a Mesopotamian-themed religious philosophy and tradition applying the spiritual technology of *NexGen Systemology*, based on Arcane Tablets.

mask : a covering to conceal or protect the face; anything that conceals or disguises; a molded likeness of a face; a grotesque representation of a face, worn to amuse or frighten.

masquerade : a ball or party at which masks and fancy costumes are worn; a disguise; acting under false pretenses.

memory (imprint) : energetically encoded imprints that the Self calls *experience*, which serves to store self-validating reality programming, controlling all beliefs, thoughts and ability to recall.

mesopotamia : "land between the rivers"; the ancient Near East; a region where ancient Sumerians and Babylonians resided.

metaphysics : a field of study concerning the nature of Reality in existence at a range outside or beyond the 'normative range' of the Human Condition.

methodology : a system of methods (and method of systems) that organizes or orders the system as a fundamental underlying aspect.

monistic continuity : a NexGen Systemological standard model that illustrates the ideology of a singularity force demonstrating *total system* inter-connectivity 'above' and 'below' the observation of any apparent *parameters* along a *continuum.*

moroi (moroii, pl.) : *Vampyres* with a conscience; *Vampyres* that feed respectfully; *Living Vampyres* who practice magic and have vampyric affinity prior to *First Death*; a partial *Vampyre;* self-directed *Vampyres* of the *Zeper Legacy* by the *Moroii ad Vitam Paramus;* sometimes assisted by *Dhampyr.*

moroii ad vitam (mission) : "To Evolve, To Become, To Protect."

moroii ad vitam paramus : literally: *"Living Vampyres Preparing For Life"*; the full name for the self-directed system for *Moroii ad Vitam.*

mortal : a person who spends their existence preparing for their *Final Death;* someone who treats "this" *Life* in the Realm as all there is.

mundane : a mortal without *Darksider* tendencies; a close-minded unawakened mortal; that which is ordinary or the "norm" in the *Realm;* a "cowan" or uninitiated individual.

mystery school : an organization preserving the Quest of the Unknown and operating apart from, outside of, or beneath the 'surface' Realm, imparting knowledge to a chosen few 'initiates' who directly and covertly engineer Reality; a school educating initiates (students) in the arts of *Self-Directed 'mysticism'*.

NABU : *"Prophet"* or *"Messenger"* of the Babylonian gods, esp. *Marduk*; heir-son of *Marduk*; husband to Tasmit (Teshmet); developer of refined Babylonian cuneiform and its stylus pen; patron of the Mardukite Scribe-Priests and Magicians in *Borsippa* (near Babylon).

neurotransmitters : a chemical substance released at a physiological level, bridging the *mind-body* transmission of energetic communication using the *nervous system* of the *'physical body'*; biochemical amino acids and peptides (neuropeptides), peptide hormones, etc.

paradigm : an all-encompassing standard by which to view the world and communicate Reality; a standard-model of reality systems used by the Mind to filter, organize and interpret experience.

parameters : a defined range of possible variables within a model, spectrum or continuum.

passive ambient feeding : tapping energy that a group is sending to an *Active Ambient Feeder*.

perturbation : the deviation from a natural state, fixed motion, or orbit system caused by another external system; disturbing or disquieting the serenity of an existent state; inciting observable apparent action using indirect or outside influence; the introduction of a new or unseen element or facet that disturbs system equilibrium.

plasma : star-stuff; pure fundamental energy within all stars; visible phenomenon otherwise known as *lightning*.

potentiality : the total *'sum'* (*collective amount*) of latent (*"dormant"* – present but not apparent) capable or possible realizations; used to describe a state or condition of what has not yet *manifested*, but which can be influenced and predicted based on *patterns*.

probability : causal likelihood of something to 'result' or ' manifest' in and as a certain way, manner or degree based on *'observed evaluation'* of programming and tendencies that follow *cosmic coding* and *'Universal Law'*.

probability patterns : observation of cycles and tendencies to predict a causal relationship or determine the actual condition or flow of dynamic energy using the holistic system as opposed to the understanding of Life, Reality and Existence in isolation or exclusion of perceived parts being separate from other perceived parts.

radiant feeding : absorbing directed attention when large amounts of "*Attenergy*" are present from use of media, hobbies, personal excitement, etc.

rays of light : fragmented *etheric* waves or beams of *Starfyre;* unique vibrational degrees of *Starfyre* when considered on a spectrum.

realm : the world of lights that you can see; the human world; a material degree of existence within the sensory range of the human condition.

revenant : an animated corpse; a manifested spirit or ghost; a person who has returned from the dead.

semantics : a philosophic school of thought focused on the meaning and truth carried in language and effect of language on the mind and behavior; the meaning of language and symbols used as conceptual representations in a paradigm model.

starfyre : raw energy of creation; essence of Life; singular all-encompassing energy; the Universal Agent; a Moroii ad Vitam term for "lifeforce" equal to *ch'i, ki, qi, prana, vril,* or ZU.

strega : a female witch, vampyre, werewolf or gypsy. [*Italian*]

stregheria : witchcraft and magic. [*Italian*]

strego : to enchant, bewitch or glamour [*Italian*].

stregone : a male witch, vampyre, werewolf or gypsy. [*Italian*]

strigoi : a vampyre, werewolf or gypsy. [*Romanian*]

strigoii morte : ancestors of a witch, vampyre, werewolf or gypsy bloodline. [*Romanian*]

thought (wave) : a proactive *Self-directed action* or reactive-response *action* of *consciousness* (*Awareness* activity); the process of thinking as demonstrated in wave-form; the activity of *Awareness* within the range of thought vibrations and frequencies.

thought-form : apparent manifestation or existential realization of thought-waves as "solids" even if only apparent as Reality agreements of the Observer (creator); the treatment of thought-waves as permanent imprints obscuring Self-Honest clarity of *Awareness* when reinforced by emotional experience as a "belief."

TIAMAT (TI.MA.TU) : "*Life-Giving Mother*" in the Babylonian (Mardukite) Epic of Creation (*Enuma Elis*); the first cause; primeval "dragon" of primordial age, equiv. to Sumerian *Kur*; Ancient One of the Anunnaki; *Ialdaboaoth* in Gnosticism and Judaic mysticism (also *Tehom*); the name appears later on epic tablets as wife of *Adamu* (*Adam*); the proto-Judaic *Eve*.

universal agent (UA) : pure, raw, primordial 'divine' or' All-as-One unified Source-Substance that reflects the *Force-principle* ('energetic current') that projects from the All-as-One in All directions as One (and recursing back upon itself (as an infinite loop). According to Eliphas Levi in '*Doctrine of Spiritual Essences*': "A substance diffused through infinity, that single substance which is heaven and earth, fixed according to its degrees of polarization. It is at once matter and motion, a fluid and perpetual vibration." [This is also treated as "ZU" in Mardukite Systemology.]

universal arcanum (great magical arcanum, GMA) : universal semantic-symbol singularity (unified) expression of ALL (All-as-One) that is everywhere the same (only fragmented based on existential perception) and everywhere carefully concealed; Infinity.

vampire : traditionally a fictional being with vampyric characteristics; a blood-drinker or feeder.

vampirism : in pathology, a medical condition of *haematophagy* blood-drinking and/or *porphyria* or a belief of psychotic unstable persons that they personally are a vampire. The spelling is used to distinguish it from the occult practice of vampyrism.

vampyre : a practitioner of vampyrism; someone inflicted with a *darksider* disease or condition that also carries an affinity to vampyrism. [*Olde English*]

vampyric : possessing *Vampyre* traits; things pertaining to *vampyres*; sometimes a reference to traits of neurological *vampirism*, such as drinking blood from victims of violence, etc.

vampyrism : the practice or occult field of *Vampyre* activity.

zeper legacy : the official *Legacy* of the *Moroii ad Vitam* as presented in the *Vampyre's Bible* and *Cybernomicon* (and collected for this edition of the *Vampyre's Handbook*) by Nabu, Joshua Free, "*Zeper*."

WOULD YOU LIKE TO KNOW MORE ???

Your
Pathway to Self-Honesty
continues with books and courses by
Joshua Free

NEW MATERIALS FORTHCOMING IN 2020

from
the NexGen Systemological Society (NSS)
and
International School of Systemology (ISS)
a division of the
Mardukite Research Organization

stay tuned!

SYSTEMOLOGY
The Pathway to Self-Honesty

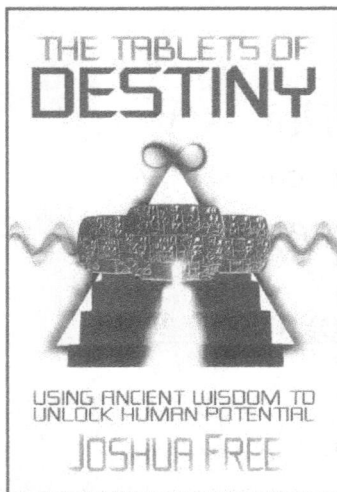

THE TABLETS OF DESTINY
*Using Ancient Wisdom
to Unlock Human Potential*
by Joshua Free

(Mardukite Systemology Liber-One)

A rediscovery of the original
System of perfecting the Human
Condition on a Pathway which
leads to Infinity.
Here is a new map on which
to chart the future
spiritual evolution of
all humanity!

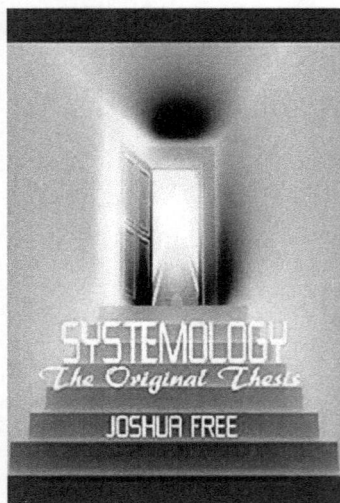

**SYSTEMOLOGY:
THE ORIGINAL THESIS**
*An Introduction to
21st Century New Thought*
by Joshua Free

(Mardukite Systemology Liber-S-1X)

A collection of the original
underground discourses released to
the "New Thought" division of the
Mardukite Research Organization
and providing the inspiration for
rapid futurist spiritual technology
called "Mardukite Systemology."

- - - - - - - - - - - - - - - - -**ALSO AVAILABLE**- - - - - - - - - - - - - - - - - -
- Systemology: Truth Seeker's Adventure Journal & Flight Log
- Systemology: The Pathway to Self-Honesty: Pilot's Flight Log
- Systemology: The Pathway to Self-Honesty: Captain's Logbook

Necronomicon: The Anunnaki Bible : 10th Anniversary
Collector's Edition—LIBER-N,L,G,9+W-M+S (*Hardcover*)

The Complete Anunnaki Bible: A Source Book of Esoteric Archaeology :
10th Anniversary—LIBER-N,L,G,9+W-M+S (*Paperback*)

Necronomicon: The Anunnaki Bible : 10th Anniversary
Pocket Edition—(*Abridged Paperback*)

*Gates of the Necronomicon: The Secret Anunnaki Tradition of
Babylon* : 10th Anniversary Collector's Edition—
LIBER-50,51/52,R+555 (*Hardcover*)

The Sumerian Legacy: A Guide to Esoteric Archaeology—
LIBER-50+51/52 (*Paperback*)

*Necronomicon Revelations—Crossing to the Abyss: Nine Gates
of the Kingdom of Shadows & Simon's Necronomicon*—
LIBER-R+555 (*Paperback*)

*Necronomicon: The Anunnaki Grimoire: A Manual of Practical
Babylonian Magick* : 10th Anniversary Collector's Edition—
LIBER-E,W/Z,M+K (*Hardcover*)

*Practical Babylonian Magic : Invoking the Power of the Sumerian
Anunnaki*—LIBER-E,W/Z,M+K (*Paperback*)

*The Complete Book of Marduk by Nabu : A Pocket Anunnaki
Devotional Companion to Babylonian Prayers & Rituals* :
10th Anniversary Collector's Edition—LIBER-W+Z (*Hardcover*)

*The Maqlu Ritual Book : A Pocket Companion to Babylonian
Exorcisms, Banishing Rites & Protective Spells* :
10th Anniversary Collector's Edition—LIBER-M (*Hardcover*)

Necronomicon: The Anunnaki Spellbook : 10th Anniversary
Pocket Edition—LIBER-W/Z+M (*Abridged Paperback*)

*The Anunnaki Tarot : Consulting the Babylonian Oracle of
Cosmic Wisdom (Guide Book)*—LIBER-T (*Paperback*)

*Elvenomicon—or—Secret Traditions of Elves & Faeries : The Book of
Elven Magick & Druid Lore* : 15th Anniversary Collector's
Edition—LIBER-D (*Hardcover*)

The Druid's Handbook : Ancient Magick for a New Age
20th Anniversary Collector's Edition—LIBER-D2 (*Hardcover*)

Draconomicon : The Book of Ancient Dragon Magick :
25th Anniversary Collector's Edition—LIBER-D3 (*Hardcover*)

The Sorcerer's Handbook : A Complete Guide to Practical Magick
21st Anniversary Collector's Edition—(*Hardcover*)

SYSTEMOLOGY
The Pathway to Self-Honesty

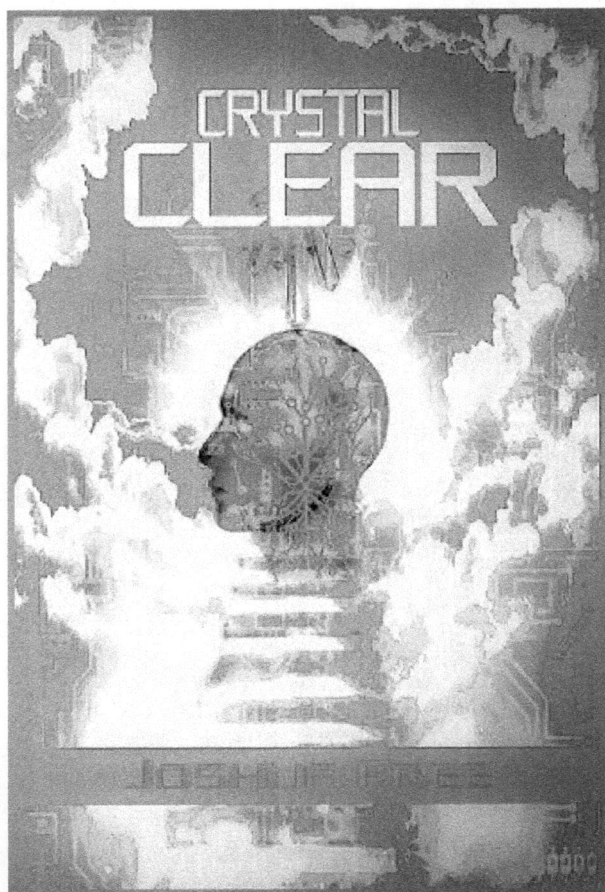

**CRYSTAL CLEAR : THE SELF-ACTUALIZATION MANUAL
& GUIDE TO TOTAL AWARENESS
by Joshua Free**

*The Systemology Crystal Clear Self-Defragmentation Course
Hardcover Textbook and Paperback Editions Now Available!*

NABU—JOSHUA FREE ("Merlyn Stone")
Chief Scribe & Librarian of New Babylon
Bard of the Twelfth Chair at New Forest
Mardukite Zuism & Systemology Founder